SOCIAL ECOLOGY
AND SOCIAL CHANGE

SOCIAL ECOLOGY
AND SOCIAL CHANGE

EDITED BY EIRIK EIGLAD

new-compass.net

Social Ecology and Social Change
2015 © by New Compass Press

ISBN 978-82-93064-34-3
ISBN 978-82-93064-35-0 (ebook)

Published by New Compass Press
Grenmarsvegen 12
N–3912 Porsgrunn
Norway

Design and layout by Eirik Eiglad

The editor received a grant from the Norwegian Research Council.

New Compass presents ideas on participatory democracy, social ecology, and movement building—for a free, secular, and ecological society.

New Compass is Sveinung Legard, Eirik Eiglad, Peter Munsterman, Mat Little Kristian Widqvist, Lisa Roth, Camilla Hansen, and Jakob Zethelius.

new-compass.net
2015

For Murray,
friend and comrade.

CONTENTS

ACKNOWLEDGEMENTS

IN SEPTEMBER 2014, an international conference on ecological politics was organized in Oslo. This conference brought together some 130 scholars and activists to discuss the social and political aspects of climate change and ecological crises.

The conference turned out to be a great success. The presenters and the panelists, the participants and the volunteers, all deserve credit for their contributions.

THE CONFERENCE ECOLOGICAL CHALLENGES 2014 was hosted by the New Compass collective and The Department for Sociology and Human Geography at the University of Oslo (UiO). We cooperated with the Oslo urban ecology journal *Bytopia*, the Swedish network Demokratisk Omställning, and Färnebo Folkehögskola, as well as with The Department for Philosophy, Classics, History of Art and Ideas at the University of Oslo.

Financially, the conference was sponsored by the Norwegian Research Council, the foundation Fritt Ord, the Department for Sociology and Human Geography at UiO, and by New Compass. Generous grants and donations made it possible to invite a broad range of international scholars and activists to present papers, organize workshops, and engage in panel discussions.

I AM GRATEFUL for the grant from the Norwegian Research Council that made this book possible.

I EXTEND MY HEARTFELT THANKS to everyone around New Compass who helps out and supports our project. On behalf of the New Compass collective—and me personally—I would like to use this occasion to send a special thanks to Camilla Svendsen Skriung, who co-founded New Compass. Her commitment was crucial in our first years of existence.

For this particular book, some deserve special mention, and that is the group of people who have helped me copyedit and proofread the book: Janet Biehl, Mat Little, and Adam Krause offered invaluable assistance, and so too did Sveinung Legard and Peter Munsterman. Thanks also to Camilla Hansen, Jakob Zethelius, Lisa Roth, and Kristian Widqvist, who help run New Compass. Above all, however, I am grateful to the authors for their contributions to this book and our common discussion.

FINALLY, I WOULD LIKE TO EXPRESS my immense gratitude to Volia, Iskra, Sofi, and Yngvild Hasvik, whose patience and love never cease to amaze me.

INTRODUCTION

EIRIK EIGLAD

Social ecology is a body of ideas that seeks to explain the interplay between nature and culture. Indeed, it seeks to explain why our age is beset with crises, why our society is at odds with nature, and how this rupture and conflict came about.

Social ecologists insist that all ecological problems are really social problems, and that the solutions to today's ecological crises are primarily social and political. According to the late American social theorist Murray Bookchin, even the very idea of dominating nature stems from the domination of human beings by other human beings. How exactly did we come to see nature as an agglomeration of resources available for plunder and exploitation? Because we live in a society that cultivates domination and exploitation.

It is from this perspective that social ecologists come to very radical conclusions. To solve today's ecological crises, we argue, we have to make our social world more egalitarian and more democratic. Indeed, we must create a nonhierarchical society based on municipal democracy and an ecological economy. Only this will allow for a full reintegration and re-harmonization of society with the natural world. The primary objective of social ecology, then, is to create an ecological society.

Bookchin developed these ideas over four decades. From the mid 1960s onward, he ventured into the fields of anthropology, history and sociology, and still further into cosmology, ethics, and epistemology. He sought to provide within a coherent framework the basic pillars for understanding society and its relationship to nature, and the prospects and preconditions for political change. Many of the central ideas that he pioneered have since percolated out into radical circles and the broader ecology movement. But in order to effectuate the social changes we need, we must form bold new movements and a new politics.

This description of social ecology is admittedly simplistic and rigid, but it does identify our political and analytical point of departure. A basic aim of the book is to demonstrate the nuances of social ecology, rather than how I've briefly presented it.

This book is a selection from the papers that were presented in September 2014 at an international conference organized in Oslo. The conference brought together scholars from a variety of disciplines and activists from a variety of movements. There we discussed some of the burning questions for ecological politics, such as: What is the role of democracy to solve environmental problems? How can we make our cities green? And how can we develop a broad and yet radical ecology movement?

The first aim I had when preparing this book was to present an overview of contemporary social ecology and some of the questions that concern our movement. Given the nature of the conference there is some thematic overlap between various essays, but I think that is a strength: it helps flesh-out these topics and show how they all relate to each other. I believe that all of these essays are great by themselves, but taken together they provide a broad overview of the quest for a social ecology and the need for social change.

A second aim is to point to areas where this theory can be developed. Where are the weaknesses and what are its strengths? What new developments have entered the historical arena and how can we develop these ideas further?

Third, I wanted to relate this theory directly to existing movements and practices. Social ecology is nothing unless it is tied to contemporary movements and current politics. We should approach new social movements both as insiders and outsiders: we should learn from these movements and help them find their direction.

This book is not meant to be a general introduction to social ecology. In my opening essay I have attempted to remedy this by giving a basic overview of the social ecology perspective. To this end I focus on how our quest for a genuinely democratic politics is rooted in more comprehensive social analyses and in an understanding of our place in nature. Democracy, I argue, is crucial for the ecology movement and not just for tactical or strategic reasons: it is fundamental to our visions of an ecological society. Dan Chodorkoff expands on this and insists that utopian visions should always guide our activism: our struggle for an ecological society is, after all, always fueled by visions of what such a society would be like, not only on possible outcomes but genuinely ethical considerations of what ought to be.

Brian Tokar delivered a keynote address to the conference, and his contribution to this volume outlines the major challenges that climate change poses for our societies. He presents a sobering analysis of contemporary climate predictions and the various environmentalist responses, and points to the prospects for democratic grassroots empowerment. Sveinung Legard approaches the question from a different angle and asks whether participatory democracy would indeed be better for the climate. He identifies, analyzes and evaluates some of the key arguments for participatory democracy within the ecology movement.

Despite the gravity of the ecological crisis, says Mat Little, we should not ignore the very real conflicts within society that have again burst to the fore. He challenges the notion that society has overcome its internal contradictions in favor of a more fundamental external contradiction between society and the natural world. In many countries and parts of the world, capitalism can no longer promise human well-being and progress. Adam Krause also approaches the current economic crisis, but more philosophically. He starts from scratch, that is to say, from the very elements of matter, and the essential features of what constitutes life and nature. His succinct evolutionary account sheds light on some of the essential economic questions that confront us today.

Under capitalism and in nation-states, citizenship is a rather hollow concept, but it can become the foundation for new political communities. Marco Rosaire Rossi discusses how classical radicalism—notably Marxism and anarchism—stressed workers and the proletariat as the primary agents of social change. Communalism, by contrast, emphasizes citizenship and a civic form of radicalism, and its role in creating a new political system that assumes responsibility for the world. John Nightingale's essay highlights the significance of solidarity for social ecology, namely that it is necessary to achieve a balanced relationship with the natural world. Nightingale explains how Bookchin and social ecologists seek to achieve solidarity in society precisely through a political reconceptualization of citizenship.

Janet Biehl, who has done so much to popularize libertarian municipalism and social ecology, traces the emergence of a car-dependent infrastructure the United States, where more than half of the population lives in suburbia. She discusses the ideas of the new urbanists, and lists some central features of an infrastructure that could support citizenship in ecological cities. Arnošt Novák gives the history of a very different development, that of Czech environmental activism. He suggests that one of the main lessons from the trajectory of Czech environmentalism is that we should try to build a broad popular movement, while also radicalizing our ecological visions, and to expand our repertoire of actions.

Jonathan Korsár returns our focus to the municipality and translates Jeremy Rifkin's ideas on a "zero marginal cost society" into a municipal setting. The future of production, energy, and community lies in new forms of creating, sharing, and caring. The main challenges for a zero marginal cost society, Korsár argues, are indeed municipal challenges:

municipalities should constitute the political framework of a new economy and a new energy system.

The analysis provided by Ersilia Verlinghieri fits well in with the preceding essays. She dissects modern planning practices and asks us to consider alternative, more radical approaches to transport planning which take into account questions of social justice, freedom of movement, and the right to the city, as well as ecology.

Salvatore Paolo De Rosa and Monica Caggiano point to another real challenge for many communities of the world today, namely that they are plagued not only by state encroachment and capitalist development projects, but also by organized crime and violence. The Campania region in southern Italy suffers from pollution and mismanagement, but the communities now organize to fight mafia culture and organized crime. Their analyses are stimulating and they point toward the radical, even revolutionary changes, we need to see. In the following essay, Metin Güven interprets the concept of revolutionary change based on the historical works Bookchin wrote on popular movements in the early modern era.

Toon Bijnens and Johanna L. Rivera discuss the emergence of an ecology movement in the Middle East, highlighting recent campaigns for water rights in Iraq and the surrounding countries, and Cağri Eryilmaz evaluates a different experience in Anatolia: the movement that arose in the conflicts over Gezi Park in Istanbul. He compares this movement, which in 2013 created hundreds of popular forums all over Turkey, to the politics of social ecology.

We should have a closer look at how a dialogue can be initiated between the theory of social ecology and the practice of new urban movements for social change, says Federico Venturini. In Brazilian cities like Rio de Janeiro, new urban movements have managed to mobilize large sectors of society against megalomaniac urban development projects; their experiences are important and valuable.

Camilla Hansen turns our attention to Hannah Arendt, looking at how her political ideas can inspire our activism. She argues that participatory democracy is the only political system that allows us to reflect publicly, as a society, on where we are going. To change our current course such public reflection is crucial.

Last, but not least, Dimitrios I. Roussopoulos ends this collection of essays with an evaluation of the status of environmental policies and the outlines for a new ecological municipalism. Few have done more than Roussopoulos to spread the practical dimensions of social ecology to an urban political setting. He gave a keynote speech that concluded the conference, and I think it is befitting that his experience and advice should also conclude this book.

These essays speak well for themselves. Still, I believe that the reader will benefit from seeing this collection of essays as a whole, as mutually enriching contributions to a common approach.

Until now, social ecology has not had an extensive outreach; usually its ideas are applied only in bits and pieces. To be sure, all of the various ways we can spread ecological consciousness, social analyses, cultural critique, and even political activism have their merit. They can all help us reach our common goals, however piecemeal. But we also need to see new social movements emerge that don't fear setting ideas into context—indeed, perhaps even a system—and launch a systematic critique of our society as a whole.

One place where social ecology has had a certain outreach is in New England, notably in Vermont, where Bookchin lived, particularly in the areas around Plainfield, where the Institute for Social Ecology was located. Some Canadian cities, notably Montréal, have also seen bold attempts to implement a social ecology program.

Here in Scandinavia, these ideas have matured since the early 1990s, when a small group of environmental activists turned to social ecology for advice and inspiration. Since then, several organizations in the Nordic countries have been committed to social ecology and its communalism. This commitment lies at the basis of the New Compass.

Recent events in Kobanê and Rojava have brought the world's attention to Kurdistan. In the chaos of the Syrian Civil War, the predominantly Kurdish regions of Rojava proclaimed free cantons based on communal self-government. In 2014, I visited the Cizîre canton with an academic delegation and was impressed with what I saw there. With an extremely difficult and, at the time I pen these lines, still precarious situation forced upon them, their accomplishments are indeed remarkable. After visiting the region and meeting with a host of movements, parties, local institutions, academies, and the militias, I am convinced that there is a genuine social revolution occurring in Rojava. I am also convinced that it is founded on communalist political structures and that women play a central role in this movement. The experiences from the revolution are extremely valuable and may complement other experiences and ideas. In this book, we unfortunately do not feature any essays or analyses of the Kurdish experiment. In the near future, New Compass intends to publish a whole series of exciting titles dedicated to the Kurdish question. They will attempt to explain and analyze this movement and its democratic confederalism in more detail.

I am convinced that these ideas are very powerful, and I believe that they can unite a series of social and political movements in a common struggle against all hierarchies, for our common empowerment, and for the transition to a free, ecological society.

This book will ideally receive a readership ready to translate these ideas into their own political setting. My hope is that this book contributes not only to the theory and politics of social ecology but also to concrete social change.

March 21, 2015
Telemark

— *Humanity is too intelligent not to live in a rational society. It remains to see whether it is intelligent enough to achieve one.*

Murray Bookchin

DEMOCRACY FOR THE ECOLOGY MOVEMENT

EIRIK EIGLAD

Half a century after the ecology movement first emerged on the political scene, there is still a pressing need to make ecology a political issue. Yes, "ecology" makes major headlines, it is on every political party program, and markets every thinkable product. Still, making ecology genuinely *political* seems to be another matter altogether. What is the political significance of ecology? What does this mean for our activism? And what is the relevance of democracy for the ecology movement?

The fact that we face grave environmental problems today becomes increasingly obvious to attentive citizens. The pollution of the soil and the waters keep apace, so too does the emissions of carbon dioxide, methane, and nitrous oxide—greenhouse gases that trap heat in the atmosphere. Indeed, today we face not only pollution of our environments and a distressful reduction of biological diversity, but also the terrifying prospect of a significantly altered planetary climate. "The warming of the climate system is unequivocal," concludes the Intergovernmental Panel on Climate Change (IPCC) in their September 2013 assessment report: "The atmosphere and ocean have warmed, the amounts of snow and ice have diminished, sea level has risen, and the concentrations of greenhouse gases have increased."

So far, political leaders have failed to rise to the occasion, and there is a wide field open for ecological activism today. Although no major new ecological movements have stepped into the breach, all mainstream environmentalists insist on the gravity of our situation. In April 2013, newspapers reported that the prominent scientist James Hansen stepped down from his job at NASA to work as a full-time activist, to pressure governments more forcefully for environmental regulations. Hansen is not at all the prototypical radical activist, and neither is Nicholas Stern, a former chief economist of the World Bank. In 2006, Stern authored the UK government-commissioned Stern Review, a report warning that the human impact on the global climate was "catastrophic." In 2014, with the hindsight of only eight years, he said, "I got it wrong on climate change—it's far, far worse" than predicted back then.

The growing awareness that we face grave environmental *problems*, however, seldom rises to a recognition that we are in the midst of a full-scale ecological *crisis*. Still, if we consider only the issue of global warming, it is worth noting the dramatic shifts in how the scientific community frames the problem. Since the IPCC was formed in 1988, every report it has published has become more explicit, not only in emphasizing the gravity of the situation, but in acknowledging that "Human influence on the climate system is clear." As probabilities and predictions turn into somber realities, it is likely that we will see a radicalization of ecology in the years to come.

Still, even when it is acknowledged that we face *an ecological crisis* today—and not merely a set of environmental problems—the *underlying causes* of the crisis are easily overlooked. Admittedly, it is far easier to focus on the symptoms of the crisis than to focus on its structural causes. It is, after all, mainly through the effects we experience the crisis. On the local level, when we become aware of certain consequences of environmentally harmful practices, it may be easy to locate its direct causes: a certain polluter or a specific practice, or perhaps inadequate legislation. But when we assess the overarching global challenges, we immediately come up against problems that are far more complex and have no simple solutions. We can seldom, if ever, assess these more fundamental ecological problems in isolation, nor are they strung together in linear causal relations—further reflection reveals how seemingly unrelated ecological issues constitute a critical *totality*, and that it is *the set of problems* rather than the sum of problems that constitute the ecological crisis we face today.

Although the crisis expresses itself existentially through its consequences, and not its causes, it is toward the causal nexus we must direct our attention. Unless we approach these root causes head on, it is unlikely that we will be able to fend off their many detrimental effects. The strength of ecology lays precisely in its focus—indeed, insistence—on holism, totality, relationships and interaction. This, it seems to me, is precisely what makes ecology so radical. In the early 1970s Arne Næss and Murray Bookchin developed their respective versions of ecological philosophy, and they both emphasized this point. While Næss underscored the distinction between "shallow" and "deep" ecology, Bookchin argued that the real distinction went between ecology and environmentalism. Both insisted that ecology went beyond single-issue activism and legislation and they both emphasized the need to rethink humanity's basic outlook and relationship to nature.

Ecology, however, is not simply a new outlook, but provides the foundations for a coherent social critique. The various environmental issues we face comprise a totality that reflects society's ability—or inability—to relate to the broader natural world. While the deep ecologists claim that we all should ask the deeper questions that will reveal the warped relationship between humanity and nature, our social analyses must not stop short by blaming "humanity" or "technology," as deep ecologists too often do; they must rather address *how* humanity is organized and *how* we use technology. Today's ecological problems have their roots in more fundamental social conditions; in how we choose to organize production, what kind of technologies we use, and what leitmotifs we allow to govern our economy. A critical role for ecology is to provide the coherent framework for interpreting the effects and the symptoms of the current ecological crises and to locate their root causes. As soon as we go beyond the shallowest forms of environmentalist tinkering, we see that the ecological crisis demands distinct social imperatives: we must change the ways we live, work, and think. This is not just a question about transformation of personal values or even of our cultural values, but about how our societies are structured and function.

We must come to recognize the full extent to which we are responsible for today's ecological crises, not simply as a collection of individuals, but as a culture and as a society. It seems to me that even the most rudimentary social analysis of the ecological crisis immediately becomes intensely political. If we just look at the climate changes we face, there is nothing politically neutral about them: they are human-induced and they are propelled by powerful structural and economic incentives. Today's excessive discharge of greenhouse gases pours out of our industrial structures and transportation systems.

To a great extent, therefore, today's ecological crisis is a *willed* development. Not only are the ecological problems sanctioned by aggressive social forces, but they are produced by strong underlying social dynamics that for the most part goes unchallenged. In a world with limited resources and fragile balances, it is important for us to denude this political will.

Furthermore, the longer it takes us to recognize the social causes of the ecological crisis, the more dramatic changes we should expect. The longer we wait, the more acutely ecology becomes a social imperative. Still, the most immediate task of the ecology movement is not merely to fight for specific issues and reforms, but, critically, to educate the public about the social and systematic causes to environmental dislocations and ecological crises. This critical role immediately becomes a political role. In providing analysis and reflection we help bring out the political implications of the question of ecology.

To grasp and evaluate the totality of our rupture with the natural world remains a critical task for ecology, and we direly need new popular movements that pick up the ecological challenge and change the destructive course our society is on. "Think globally, act locally" remains a sound adage, and to this end, I believe, democracy is decisive. Solving our ecological problems require *political* will—and action. But before we turn to just *how* the question of democracy is important to the ecology movement, let us explore further the social significance of ecology.

No matter how much contemporary culture attempts to sever our ties to our biological bases—the realm of life—a deep and fundamental relationship still exists between society and the natural world. In sharp contrast to the dominant impulses and economic practices of our time, which ceaselessly pit human beings against the non-human world, we need to recover the foundations our societies in the web of life. This does not mean that we should denigrate what is human at the expense of what is natural. Indeed, there is even a sense in which we can say that human culture is still eminently natural: it has developed out of nature and still retains a series of crucial "natural" qualities—it is not simply an aberration from evolution. However much this is ignored by our societies, we never exist apart from the natural world and, in a deep sense, our actions, values, and communities should reflect this. The relationship between society and nature, however, is neither symmetrical nor strictly proportional, and we need to better clarify this relationship in order to properly recognize the great responsibilities we humans have toward the rest of nature. Too often, unfortunately, when ecology attempts to ask the "deeper" questions, it conflates social and natural categories, and in the process diminishes society's unique responsibilities toward the non-human natural world.

How can we untangle this? First of all, we should make clear that our perceptions of the natural world always are socially mediated. This does not mean that our perceptions of nature is entirely "constructed," that nature is merely a "social construction," but as long as we have been human beings with a language and rudimentary forms of social institutions, this has been an inescapable fact. Throughout our formative years we are entirely dependent on the care of others. not only to survive but also to learn to cope with the world, and the extensive rearing and social conditioning we undergo by far surpasses all other animals. This means that however much we may cherish the individual experience of nature, nobody confronts nature as a mere individual. We need not invoke Wittgenstein's private language argument to recognize that we are essentially cultured beings. Sea turtles may live twice as long as human beings, but they never encounter the world the way we do.

More important, however, is the fact that our encounter with nature is not merely the sum of our individual human actions. On the contrary, our interaction is primarily collective and systematic: it takes the form of highly complex transportation systems, the extraction of oil, gas, and metals, or of industrial workshops, mono-crops, trawl fishing, and cruise ships. It is above all *as a society* that we relate to the natural world. Although we may—and should—individually seek to reduce or change our consumption patterns there is only so much individual changes can do. We need to move toward a society that is not only "sustainable," but genuinely ecological, and this transformation will, above all, require a vigorous collective effort.

Now, there is a crucial and inescapable relationship between society and nature, but our analyses suffer greatly if we fail to properly distinguish between the different realms in order to advance an ecological politics. There are no direct links from "ecology" to "politics"—we need to define both of these words. I will not discuss here the fact that much of what passes today as Green politics is essentially technocratic and conformist, and not ecological in any meaningful sense; I am more troubled by the fact that more radical forms of "ecological politics" often fail to develop progressive social alternatives. It seems to me that this failure stems from theoretical mistakes that, put simplistically, fall into one of two categories. The first mistake is to import too much "nature" into the social realm, to assign too great a role for biology in determining social relations. If we allow seemingly essential biological categories to define social obligations and our "human nature" we lose what is humanity's most valuable contribution to the world of life, namely our cultured rationality and capacity for ethical deliberation in human collectives. Human communities and culture allow for a whole new realm of agency that supersedes each individual's biological makeup. The fact that this capacity is to a great extent denied to most of our communities and citizens today does not invalidate the point: on the contrary, it should strengthen our resolve to reshape our societies to make room for the blossoming of ethics. But a sociobiological approach can only create real or artificial links between various individuals and their biological nature, and cannot in any meaningful sense speak about human culture and social institutions, technology, and infrastructure. For this reason it greatly diminishes our chances of developing a new ecological ethics and a new society. Sociobiology is not social ecology.

On the other hand, it is also a mistake to turn this relation on its head, by assigning social functions and qualities to bees, wolves, horses, and turtles—or to rivers, mountains, and the moon, for that matter. This is what many deep ecologists do when they seek to point out the affinities we have to nonhuman beings. But we cannot use distinct social terms—like "welfare," "rights," "education," "oppression," or "hierarchy"—to define relationships in nature, without losing much of what are distinctly human approaches to reality. This is to export too much of our social categories into the realm of nature, and would be a form of "biosociology." Too often contemporary environmental ethics, in its drive to reintegrate human beings into the natural world, commits this error. If we anthropomorphically project human qualities onto other organisms and biological communities, we also lose a sense of what are genuinely evolutionary advances in human culture, and the creative role we *can* play in the web of life. If we project what is essentially human or social terms to explain nature we not only fail to understand the organism or ecocommunity in question—on its *own* terms—but we undercut the need and the possibility of recreating our societies along humanistic *and* ecological lines. The problem here is not the benign intentions behind calling for, say, "earth citizenship," but the implicit premises that devalue the human capacity for consciously and collectively reshaping their social world.

Social ecologists claim that we need an ecological society with new political institutions to counter the ecological crises, but this does not mean that "ecology" prescribes certain political institutions that are

25

"naturally ordained." The Enlightenment got rid of the notion of The Great Chain of Being, and we don't want it back. Ecology should be critical towards "biologistic" approaches that essentialize "human nature" and claim we are on par with other life forms. We are biological beings, to be sure, but more than that, we are social beings, expressing socially determined—*and determining*—agency. We relate to nature above all as society, through a set of economic, political, and cultural practices. And, although there is not a direct relation between ecology and a certain cultural practice, we must understand just how we came to turn vast stretches of fertile land into concrete, steel and glass, or to burning oil wells and mop the sea bottom with gigantic trawls. It certainly isn't simply the result of thoughtlessness and it isn't because these practices are somehow implanted in our genes.

To say that our relationship to nature is always socially mediated, however, is not to diminish the importance of acquiring an ecological sensibility or new ecological institutions, but to assert that there are no foundations for a "biocentric democracy" or for a "council of all beings"—nor can there ever be one. Thinkers that advance these ideas debase the great democratic traditions and the hard-won rights to assemble, deliberate, and participate in political life and its institutions. There *is* no link, we need to *make* that link; but making this link cannot be simply one of extending social categories to the natural world.

So, to sum up, what is the deeper relationship between "democracy" and "nature"? There is none: we cannot find any democratic political systems in the natural world, nor can we find civic ideals or even any kind of egalitarian politics there. Only in human societies will we find democracies, republics, and monarchies. These are social terms that refer to specific sets of social relations and distinct human political institutions. The fact that there is continuity between society and nature does not warrant the direct leap from an ecological outlook to prescriptions of political ideals. If only for this reason, a straightforward comparison between "democracy and nature" is flawed.

To claim simplistically that there is an intrinsic relation between democracy and nature is misleading, but there is yet another sense in which democracy is crucial for the ecology movement. Indeed, social ecologists insist that there is a connection between political democracy and ecological activism.

Although there is no direct link between the realm of nature and our political structures, the very idea of the earth's "carrying capacity" and "limits to growth" suggests that there is something inherently anti-ecological about the way contemporary society is organized. Ecology's demands for balance and reciprocity stand in marked contrast to senseless accumulation and production for profit, the ethos of the prevailing society. In a society propelled by incessant growth, competition, and cold instrumentalism, it should be easy to discern the radical implications of ecology.

But how does this relate to democracy? Of course, there is an immediate, practical sense that the political dimension of ecology is relevant for our activism, and that concerns how popular movements can use democratic structures, traditions, and processes to educate citizens about ecological ideas as well as mobilize around ecological issues.

The institutions and processes of democracy—however broad we define it—offer a range of possibilities for popular movements who seek to mobilize support for ecological causes. It is not only a way to reach people and to throw numbers on the political scale: by appealing to the democratic tendencies and traditions within our societies we garner moral legitimacy to our movements' demands. Creative use of democracy offers not only possibilities for mobilizing on a far *broader* scale than can be done through parliamentary means and lobbyism; it offers possibilities of mobilizing in a more *profound* sense, to mobilize active citizens rather than passive voters or consumers. If we hold that every citizen is an ecological agent—that each and every one of us should reconsider our relationship to nature and contribute to social change—we should not consider citizens to be mere numbers that can be rallied behind any given cause, and this outlook should be reflected in our mobilizing practices. For popular mobilization, democracy is invaluable.

This brings us to the next point: how we should use democracy to spread an ecological culture. *Popular education* is crucial for achieving the far-reaching social changes needed to avert ecological crises or breakdown. Education, here, must mean more than formal "education," it should not refer to the mere accumulation of facts or professional training, but be understood as an intellectual and emotional upbringing, a cultured way of reorienting ourselves and developing a responsible interaction with each other and the natural world.

Our movements must seek to create an ecological culture, and to this end I believe there are inspiring historical parallels to how the workers' movement tried to cultivate social consciousness through the development of a working class culture, not only in radical Vienna or revolutionary Barcelona, but even everywhere social democracy grew strong. Here, social consciousness always went together with new social institutions. These institutions were not only concerned with production and distribution; they also engaged in education, music and sports, everything that contributed to building class-consciousness and self-confidence. Although the ecology movement should have a more sophisticated concept of democracy than social democracy ever had, there is much to learn from the aspirations and the trajectories of socialist class organization.

Now, to be sure, it is difficult to spread ecological consciousness in an age of commodification and consumerism. Stepping out of the manufactured consumer culture in "advanced" capitalist countries requires almost superhuman efforts, and we can hardly blame people for not being able to resist the massive pressure to conform. Living a genuinely ecological life today is perhaps as difficult as preaching atheism in the Middle Ages. If only for this reason, initiating the necessary social and ecological changes and policies requires a collective effort. The ecology movement needs to find new arenas for working together in community.

At the municipal and regional level, democratic institutions offer such arenas. They are not the only potential arenas for collective activism and community, but democracy, in its direct and participatory sense, is an unrivalled means for *empowering* people, even on a large scale. Making people feel that their actions actually mean something is important to create a popular culture for ecological transition. Few things are more important to generate self-confidence and empowerment than actual power. Today, in our "democracies," our political involvement mostly generates the opposite sentiment; it merely confirms how powerless we are. This experience can surely give us important political lessons, but nothing beats real empowerment: the possibility to really make a difference, and actively contribute in shaping our society's destiny.

Whenever we engage with an issue we should use democracy to mobilize, educate, and empower common people—after all, *empowered as citizens* they will play the major role in the ecological transition we envision. We need to use democratic arenas—existing ones as well as emerging ones—to raise ecological awareness and advance struggles. Indeed, we should work methodically to expand democracy wherever and whenever this is possible, and all these arenas should be exploited to create an ecological opposition in political life. We should appeal to ordinary people's will and capacity to do something about today's ecological impasse. More democracy, I believe, means that society at large will be all the more responsive to an ecological movement able and willing to engage the public arena. Now, this may sound too "tactical" to many activists in the ecology movement, and, although this approach may offer some strategic political advantages in undermining the powers that be, this is really not the main reason we should strive to invigorate and expand democracy. Democracy is vital to the ecology movement for an even more profound reason.

Beyond the practical level of education, mobilization, and empowerment, ecology must be able to catch our imagination in a tangible sense. To achieve this, we must open up society and make it possible for people to dream about what an ecological society would be like. There is a sense in which ecology must be allowed a central part in our collective dreams, and democracy will help us make this possible.

In reharmonizing our relationship to the natural world, we must never underestimate the power of our imagination. Indeed, to make ethical judgments we must be able to imagine *what ought to be*. This, of course, by no means implies a disregard for the very real material factors that condition our lives and the structural limitations to the choices we are able to make. Still, our imagination may heighten our sensitivity toward ethics, toward imagining society *as it could be* and *can become*. There is a dialectical element in all historical development. The power of dialectics lies in its systematical ethical contrast between "what is" and "what ought to be," and such a dialectical imagination will not only be important for cultivating a new sensitivity toward the world, but is an essential element of social critique, or even of critical thought as such. It was in this sense Russian radical Alexander Herzen enthusiastically termed the Hegelian dialectic "the algebra of revolution." Dialectics, to be sure, is not a magical formula, or even a rigid methodology, but it yields an ethical sensitivity toward what does not yet exist but is a latent rational possibility within a given culture and its history. Dialectics operates in the fertile intellectual borderlands of reason and imagination. From this perspective, it makes sense to claim that the whole point of culture must be to create a space for collective self-reflection, to cultivate human deliberation and creativity, and here the idea of democracy plays a role. I believe that a participatory democracy could provide an institutional framework that makes such collective intellectual cultivation possible. Democracy opens society to critical self-reflection and focuses our collective attention. To achieve this, the ecology movement is in a unique historical position: it can help raise social awareness and advance ecological struggles, and, above all, help redefine what the good life really is, and, in the process, significantly raise the bar of human expectation.

Social ecology envisions a radical transformation of social structures. Not because it is prescribed by evolution, but because it—if anything—is "prescribed" by the history of human society itself. We believe in an ecological transformation of society, but one that is fueled by eliciting and evaluating progressive and civilizing traits in our common history. Paradoxically, then, we seek to make society become more ecological precisely by making it more social and distinctly human. Underlying this is a sense that society is less than rational today, that we are less than human.

It is from this social analysis that we draw a radical political program that advances both structural changes as well as a liberatory agenda in its own right. Still, social ecology is not a creed, a doctrine that sets it squarely off from the rest of the ecology movement. As I see it, it certainly is a distinct way of *approaching* ecological issues, but the whole ecology movement is potentially social if it acknowledges and analyzes the social roots of the ecological crisis. What is distinct, however, is our vision of an ecological society. We hold that an ecological society would be a fundamentally *ethical society*, and it seems we can only shape an ethical society by learning from the history of human consociation. In order to nurture social ecological reintegration, we seek to bring ethics to the forefront of society, which means that we seek to cultivate reason, dialogue, and common moral concerns.

Still, to be very specific, there are two areas that may provide concrete arenas for ecological activism; arenas that have value in themselves and that can be expanded in a broader democratic sense. First, as I have already indicated, we need to defend and expand political systems that allow for civic commitment, responsibility, and deliberation: in short, we need *democracy*. It should be redefined, to be sure, but it will provide the structure for an open and generous society. The idea here is not only to give us a better position on the game board, but also to change the very rules of the game.

Second, we need to defend and expand *the commons*. As with political democracy, all countries have different traditions in this regard, but there seems to me there are something to build upon in every region of the world. Garret Hardin's much-maligned "tragedy of the commons" presupposes that the commons are cultural wastelands, accessed by purely self-serving individuals. But this is not what the commons usually are. They are natural and cultural assets that can and should be placed under political control. Moreover, to politicize the commons is not to deny them their importance, quite to the contrary. Expanding the commons will increase municipal or regional control over natural resources and greatly bolster a burgeoning direct democracy. Democracy should not only signify the political institutions of a given society, but also its capacity for controlling its economic life. In this sense it is important that the ecology movement also seek to reclaim popular control over the means of production, of natural resources, and society's technological capacities.

In furthering this dialogue, we should encourage citizens to become involved in advancing the ecological agenda. This does not mean that we should naively believe that we are "all in the same boat." Many work actively against an ecological transition. Furthermore, it seems obvious to me that if our ecological problems are caused by structural dynamics and social organization, then the defenders of these structures and this organization are morally responsible for the ecologically destructive consequences. Some have vested interests in the economic and political system, or benefit in other way from social injustice and exploitation. Creating popular assemblies and regional councils does not remove conflict from society, nor should we ever want that. Again, we seek to advance democracy in order to bring these conflicts to the front of social development, to make the issues and choices we face plain for all to see. Society must be rearranged so that civic and ecological movements and initiatives can come forward, bring the discussion to the forefront of society's agenda, and wrest power away from the powerful elites that sanction today's destructive course.

A basic tenet in social ecology is that our idea of dominating nature will not end before we end social domination. It is now possible to imagine a world that is free of material want *and* free of social oppression and exploitation. *But* it will require a *social* ecology movement, a movement that insists on both the ecological dimension of its social program and the social dimension of its ecological program. It is by becoming genuinely social that the ecology movement can contribute to reharmonize the relationship between society and the natural world.

Ecology may be all over the news, but it has yet to come to the *center* of public attention; it has yet to be the defining feature of our society and its policies. Although ecology may be "popular" in a superficial sense, we need to ensure that it becomes meaningful in a profound ethical as well as political sense. This, I believe, can only be done if we work to change our society in a way that makes ecological concerns directly meaningful to people where they live and work. To be sure, we need to combat ecological degradations and impose firm restrictions on pollution and exploitation, but we can only advance genuine ecological reintegration of our societies if we implement these changes on a regional level, and as part of a broader program for social emancipation, where people are recognized as ecological agents and empowered in a way that makes it *at all possible* for them to take responsibility for our common future.

These solutions may be radical, but their relevance cannot but increase. The further we postpone social change and allow the crisis to unfold, the more drastic the social imperatives will become. It seems to me that the exponential nature of the ecological crisis necessarily will radicalize itself and demand fundamental changes not only in our values and behaviors, but also in how our societies are structured. In this respect the political significance of ecology cannot be overestimated.

Unfortunately, however, we have no guarantees that such a radicalization will lead to social emancipation. Ecology may instead inform a dystopian social vision, one that eschews democratic solutions. "Ecology" may come to mean "necessitarian," and "collective" may come to mean "totalitarian"—this happened to socialism, and the historical analogies here are striking. Indeed, the above-mentioned Stern Review concluded that even from a conventional economical perspective it will simply be *too expensive* for our societies to go on with politics as usual: it argued that the increasing ecological dislocations will eventually throw our societies into deep recessions and economic crises. The outcome of these crises is not given—they may give rise to socialisms as well as fascisms, and to democracies as well as dictatorships. The ecology movement must therefore have inscribed on its banners more than an end to our exploitation of the natural world and a restoration of ecological balance—it must place trust and collective responsibility in new participatory, civic institutions. If we want our notions of ecology to be guided by the fecundity, generosity, and diversity of the natural world, I believe we must work to ensure that democracy remains at the forefront of the ecology movement.

The question of democracy is also relevant for the ecology movement on a more practical level, in ensuring the transition to an ecological society. It is interesting, here, to note that among the four scenarios that were presented in the Millennium Assessment Report, the one scenario, in its prognoses, that yielded the most positive pragmatic results—the "adapting mosaic" scenario—was also the one that was the most democratic; indeed, it comes very close to a social ecological vision of regional development. This scenario and this vision, however, exists only in the prognoses and is not yet on the political agenda. Additionally, the Millennium Assessment Report points to two things that we must have in mind. First, that we need to be most conscious about the actual alternatives our societies face *before* the crises intensify. Second, that the most promising perspectives, like that of the "adaptive mosaic," will not come about by themselves. While the technocratic, elitist, and "free trade" solutions may all be implemented far above our heads, the development of such an adaptive mosaic model, at least one that is compatible with a participatory democracy, will to a great extent depend on *our* actions and our involvement.

In order to combat ecological—and social—degradation, it could very well turn out that democracy is the most important "political tool" we have at our disposal. Indeed, I would insist that the more successful we are in advancing a liberatory social program, the better suited we will become to counter the demands of the ecological crises. The crises will demand their toll, and we are best equipped to meet these challenges *together*, as a genuinely democratic—and ecological—society.

EVERYTHING DEPENDS ON WHAT PEOPLE ARE CAPABLE OF WANTING

DAN CHODORKOFF

Social ecology is a utopian project. But we believe in the reality of utopia. Of course, social ecologists use the word in part as a provocation. For most people, I think, utopia is a pejorative term. In common usage we may say that something is utopian and mean quite simply that something is impossible, it's unachievable; it's a cloud cuckoo land, a total fantasy. This common use of the term makes it is very easy to fall into that mindset and dismiss utopia as unrealistic and irrelevant.

But when social ecologists use the word utopia, we use it in a very different sense. To understand the utopian dimension of our project, we need to go back to the etymology of the term. Sir Thomas More coined the word in 1516, when he wrote the book *Utopia*. He was someone who loved wordplay, and he identified the word utopia as having two sources, both from the ancient Greek. The first was the word *outopia*, which means "no place." This is the sense in which the word is primarily used today. But the other was the word *eutopia*, which means "the good place." It is in that second sense we should use the word, and I would urge us now to rehabilitate that term. Ever since the ancient Greeks, utopia as the idea of "the good place" has played a very important role in social thought; it has been the standard against which the existing society is judged, and something worth striving for. That is to say that utopia has been both a form of thinking about current social problems and critiquing existing conditions and about projecting into the future a good place, a better society.

Of course, it is not difficult to find many problematic aspects within the history of utopias and utopian literature. One can review them and see that many of them indeed represent the old adage that one person's utopia is another person's hell. Utopian visions tend to be very idiosyncratic; they may reflect the likes and the dislikes of a given historical individual. At the same time, to be sure, these literary utopias may, and often do, incorporate many progressive elements, but they nonetheless come from the mind of one person. There is, however, another tradition of social utopias that are born out of the experiences of a group of people working together not just to imagine a new future but to actualize that future, and that's the utopian tradition I would like to connect us to.

Utopia is important because it is a way of thinking about the future that transcends the given. It enables us to think beyond what *is* and conceptualize what *could* be, or even what *should* be. There is of course a danger that we may overfly in that process, that we let our imaginations run wild, and design a utopia that defies the laws of physics, or of chemistry or of biology. We can even prophesy, as Charles Fourier famously did, that the seas would eventually lose their salinity and turn to lemonade. But at its most profound, utopia is an expression of real, existing potentialities in our own society.

These potentialities may be difficult to see because so much of our experience is colored by the hegemonic nature of our own culture. Today, it is hard to even think beyond, say, our notion of human nature. We live in a capitalist society where we are told the essence of our human nature to be greedy, acquisitive, and violent, and that these are all innate human traits. Capitalism, it is argued, is a system that allows us to express these very natural tendencies and to be competitive. Well, these capacities are certainly part of the broader human potential, or of human nature, if you like. But anthropologists no longer speak of a narrowly defined human nature. Nowadays, anthropologists use concepts that refer to a broad spectrum of behaviors that represent the human potential, and we determine that by looking not just at our own society, but also at societies that preceded us. These societies would often allow other aspects of the human potential to come to the fore, and we still see those elements present in our own society. Nurturing, caring, sharing, and mutualism; they are all part of our heritage, part of our common humanity. Today, our particular society de-emphasizes those elements, but if we are thinking in terms of a utopia that seeks to actualize real existing potentialities we can draw on those elements and develop them socially. They make it possible for us to think about a world organized along very different lines.

Furthermore, to address the ecological crisis that we find ourselves in, I would argue that we have to recognize first of all that it is a social crisis. It is not a crisis that was created by non-human nature; it is a crisis that was created by the institutions and organizational forms we allow to dominate our society. The economic and political institutions that govern our lives cause this crisis, and we have a responsibility to change them, we can choose to change this society.

The Italian anarchist Errico Malatesta said, "Everything depends on what people are capable of wanting." There is a basic truth to this statement. Today, we are so limited in our ability to think about what we want by what is, that we often forget what could be. And we need to recapture that sense of what could be; we need to recapture an imaginary that can help to guide us toward a more ecological and just future. If we fail to do that, I fear we face a very bleak future. If we take the approach of systems theory, which most futurists follow, in simply projecting what is out into the future, we look at a very dismal picture. But if instead we look at elements in our society today that could be teased out, that could be elaborated and made real, it is not that hard to imagine a very different future. And, with that vision in mind, we can begin to create that different future. This is, ultimately, what utopia is all about: it is about not just imagining, not just theorizing, but of actualizing a new society. In light of the current crises, social ecologists suggest that this should be a society based on a very different set of principles.

Social ecology has a very specific view about how those principles should be derived and what they should be. The vision of social ecology is to re-harmonize people and society with the rest of the natural world. We understand people as a part of the natural world, but we have specific characteristics that give us the ability to influence the environment, to effect and even change the environment in either constructive or destructive ways. This capacity differentiates us from the rest of the natural world.

But when we look at natural history and the process of evolution—which for social ecology is how we constitute nature—we can tease out a series of principles that may help us. Indeed, I believe there are some tendencies in nature that need to inform our vision of the future, if our goal is to re-harmonize people and nature. Those principles should be founded on the fact that in ecosystems there are no hierarchies; nature is non-hierarchical. It is more appropriate to say that nature is mutualistic and that there are interdependencies throughout the natural systems. When we speak of the lion as the "King of Beasts" or the ant as "the lowly ant," we are really projecting our own social structures onto nature, they don't exist there. In a very fundamental sense, these are mutually dependent organisms. Ants help decompose all of the vegetable matter and they play a crucial role even in the rain forests: a wealth of ant species provide the nutrients for the plant life that then support the herbivores which in turn are preyed by the carnivores, by the big cats. The fact is that the lion couldn't exist without the ant. And none of us could exist without the blue-green algae in the oceans that produce 80 percent of the oxygen on our planet. So that very interdependency, that mutualism, very clearly comes through our observations of the natural world, and it should inform our visions of an ecological society.

Within nature we also see a principle called unity in diversity. We can see that the natural eco-systems that have the greatest possibility of thriving and surviving are systems that have the greatest number of species interacting. If we look at a rainforest or an estuary, or a corral reef, they are very complex eco-systems with many different species at every trophic level. In these environments we see that even if one of those species should experience a tremendous decline or even extinction, there are other species that can take over the role that it played. Complex eco-systems maintain balance and in that way. Unity in diversity is a very important ecological principle, because it allows for ecosystems to enrich themselves and support many different kinds of life.

We also see a related tendency toward diversity in natural evolution; to be sure, there has been not a steady incremental movement, and there have certainly been ups and downs, but overall, there has been an undeniable increase in diversity and complexity. According to the general idea of Darwinian evolution, life began as single-cell organisms and has elaborated out into much more complex forms of life. This suggests that within nature, within the course of natural evolution itself, there is a distinct tendency toward ever-greater diversity, ever-greater complexity, and ever-greater degrees of self-consciousness, and ultimately, freedom. These are all principles that social ecology draws on to inform its utopian vision, keeping in mind that our goal is to re-harmonize people and nature. I believe that this gives us a solid basis for creating a set of principles that we can orient our actions toward, but I would, however, suggest that the concept of utopia is most powerful when we understand it not as a blueprint, not as a design in which every detail is worked out, but rather as a set of principles. The principles suggested here can then be used to orient our actions here and now.

Utopia plays a very important role; indeed, it plays a number of important roles. First of all it gives us a vision of what we might want to achieve some day. That is crucial because without a vision of where we want to go, we will have no way of knowing whether we are moving in the right direction or not. This is another aspect of utopia that is very important, it allows us to analyze our actions, the seemingly small steps that we begin to take today. Obviously it will be in process of one step after another that moves us toward utopia, but it allows us to understand whether those steps are taking us in the direction we want to go or are actually moving us somewhere else. Having a vision is also important because it provides a point of inspiration. It's important for people to have something that represents their highest aspirations, rather than having to accept the lowest common denominator that our society hands us today. We need to be able to want something worth wanting. We should take Malatesta's words to heart and be bold when we set our social aims. To create a genuinely ecological society, we need to want something qualitatively different from what we have today and utopia can help us maintain that vision. It can inspire us to maintain our efforts over the long haul, which is necessary because we are not involved in a short-term project: after all, we are never going to actually achieve utopia. Indeed, with all this in mind, we can deal with the concept of utopia on a more mature level and then I definitely think it is worth also retaining the other aspect of utopia—that it is "no place"— that it is unachievable, and I am convinced that this is actually one of its strengths. We are not going to achieve some ultimate end. As we approach our vision, this vision, hopefully, recedes to a new horizon; it evolves and becomes more sophisticated. From the perspective of social ecology, utopia is not something static, it is not a final state, and it can never be fully achieved.

Social ecology does have a particular utopian vision, and that is a non-hierarchical society based on the principles of communal self-management, participatory democracy, and cultural diversity. We envisage a decentralized and balanced society, where all the various social functions that are now compartmentalized, specialized, and blown up to a gigantic scale, would be integrated into a community life. Our vision of an ecological community is one that integrates agriculture, industry, art, spirituality—indeed, all aspects of society—on a scale that is accessible to all and encourages genuinely democratic forms of government.

I know these ideas may sound like a complete fantasy, and perhaps as the unachievable cloud cuckoo land of utopia. But if we begin to think through these ideas carefully, and if we begin to work systematically, I am sure we will come to see their relevance. If we start to transform our communities and work toward an ecological society, we need an approach that can meld bold utopian theories with real political practice.

We need to meld theory with practice, and that practice has to develop on a variety of levels. Very importantly today, we see the need for protest and resistance. We need to raise our voices and say "no!" to those who will befoul the planet, to those that would pollute the oceans, to those who would bring about climate change. We have to be willing to confront the powers that are responsible for those developments. Those who hold power—economic and political power—determine the course of the world today. We must be willing to confront them: the politicians and the political system, the vested interests and the corporations. It is simply not true that we are all greedy consumers and that's why we are in this mess. In fact, there is a corporate agenda that has given us very few options in terms of consumption and production patterns; it has determined for us the kinds of actions we can take. While it is vitally important that we all take personal responsibility for our actions, there are larger actors out there who have much greater responsibility, and they should be confronted. At the same time, is not enough to just say no, we also have to create social and political alternatives. We must have a vision of what should be, but we also need to start building what should be, beginning today, where we are now. To achieve this, we also need to operate on the political level, to systematically create a new form of politics.

Once we start to get politically involved our own communities with the aim of creating an ecological society, we are already engaging in a dauntingly ambitious project. It may seem unnecessary and counterproductive to move our ultimate political aspirations even further away from the actual society in which we live. But I believe that a sober utopianism would make our burden easier to carry, it would be far easier for us to cope with the fact that what is does not at all correspond with what should be. The realities we have to politically orient ourselves in today do not have to shackle our dreams and fetter our aspirations: we *can* create a better future.

Social ecologists seek to create a politics that not only mobilizes people, but that also engages their imagination and their aspirations. Our utopia is not any one individual's blueprint: it will emerge from a collective process. We should all help define what the good society would be like, and how we can possibly achieve it. Together. Because everything depends on what people are capable of wanting.

CLIMATE CHANGE AS A DEMOCRATIC CHALLENGE

BRIAN TOKAR

n September of 2014, 400,000 people filled the streets of New York City, demanding a more urgent response to the global climate crisis. People of all ages and ethnic backgrounds, and from many diverse walks of life, were among the exuberant and determined participants in this historic gathering, deemed the People's Climate March. It was the largest political demonstration in the US since President George W. Bush was preparing to invade Iraq in 2003, and by an order of magnitude the largest environmental protest in more than forty years.

Busloads of marchers came to New York from every part of the US on that inspiring day; there was even a train to bring people from the West Coast. Many came prepared with homemade signs, and some with elaborate costumes and parade floats, seeking to dramatize the ways their communities are affected by climate disruptions, as well as the particular solutions they favored. Indigenous peoples, peace activists, advocates for women's rights, opponents of fracking for gas and oil, and adherents of several religious traditions were only a few of the most prominent contingents.

One significant bloc, including representatives of organized labor, gathered around the slogan, "System Change, Not Climate Change," which had first appeared on the streets of Copenhagen five years earlier during a rather more optimistic time in the evolution of global climate policies. On the Monday morning following the march, thousands of activists with a view toward the underlying, systemic roots of the climate crisis converged near Wall Street to obstruct business as usual in New York's fabled financial district. Both events demonstrated an increasing breadth and depth of climate concern among the population of a country that has long been a significant obstacle to international climate diplomacy.

It has become a matter of everyday wisdom for scientists and activists alike that global climate change is the defining issue of our time. Disruption of the earth's climate patterns, mainly due to over a century of emissions of carbon dioxide from fossil fuel combustion and related technologies, has become a central challenge for human societies worldwide, and also for the continued practice of democracy. Indeed, with some weather extremes exceeding anything experienced in the entire history of human civilization, several prominent voices have come to question the survival of civilization itself.

In the US, advocates for a "Deep Green Resistance" argue that the preservation of biodiversity is inherently incompatible with civilization as we know it. In the UK, a group known as Dark Mountain offers a more contemplative outlook, but similarly suggests that human civilizations are likely doomed to collapse. Even Noam Chomsky, the world-renowned scholar and social critic, argued in a recent column that the coincidence of massive climate disruptions and an increasingly out-of-control militarism suggests a fundamental challenge to civilization such as we have not experienced since the Middle Ages or even mythical times.[1] In a cultural climate of widespread despair, and a pervasive dystopianism in popular culture, it is often challenging to identify more promising and politically forward-looking approaches.[2]

When mainstream media address the issue, the focus is most often on the ever-increasing scientific evidence for anthropogenic climate disruptions. Studies of melting glaciers, rising sea levels, and threats to charismatic Arctic species such as polar bears still tend to dominate the headlines. As essential as it is for the public to remain abreast of such developments, the climate dimensions of more immediate human problems often remain hidden. Most notable among these is the dramatic rise in extreme weather events, which have become the "new normal" worldwide and now threaten ways of life that some cultures have sustained for millennia.

Over the past decade, devastating patterns of floods, droughts, wildfires and other catastrophic weather events have disrupted life on every continent. They disproportionately impact the people who are most vulnerable, and who also contribute the least to the excessive emissions of greenhouse gases that lie at the heart of the problem. This is the core, underlying message of climate justice, a theme to which we will return shortly. Accelerating weather catastrophes mainly affect the earth's most remote regions, but in recent years they have begun to affect people and ecosystems nearly everywhere.

The names of some of the most notable events lie deep within everyone's memory now; in the US these include Hurricane Katrina, which drowned the city of New Orleans in 2005, and Tropical Storm Sandy, which devastated coastal communities in the New York metropolitan area and beyond in 2012. Droughts and massive wildfires have become an annual occurrence in much of the American West: the agricultural zones of California are rapidly running out of water and frequent, sometimes untamable wildfires have spread from the desert Southwest into the temperate rainforests of the Pacific Northwest.

The consequences are far more severe throughout the global South. The California drought pales in comparison to the drought that has plagued the Horn of Africa for many years now, forcing hundreds of thousands of people to flee their parched fields for refugee camps and urban slums in Kenya and beyond. When the Indus River in the heart of Pakistan overflowed its banks in 2010, it flooded a fifth of that country's landmass. Neighborhoods in major South Asian cities, from Bangkok to Jakarta, have flooded in recent years. On the eve of 2013's UN climate conference in Warsaw, Typhoon Haiyan became the most powerful tropical storm ever to reach landfall, devastating scores of Philippine islands. Catastrophic early December typhoons in the Philippines have become a nearly annual occurrence.

Of course there still remains some scientific uncertainty around the climate dimensions of specific weather events; the analysis required to determine how particular events are shaped by longer-term trends is exacting and often still controversial, even among climate scientists. But a few basic facts are clear. First, it is a fundamental physical fact that warm air holds more moisture. Atmospheric water vapor has increased by 4 percent since the 1970s, amplifying precipitation and storms by 5-10 percent.[3] Clouds accumulate more water over a longer period of time and have more water to release when conditions are finally ripe for rainfall. The 2014 US National Climate Assessment reported that a consistently higher proportion of precipitation now falls in the form of very heavy storms, up to a 71 percent increase in the northeastern US compared to twentieth century norms.[4]

Second, the turbulent weather we are now experiencing is precisely what climate scientists have been predicting for several decades, based upon increasingly sophisticated computer models of the global climate. Climatologist James Hansen describes the continuing shift away from the relatively stable climate state that prevailed for much of human history as analogous to playing a game with loaded dice.[5] Nearly thirty years have passed since the world has experienced a single month that averaged below normal in temperature based on twentieth century norms.[6] The parallel and consistent predictions of various climate models strengthen the case that extreme weather is significantly the result of a changing climate.

Third, several studies have set out to precisely calculate the actual contribution of global climate shifts to specific weather events. One of the first detailed studies, which appeared in the prestigious journal *Nature* in early 2011, examined the climate component of a series of catastrophic floods in England and Wales during the autumn of 2000. The study took ten years to complete and mobilized a vast network of volunteers to offer surplus time on their home and office computers in order to run thousands of forecast scenarios and complete the required calculations. The researchers, based in the UK, Switzerland and Japan, determined that recent climate changes indeed made those severe storms far more likely, with a high level of statistical precision.[7] A 2014 study of recent heat waves in Australia, Europe and east Asia confirmed an unambiguous climate link.[8] On the other hand, studies of the continuing California drought agree that climate change has worsened its impacts, but scientists are still divided as to whether human-induced warming is the main underlying cause.

While detailed knowledge of climate science and its approach to understanding weather extremes varies widely, even among climate activists, the broad outlines of this analysis are generally well known. What is far more lacking, however, is any clear agreement about what we can do. From the earliest mainstream writings about global warming, people have suggested that a failure of adequate preventive actions will raise the likelihood of an authoritarian response to climate instability. Most notably, in his 1992 book, *Earth in the Balance*, soon-to-be US Vice President Al Gore recounted the history of societal responses to past weather catastrophes, which in his view paralleled the rise of "the bureaucratic, administrative tendencies of the modern state." If societies are unable to anticipate and prevent climate-related disasters, we could see, in Gore's words, "a new worldwide bureaucracy to manage the unimaginable problems caused by massive social and political upheavals."[9] Gore's suggestion was to instead launch a "Global Marshall Plan" for renewable energy development, driven by a largely imaginary US technological and organizational superiority.

When Gore's book came out more than twenty years ago, it was already clear that this was not going to happen, as the US had already fallen far behind Europe and other regions in advancing solar and wind technologies, and was also in the forefront of a neoliberal world order that would systematically undermine ambitious public sector initiatives. The subsequent evolution of international climate diplomacy has been one of steadily declining expectations, significantly driven by the obstinacy of both Republican and Democratic US administrations.

Meanwhile, many cities, towns, and a few entire countries have advanced more forward-looking climate measures, seeking to compensate in part for the lack of progress on a global scale. Simultaneously, an emerging climate justice movement echoes the voices of the most vulnerable peoples and is challenging an expansive new wave of high-risk fossil fuel extraction. Let us trace the evolution of those differing approaches to the climate crisis, and then consider some potential paths toward a more comprehensive democratic resolution.

Global climate diplomacy was launched on a relatively hopeful note at the 1992 "Earth Summit" in Rio de Janeiro, with the drafting of the original UN Framework Convention on Climate Change (UNFCCC). Most notable in that founding document was an acknowledgement that the world's peoples have a "common but differentiated responsibility" for the unfolding climate crisis. Some countries have produced massive quantities of carbon dioxide and other greenhouse gases over many generations, while others have contributed relatively little to the problem. The document acknowledged from the outset that the major industrialized countries should be chiefly responsible for reducing their emissions, developing non-polluting energy sources, and sharing new technologies with poorer countries.

In many ways, that initial global summit was the high point of the process to date. The first round of efforts to implement the climate convention's terms culminated in Kyoto in 1997 with the first internationally agreed-upon targets for reducing greenhouse gas emissions. But the US delegation, representing the administration of Bill Clinton and Al Gore, threatened to derail the proceedings by refusing to accept mandatory emissions cuts. Gore flew to Kyoto, supposedly to "save the day," but his intervention altered the discussion in ways that significantly undermined the emerging global consensus. Gore offered that the US would agree to emissions reductions only half as stringent as were previously on the table. To implement these reductions, he proposed a global market in tradable carbon emissions credits and the transformation of a proposed "Green Development Fund" into yet another market mechanism, whereby companies would offset their own carbon dioxide emissions by investing in nominally low-carbon projects in the global South.[10] Even with these changes, the US Congress refused to ratify the Kyoto Protocol, but the rest of the world has had to live with the consequences of a cumbersome and inherently inadequate carbon trading system that has thoroughly failed to bring needed pollution reductions.

Since the Copenhagen climate summit in 2009 failed to launch an anticipated second round of emissions reductions by developed countries, the always-shaky diplomatic consensus around mandatory cuts in greenhouse gases has essentially collapsed. The US delegation arrived in Copenhagen with a plan to replace international emissions standards with a patchwork of voluntary, country-specific pledges to reduce global warming pollution.[11] In subsequent years, most countries outside of Western Europe that were subject to Kyoto's original emissions limits formally withdrew from the Protocol, including Japan, Australia, Canada, Russia, and New Zealand. Dialogue between countries of the global North and South became increasingly polarized as the US moved to dilute the long-standing focus on "common but differentiated responsibilities" and remove all explicit references to climate equity from the UNFCCC process.

As the world's elites edge toward a new climate agreement, scheduled to be signed in Paris at the end of 2015, the focus has shifted entirely toward the US-initiated proposals for voluntary national "mitigation commitments." At the 2013 climate conference in Warsaw, the language was further diluted from commitments to "contributions," and legal status of pledges by various national governments remained undefined. At one point, global South delegates walked out *en masse* from the proceedings to protest wealthy countries' dismissal of their concerns. A year later, in Lima, Peru, the last major UN climate conference before Paris ended with an agreement to move forward with "Intended Nationally Determined Contributions" to climate mitigation, but without any clear benchmarks, timetables, transparency rules, nor agreed-upon financing mechanisms.

In a speech in the UK during the lead-up to the 2013 climate conference, the US chief climate negotiator Todd Stern brushed aside the issue of compensation for present-day climate damages, put forward by global South delegates, as merely an "ideological narrative of fault and blame," and insisted that no significant public funds for international climate aid would be forthcoming beyond the meager $2.5 billion that the US has committed annually since 2010; in Copenhagen, US officials had promised to raise $100 billion a year from Northern countries in order to win acceptance for the voluntary approach to emissions cuts. Further, Stern dismissed the long-standing principle of responsibility for historic CO_2 emissions, declaring with unsurpassed arrogance that, "It is unwarranted to assign blame to developed countries for emissions before the point at which people realized that those emissions caused harm to the climate system."[12] Of course this completely overlooks the fact at least half of all cumulative emissions have occurred since 1980, with a much larger share occurring since the very first observations of rising atmospheric carbon dioxide levels in the late 1950s.

With global climate diplomacy continuing to falter, many activists and public officials have turned toward implementing climate measures at the local and sometimes national levels. While some of these policies might be folded into countries' national "contributions," local climate measures are widely viewed as a means to overcome diplomatic inertia and reclaim a sense of local initiative, while demonstrating the feasibility of more ambitious steps forward. Countries such as Germany and Denmark have received the most widespread attention for their efforts to rapidly increase the renewable portion of their electricity supplies to 30-40 percent, aiming for a complete conversion within a few decades. In Germany, this is largely the outcome of four decades of effective anti-nuclear activism, which eventually pressured the ruling Christian Democrats to phase out nuclear power in the aftermath of Fukushima.[13] The most ambitious national projects are often the cumulative result of policies that mainly emerged from the local level.

Despite the Obama administration's continuing preference for voluntary measures, several US cities and states have mandated energy-saving and renewable energy enhancing initiatives similar to those that have succeeded in Europe, albeit on a more limited scale. These include "renewable portfolio standards" that require utilities to obtain a rising share of their power supplies from renewable sources, net metering and feed-in tariffs to help subsidize home- and farm-scale producers of solar and wind energy, and measures to attach loans for fuel-saving equipment to home mortgages to facilitate easier financing. Cities are advancing zoning changes to encourage higher downtown population densities to limit urban sprawl, strengthening building codes to mandate energy savings, building infrastructure to charge electric vehicles, and supporting urban farms and relocalized food systems.[14] A few US cities are even expanding their public transportation systems despite continuing pressures toward fiscal austerity. Such local measures clearly demonstrate the feasibility of various alternatives, but by themselves are far from sufficient to prevent accelerating climate chaos.

To realize more ambitious goals will require the continued evolution of a bold and effective climate movement, led by organizations committed to a justice-centered perspective. Climate justice, as we have seen, highlights the experiences and demands of people around the world who contribute the least to excessive greenhouse gas emissions, but live with the most severe consequences of accelerating climate chaos. As an emerging movement, climate justice unites three distinct elements, with roots in particular regions of the world. Some of the most compelling voices are those of indigenous and other land-based peoples, mainly in the global South, who have raised crucial demands at the UN and other settings emerging from their communities' unique vulnerability to climate disruptions. In North America, organizers for racial and environmental justice bring the experience of their historical roots in the civil rights movement, a lived understanding of the effects of climate change on marginalized communities, and essential links to other justice-based movements around food, healthcare, transportation, and other basic social needs.

In Europe and beyond, explicitly anti-capitalist formations contribute an essential critical dimension, with origins in the global justice movements of the late 1990s and early 2000s and a focus on the systemic nature of the climate crisis. In the aftermath of the Copenhagen debacle,

European climate justice activists declared that "Climate Justice means linking all struggles together that reject neoliberal markets and working towards a world that puts autonomous decision making power in the hands of communities."[15] Internationally, groups from the Indigenous Environmental Network to the youthful direct action network known as Rising Tide bring an added focus upon the many corporate-driven false solutions to the climate crisis, including nuclear power, biomass incineration and biofuels, as well as the continued reliance on carbon markets to achieve—more often to evade—internationally mandated emissions reductions. And today, climate justice activists are in the forefront of challenging what may be the largest expansion of fossil fuel infrastructure since the post-World War II era.

With more easily accessible sources of fossil fuels rapidly diminishing, energy companies have embarked on an all-out effort to extract oil, gas and coal from previously inaccessible locations, using increasingly extreme forms of extraction. Industry projections for the future of fossil fuels are increasingly tied to so-called "unconventional" sources such as tar sands, shale gas, and oil drilled from miles beneath the oceans, including the far reaches of the Arctic, and each of these has been the focus of a renewed opposition by affected communities around the world. The emergence of new communities of resistance to tar sands oil, fracking for oil and gas, and the construction of new pipeline networks may be the most persistent contribution of the evolving climate justice movement. Indeed South African scholar and activist Patrick Bond aptly describes the current state of climate justice as one of "global pessimism and local optimism," with a growing movement from below in response to "paralysis above."[16]

This movement has an impressive record of accomplishments at the local level. In the US, local activists, aided by the national Sierra Club, have prevented the construction of more than 170 proposed new coal-fired power plants and shut down many existing ones. In western Canada, a month-long encampment led by indigenous First Nations along the route of a major proposed tar sands pipeline, forced the company to pack up and leave the area. Scores of cities, towns, states and regions have voted to ban fracking for gas and oil, and local protests have helped force the cancellation of plans to build several new export terminals for fossil fuels from the US. Naomi Klein reports in her recent book that successful grassroots campaigns against fossil fuel expansion have even spread to India and China.[17]

Local activists are also looking forward toward a different kind of energy future, and ultimately a different economic system that could encourage rather than undermine meaningful climate solutions. Beyond the incremental policy measures already mentioned here, visionary architects and planners are working to redesign cities to reduce commuting and minimize energy use. Permaculture activists are bringing ecologically designed, edible landscapes into communities, while saving both water and energy. A youth-initiated rebellion against rising transit fares in Scandinavian countries sparked a global movement for free public transportation.[18] Food and farm activists are reinvigorating urban farming around the world, demanding genuine food sovereignty, and advancing local alternatives that save energy, improve public health, empower marginalized communities, and challenge the hegemony of global agribusiness.

Improvements at the local level are not sufficient, even though they do offer a wealth of benefits relative to more top-down measures. Local solutions are far more likely to be democratically structured and accountable to those who are most affected by the outcomes. They help build closer relationships among neighbors and strengthen the capacity for self-reliance. They enable us to see that the institutions that now dominate our lives are far less essential for our daily sustenance than we are often led to believe. But how do we spark a broader transformation that is ultimately more than the sum of its dispersed local expressions? In the face of still-rising emissions of greenhouse gases worldwide, we clearly need to reach beyond the existing pockets of local consciousness toward a global movement that can address the full magnitude of the present crisis, overturn the status quo, and usher in a different kind of world. Changes are necessary in the technological, social and political spheres that go far beyond what is presently considered feasible.

In the realm of technology, we know the means already exist to supply our energy needs with renewable technologies that rely on the sun and wind, and that agroecological farming methods are far more resilient in the face of a changing climate than those advanced by agribusiness corporations. Analysts such as Mark Jacobson as Stanford University and Amory Lovins of the Rocky Mountain Institute have demonstrated the feasibility of a rapid conversion to a fundamentally different energy system, but such analyses rarely address the underlying problem that social ecologist Murray Bookchin described as the "social matrix" of technology. We need to consider all the ways in which technological developments reflect, and ultimately reinforce, the social contexts from which they emerge and then approach the problem of technological change in a manner that accurately reflects this systemic understanding.[19]

While mainstream accounts celebrate the reality that solar and wind projects are finally reaching "price parity" with fossil fuel energy, commercial investors are losing interest. Investments in renewable energy began to decline over the past year or two, as they rarely achieve the mega-profits still obtainable from fossil fuels. And corporate developers are generally far more interested in large-scale projects that promise higher profits, rather than the locally-scaled and community-owned solar and wind power installations that can point the way toward a genuine alternative. One recent study suggests that the vast majority of new non-fossil energy is adding new capacity to the system rather than replacing fossil-derived power.[20] Indeed fossil fuels are so central to the history of capitalism that the energy and economic systems have become virtually inseparable. As a recent study from the British research group, The Corner House, states:

> The entire contemporary system of making profits out of labor depended absolutely on cheap fossil carbon [and therefore] there is no cheap or politically-feasible substitute for fossil fuels in the triple combination of fossil fuels-heat engines-commodified labor that underpins current rates of capital accumulation.[21]

In the social realm, however, we are seeing the re-emergence of traditional modes of community control and governance around the world, partly in response to the rise of neoliberal and extractivist policies. This renewal of the commons in the face of hegemonic state and corporate power has been noted by scholars and activists alike, and can be seen as a popular, grassroots alternative to capitalist models of so-called "sustainable development." The reclaiming of the commons invokes some quite ancient modes of local governance that often transcend conventional notions of public or private ownership. But the idea of the commons also arises in uniquely contemporary instances, such as resistance to the neoliberal privatization of public assets and defense of wholly new kinds of commons, from communications airwaves and the Internet to the integrity of living cells' genetic sequences.[22] Scholars of the commons celebrate cooperative enterprises and various models of workers' control, but also the traditions that have established many indigenous communities as the most consistent and reliable stewards of the land. As the former editors of *The Ecologist* magazine explained in a pioneering 1993 book:

> The evidence is overwhelming that local-level institutions in which power is limited and the common right to survival is the preoccupation of all, are the best means of repairing the damage done through enclosure. Equally overwhelming is the evidence that "non-local, state-management systems are both costly and ineffective."[23]

In the political sphere, social ecology's strategy of confederal municipalism presents a uniquely promising way forward.[24] This strategy proposes a revolutionary, community-centered politics, rooted in democratic citizen assemblies, regional confederations and cooperative economic practices. Social ecologists envision confederations of free communities contesting political power, overturning dominant institutions, and rooting their political praxis in long-standing ethical principles of reciprocity and complementarity.[25]

Kurdish communities in some areas of Turkey and Syria are today actively implementing this approach, which they describe as a "democratic confederalism." One recent study describes the Association of Communities in Kurdistan (KCK) as a bottom-up organization governed by local citizen assemblies. "In its founding text, the *KCK Contract*," the authors write, "its main aim is defined in terms of a struggle for the expansion of a radical democracy which is based upon peoples' democratic organizations and decision-making power."[26] This approach has enabled many Kurdish communities to move forward with ambitious programs to achieve gender equity and ecological reconstruction, even in a region wracked by sectarian warfare and persistent religious violence.

The reconstructive social and political outlook of social ecology is reinforced by more traditional anti-authoritarian approaches to social movement organizing, looking to the emergence of a "movement of movements" to achieve systemic changes that may lie beyond the scope of current possibilities. This historical outlook was revived by the worldwide global justice movement that successfully challenged international financial institutions during the late 1990s and early 2000s. While that movement sometimes embraced older community-based organizing efforts more in rhetoric than in its praxis, its horizontalist organizing methods were further developed and expanded in recent years by the dynamic global movement that staged massive occupations of public squares in major cities around the world. Activists challenging austerity policies and rising social inequality continue to develop strategies that combine resistance to the status quo with the creation of local, grassroots alternatives. In the realm of public policy, these movements often adopt a strategy of seeking "non-reformist reforms" that can serve to actively advance more fundamental and systemic changes, an approach that is rooted in the history of many of the last century's most dynamic community-based movements.

Of course not all social movements that are organized at the local level seek positive, reconstructive changes. In both Europe and North America, forces of the far right have adopted the rhetoric of local control to further regressive, ultra-nationalist and often extremely racist ends. For example, when the fast-growing UK Independence Party proclaims that "real decision-making should be given to local communities," they seek to further marginalize immigrant populations, oppose renewable energy developments, and even try to ban discussions of climate change in local schools.[27] Racist organizations in the American South have long hidden behind localist rhetoric. Murray Bookchin always insisted that a more consistently liberatory localism would emerge from the practice of direct democracy, with communities acting as "a school for creating a new kind of citizenship," rooted in participatory self-governance and an expansive ecological ethics.[28]

Still we cannot predict whether current movements for climate justice and community empowerment will be able to achieve the revolutionary changes we seek. We know there are significant political differences, even among those who share a liberatory anti-authoritarian outlook. Some adopt a pragmatic stance toward the nation-state, seeking to expand the scope of necessary public sector initiatives within the limits dictated by current political structures, while others advocate a principled rejection of statecraft. But we can unite around the desire for more expansive models of community-centered governance and a thoroughgoing social and political reconstruction. There is little doubt that the coming decades' climate changes will be disruptive and difficult, but we still may be able to prevent them from becoming catastrophic and extreme. We will need to keep our eyes on the prize and continue discovering new ways to challenge the systems that dominate our lives.

NOTES:

1. Noam Chomsky, "The End of History?" *In These Times*, September 4, 2014.

2. For a fuller discussion of contemporary dystopianism and its possible antidotes, see Chapter 5 of Brian Tokar, *Toward Climate Justice: Perspectives on the Climate Crisis and Social Change*, revised edition (Porsgrunn, Norway: New Compass Press, 2014).

3. Kevin Trenberth, "Framing the way to relate climate extremes to climate

change," *Climatic Change* 115:2 (2012), 283-290.

4. *Climate Change Impacts in the United States: Overview and Report Findings* (Washington, DC: US Global Change Research Program, 2014), 9.

5. James Hansen, Makiko Sato, and Reto Ruedy, "Perception of climate change," *Proceedings of the National Academy of Sciences* 109 (2012), 14726-14727.

6. James Samenow, "February caps 29-year streak of warmer than normal months on Earth," *Washington Post online*, March 19, 2014.

7. Pardeep Pall, et al., "Anthropogenic greenhouse gas contribution to flood risk in England and Wales in autumn 2000," *Nature* 470 (2011), 382-86.

8. Justin Gillis, "Scientists Trace Extreme Heat in Australia to Climate Change," *New York Times*, September 30, 2014.

9. Al Gore, *Earth in the Balance: Ecology and the Human Spirit* (Boston: Houghton Mifflin, 1992), 73, 79.

10. See Tokar, *Toward Climate Justice*, 104-6.

11. Ibid., 57-59, 62-64.

12. Todd D. Stern, "The Shape of a New International Climate Agreement" (London, October 2013), at http://www.state.gov/e/oes/rls/ remarks/2013/215720.htm.

13. Critics appropriately point out that Germany has simultaneously increased coal use; German activists assert that this is due to policies independent of their country's renewable energy transition, and which they are actively opposing. See Naomi Klein, *This Changes Everything: Capitalism vs. the Climate* (New York: Simon & Schuster, 2014), 138.

14. For a detailed description of these various measures, see T. Linstroth and R. Bell, *Local Action: The New Paradigm in Climate Change Policy* (Burlington: University of Vermont Press, 2007).

15. "What does Climate Justice mean in Europe? A Discussion Paper," via Climate Justice Action email list (March 26, 2010).

16. Patrick Bond, "Is the Climate Justice Movement Ready to Scale-Jump Our Politics?" *Telesur TV online*, December 4, 2014.

17. Klein, *This Changes Everything*, 350-52.

18. See http://freepublictransports.com.

19. Murray Bookchin, *The Ecology of Freedom: The Emergence and Dissolution of Hierarchy* (Palo Alto, CA: Cheshire Books, 1982), Chapter 11. On the

contributions of Jacobson, Lovins, and other contemporary writers on technology, see Tokar, *Toward Climate Justice*, 125-127, 153-154.

20. Richard York, "Do alternative energy sources displace fossil fuels?" *Nature Climate Change* 2 (June 2012), 441-443.

21. Larry Lohmann and Nicholas Hildyard, *Energy, Work, and Finance* (Dorset, UK: The Corner House, 2014), 18, 38.

22. Author David Bollier has written extensively about these new commons; for example see his *Silent Theft: The Private Plunder of Our Common Wealth* (New York: Routledge, 2002).

23. The Ecologist, *Whose Common Future? Reclaiming the Commons* (Philadelphia: New Society Publishers, 1993), 193. The book's contributors include the Corner House authors cited above (supra note 21); the embedded quote is from a 1989 UK study cited therein (p. 211, note 34).

24. This approach is also known as "libertarian municipalism," drawing upon traditional, anarchistic uses of the word "libertarian," prior to its more recent appropriation by the propertarian right.

25. Bookchin describes "complementarity" as a traditional ethical principle through which communities seek to compensate for differences among their members.

26. Joost Jongerden and Ahmet Hamdi Akkaya, "Democratic Confederalism as a Kurdish Spring: The PKK and the Quest for Radical Democracy," in Mohammed M.A. Ahmed and Michael M. Gunter, editors, *The Kurdish Spring: Geopolitical Changes and the Kurds* (Costa Mesa, CA: Mazda Publishers, 2013), 179.

27. Rob Hopkins, "Four reasons why too much local democracy can be a bad thing," at www.transitionnetwork.org (May 2014).

28. Murray Bookchin, "Market Economy or Moral Economy?" in *The Modern Crisis* (Philadelphia: New Society Publishers, 1986), 95.

WOULD PARTICIPATORY DEMOCRACY BE BETTER FOR THE CLIMATE?

SVEINUNG LEGARD

Most environmentalists think democracy should be deepened to deal with global warming. Some believe that this democratization can take place by improving the democratic qualities of existing institutions, while others think these institutions should be replaced with participatory democracies. Would participatory democracy really be better for the climate? How strong is the case that such institutions would actually make us more eager and better equipped to find permanent solutions to global warming than those which dominate our world today?

To discuss these questions I sketch out what I see as the main arguments for participatory democracy found among environmental activists and ecological thinkers. Although it is unlikely that the reader will encounter the arguments I present in this form in any particular text, it is not my intention to distort others' arguments or create more easily criticized straw arguments. Rather, I wish to present a huge diversity of claims in a more orderly, simplified, and sometimes exaggerated manner to assess their strengths and weaknesses more clearly. Therefore, I have avoided citations throughout the text.

There are many definitions of *participatory democracy*. Social ecology, to which this book is dedicated, provides one of them. I use the term "participatory democracy" here to signify the direct involvement of citizens in important decision making processes, along with an egalitarian distribution of economic and political powers. I have chosen not to provide a more precise or elaborate definition than this, because I simply want to explore the *idea* that a participatory politics would be better for the climate than the one we have today.

I will not provide "proof" that participatory democracy will reduce carbon emissions more than our current system, nor any "proof" to the contrary. Instead, I assess whether some of the most common arguments in favor of participatory democracy provide a compelling case, if there are contradictions within them, if they overlook important counterarguments, or are otherwise flawed.

Perhaps the most common argument for participatory democracy found among environmentalists is *the anti-capitalist argument*. It exists in numerous versions, and goes something like this:

The climate crisis is a systemic crisis stemming from the way our economy works. Relentless expansion and growth—the imperatives of capitalism—are changing the Earth's climate. Furthermore, wealth and power in capitalism are concentrated in the hands of the few. As such, capitalism is both antithetical to democracy and at the heart of the climate crisis.

The strength of this argument is that it shows how the climate crisis is not the result of ill judgment or ignorance, but is a crisis of systemic nature. The main aim of capitalist enterprises is to increase the profits of its owners, and if they cannot expand and grow they will be eaten by others in the marketplace. Left unregulated, capitalism will sacrifice collective environmental concerns for individual wealth accumulation. It has to be noted, however, that it is capitalism in a specific form, where relentless economic growth is combined with the burning of fossil fuels such as coal, oil, and gas as the main sources of energy that drives global warming.

For environmentalists, the main enemies in the struggle to implement carbon taxes or emission cuts are multinational corporations and powerful business groups from the energy sector, often backed by governments afraid to endanger their international competitiveness. Fighting these corporations and governments has led many environmentalists to link democracy, anti-capitalism, and climate change.

This argument usually implies that ecological economics also have to be democratic, with economic resources more evenly distributed. But there are two problems with this assumption. First, it is not unthinkable that capitalism could be replaced by an even more authoritarian system. Second, even if we are able to create a democratic alternative to capitalism, there is nothing in this argument that tells us why a democratic economy would be better for the climate than the one we have today. Even if we agree that our current economic order has to drastically change to tackle global warming, we still have to make the case for why a participatory economic order would be an ecological one.

Another argument that makes the connection between democracy and the climate is *the global justice argument*:

The world's poorest farmers, land-workers and urban slum dwellers will face the worst effects of global warming. The rich will be able to pay their way out of the crisis. Change will not happen until the poor and exploited of the world regain control of their lives and the forces affecting them. This means democratizing control of economic resources on a global scale.

The more radical version of this argument holds that the communities most affected by climate change have to be reimbursed by the biggest carbon dioxide polluters—such as industrial nations and multinational corporations—for losses to their livelihood and quality of life. The democratic aspect of this proposal is that these communities should also be given a central role in decision-making processes concerning how resources can be used sustainably.

A more moderate version of the climate justice argument focuses on "giving voice" to vulnerable populations within UN climate negotiations. Proponents of this more moderate version basically advocate improved *representation* of affected communities and populations in relevant decision-making processes.

In either version, this argument does not require that affected communities are organized in a participatory manner. Many communities affected by climate change are organized hierarchically, but still deserve a special place in climate negotiations. And even if these communities are organized according to participatory principles, it does not mean that the rest of the world participating in these processes will be.

A fair distribution of economic resources globally is not the same thing as a democratization of the economy, as a redistribution of economic resources between countries does not necessarily entail a redistribution within them. Moreover, democratizing the economy does not automatically lead to climate change mitigation. Nations or communities with newfound revenues may voluntarily choose fossil fuel based energy resources to boost economic development.

Another phenomenon that environmentalists connect to participatory democracy is social movement mobilization. I call this *the pressure-from-below argument*:

> *Most major advancements in environmental legislation and policy have been the result of grassroots pressures—not government or corporate initiative. Normally, states and corporations are forced to change to more environmentally friendly practices because of pressure from outside movements. Instead of top-down solutions, climate change mitigation will have to come from the bottom-up.*

Like the two previous arguments, this one also presents an ecological critique of the current political order. Capitalism not only gives corporations disproportionate influence in decision-making processes, but forces national governments to place international competitiveness before environmental concerns. Therefore, increased civil society and social movement participation in government is necessary to deal with global warming.

However, it is difficult to see this as an argument for participatory democracy. For one, the social movements that have led to advancements in environmental legislation and policy constitute a minority in society. Not only are such movements more progressive than governments and corporations, they are also more progressive than the general public. If an environmentally progressive social movement that strove for participatory democracy was politically successful, it could actually face the paradoxical situation of dealing with a citizenry that wanted to continue with current carbon emission levels. Many environmentalists are acutely aware of this—especially when it comes to global warming— which is why the pressure-from-below argument is sometimes used against, and not for, participatory democracy.

Furthermore, it is problematic to equate democracy within social movements with a potential society-wide participatory democracy, as some people do. Even if movements practice a strong internal democracy that "prefigures" non-hierarchical structures that may exist in the future, a movement is not the same thing as a government. Unlike movements that fight for a limited number of demands and organize participants around activities that encompass only parts of their lives, governments are involved in an almost unlimited number of issues, as well as the coordination and regulation of most activities. Social movements cannot "prefigure" or replace such a political structure. But even if movements cannot prefigure entire governments, there remains an undeniable element of path clearing to which social movements can contribute.

The arguments mentioned so far primarily critique existing institutions on ecological grounds. Other arguments contend that there could be environmental benefits from participatory democracy. The first of these is *the majority interest argument*.

The continual destruction of the natural environment is not in the interest of the majority of the world's population. This destruction is due to economic and political processes that benefit only a few. The majority depend on healthy and functioning ecosystems for their livelihood, well-being, and survival. In a participatory democracy, the interests of the many will be prioritized, and this will likely include climate change mitigation.

However, there are a few notable objections to these claims. First, they overlook potential conflicts of interest on environmental issues such as climate change. The fallout of global warming is unevenly distributed globally in ways that both affect certain minorities adversely and most majorities differently. As one example, this can be a source of conflict over the extent of fossil fuel use in the transition to renewable energy sources. Second, the argument implies that majorities automatically act rationally in the pursuit of their interests. Like individuals, majorities can also fall prey to irrational proclivities and choose immediate benefits over long-term gains, such as using fossil fuels to achieve short term growth, even if it has negative long-term consequences.

Like any other political system, a participatory democracy will need institutions that prevent, negotiate, and resolve conflicts between geographically dispersed majorities. Proponents of participatory democracy often suggest confederal structures that facilitate economic interdependence and cultural exchange between people settled in different areas.

Advocates of participatory democracy are also aware of the dangers of collective irrationality, and maintain that participatory institutions have to follow practices of "deliberative" democracy in order to arrive at the best possible decisions. Although deliberative practices, such as informed and balanced discussions, or civility and respect among participants, can also be achieved with representative institutions, conditions for "ideal" deliberation—such as formal equality between participants, and the absence of social, cultural, and economic hierarchies that informally limit the participation of some citizens—are better satisfied in a participatory system where power is evenly distributed.

However, there is a third and more challenging objection to the majority interest argument, which is concerned with the interests of future generations. It is only possible to equate the interests of majorities living today with those that will inhabit the future if we assume that most people have an interest in healthy living-conditions for their children and grand-children. But this becomes murkier if we think several centuries into the future, as we have to do when it comes to global warming.

A related objection against participatory democracy, is that ordinary citizens are ultimately too selfish, apathetic and unwilling to make the changes required to achieve ecological balance. Hence, climate change would become worse if the majority ruled. Here, another argument, *the responsibility argument*, comes to the aid.

Representative democracy fosters egoism and inertia among citizens, as they are only expected to participate in politics during elections and otherwise stay passive. Instead of taking control of their consumption, transportation, and living patterns, citizens react to incentives and directives issued by elected leaders. Participatory democracy, on the other hand, fosters a greater sense of responsibility for the climate among citizens, since they are directly involved in making choices that impact the environment.

This argument both identifies incentives for environmentally negative behavior within a representative system, as well as for environmentally positive behavior within a participatory one. The only significant power assigned to the general population in a representative system is to hold their leaders accountable in elections. It therefore encourages citizens to renounce responsibility for the consequences of their leaders' choices. A participatory system, on the other side, forces citizens to consider the environmental impacts of their choices, and to deal with the consequences of environmentally negative private actions, since these eventually become political problems.

A representative system encourages citizens to think and deliberate publicly during short election periods, but a participatory system encourages them to do so permanently. Public thinking and deliberating requires citizens to consider others' perspectives and the wider impact of political and private choices. Direct democracy entails an omnipresent possibility of being held accountable for these. Since the climate crisis has to be solved with a common effort in a variety of arenas—both private and political—the ecological advantage of such a system could be crucial.

However, we should not equate taking responsibility with taking the right type of action. Even though a sense of responsibility for the well-being of present and future generations is important in dealing with the causes of global warming, it does not automatically translate into effective solutions to the problem. There are also restraints to citizen participation. One of these is time, which prevents many types of discussions and decisions to be taken in common by all citizens. To have a functioning democracy, it is necessary to balance direct participation with both institutional differentiation (where different institutions have different tasks) and forms of representation (where certain people are delegated decision-making powers). The questions of accountability and the danger of disclaiming responsibility remain present in a participatory democracy.

Decentralization is another phenomenon which is related to both democracy and climate change.

Increased local self-determination enables communities to protect themselves from outside forces who wish to extract resources located within their borders in ways that destroy the environment and place undue risks on its inhabitants. Increased local food and industrial production makes communities more dependent on local ecological resources, and therefore increases their awareness of potentially negative environmental consequences of their activities. Moreover, a successful transition to solar, wind, and water power depends on the active engagement of communities.

One of the advantages of *the decentralization argument* is the attention it gives to the role of local communities in the transition to an ecological society. Increased self-determination is important strategically to stop environmentally predatory practices conducted by companies backed by centralized governments. In a long-term perspective, it can also act as a safety valve against majorities who wants to impose similar practices on minorities. However, this argument is more relevant to cases of local pollution than to global warming. CO_2 emissions normally have tiny impacts on the immediate environment, but much more globally. Therefore, self-determination without self or externally imposed restrictions could lead to high levels of CO_2 emissions from communities with abundant access to fossil fuel resources. Even though increased self-determination can be important in tackling "dirty" fossil fuel extraction, such as open pit coal mining or tar sand oil extraction, it is not a solution to global warming.

The material aspect of the argument is more relevant to climate change. Local renewable energy resources can match the cost-effectiveness of large-scale, centralized installations, and avoid energy spills associated with transferring energy over long distances. The implementation of such technologies is also dependent on the communities that are going to use them. But this type of community involvement is not necessarily an argument in favor of participatory democracy, and in both theory and practice it often only means the active participation by community representatives. If the decentralization argument is going to be considered as an argument for participatory democracy, it has to be coupled with other arguments.

Such coupling is often made with the knowledge argument, which stresses the need to utilize the skills and expertise of community members to find ecological solutions to food, industrial, and energy production.

An ecological transition demands immensely diverse and carefully tailored solutions which bureaucratic and centralized institutions are not able to carry out. It has to involve an active citizenry with intricate knowledge of the potentials and needs of their own localities.

The knowledge argument takes up a seminal criticism of centralized government made by environmentalists. When such bureaucracies manage the environment, there is a tendency to simplify and standardize complex ecosystems, often with detrimental results. Participatory and non-hierarchical institutions, on the other hand, bring forward a wider array of views and experiences, and potentially yield balanced and variegated solutions that mimic the complexity of the ecosystems themselves. Unlike centralized, hierarchical institutions where the experience of environmental effects is rarely felt by the political actants who cause them, the decision makers in participatory democracies are immersed in the environments where the effects are experienced. The distance between action and experience becomes shorter.

It is problematic, however, to assume that knowledge or experience of the environmental consequences of political actions will always produce improved decisions. People are not just guided by ecological motives, and may attempt to accomplish other goals, such as economic growth, that they know will have negative consequences for their environment. Local community knowledge is not always advantageous for the environment, because ecologically unsound practices can establish themselves as parameters for how communities think about their relationship to nature. It is especially easy to overlook long-term effects if one does not have sufficient scientific knowledge to understand how the environment works. This is especially true for the climate.

It is not enough to know the potentials and needs of one's community or environment. It is also necessary to possess *technical* knowledge in order to produce food, industrial products, or sustainable energy. This type of knowledge is neither the same as community knowledge, nor is it evenly distributed in the population. Communities normally have to use outside, professional expertise to develop sustainable practices. The utilization of renewable energy sources is a complicated issue, and even though local knowledge can be useful in finding good ways of implementing such technologies, it is insufficient in implementing it most effectively. This is not to say that the relationship between experts and citizens cannot be organized democratically, but rather that the knowledge argument is just too simplistic to make a full justification for participatory democracy.

On the other hand, one can argue that technical knowledge is insufficient if we culturally and politically persist in a mindset that obscures or legitimizes the current destructive extraction of natural resources. This is the core of *the mentality argument.*

Moving away from an anti-ecological mentality that emphasizes humanity's right to dominate and exploit nature, demands a move away from a social mentality that legitimizes the exploitation and domination of humans. This means changing the hierarchical structures that underpin this mentality, including political institutions that divide us into leaders and followers.

The mentality argument shows that our thinking about nature and our place in it is not arbitrary, but fundamentally influenced by the way our society is organized. To put it simply, societies that produce people who prioritize their own interests and are willing to exploit others and disregard their needs and suffering, is prone to produce people who disregard the often catastrophic consequences of climate change suffered by other people, other species and whole ecosystems.

However, the relationship between social institutions, mentalities, and practices is more complicated than portrayed here. For example, it is possible to hold very egalitarian social views and still disregard the suffering of other species or the environmental consequences of one's actions. It is also possible to hold authoritarian political views and to be concerned with other species or the environment. The classical example of this is the high number of leaders in the German Nazi party who were vegetarian, but it is also possible to imagine a scenario where global warming is remedied within more authoritarian political structures. It was pointed out at the beginning of this article that it is the relentless growth of capitalism *combined* with the burning of fossil fuels that is the main cause of global warming. A capitalist system based on sustainable energy sources that did not harm the climate is an option, even if it continued to be ecologically harmful in other ways.

The strength of the mentality argument is that it points out that our current hierarchical society will continue to wreak havoc on the natural world. Ending this destruction will necessitate creating a free and just society—one that likely includes a participatory democracy. On the other hand, there is no *necessary* relationship between the two endeavors. All environmental problems are not equal. It is possible to solve one but ignore others. We can be as non-hierarchically minded as can be, but we still have to *know how* to produce food, industrial products, and sustainable energy.

The first three arguments presented in this article—the anti-capitalist, global justice and pressure-from-below arguments—are primarily ecologically based critiques of a non-democratic global order. Alone they provide only ulterior motives for participatory democracy, but combined with the others they make more sense as they point to a positive relation between democracy and climate change mitigation. There are, however, important objections to the majority interest, responsibility, decentralization, knowledge and mentality arguments, and none of these provide a strong case for participatory democracy alone. Combined, on the other hand, they fill in some of the blind spots of the others and jointly grow stronger. And in all fairness, it is rare to see these arguments in isolation, as they are usually mixed together by environmental advocates of participatory democracy.

A stronger line of reasoning that mixes the arguments can be formulated as follows:

Global warming is caused by a global, capitalist, and unjust order, where economic and political power is unequally distributed, and relentless growth for the benefit of the few is realized at the expense of the majority of the world's population and the environment. It is highly unlikely that climate change mitigation will happen unless power and economic resources are more evenly distributed between and within societies. A participatory democracy based on sound deliberative practices, community self-management, and institutions that coordinate, negotiate, and delegate actions on a larger scale, is a better framework for dealing with global warming than the present representative system. It increases the likelihood that majority interests for a sustainable climate will be satisfied, that citizens will take responsibility for the environmental consequences of their private and political actions, that climate friendly solutions to agriculture, industry and energy will be more efficiently implemented, and that people will consider the health of local, regional, and even global ecosystems in their everyday lives to a greater extent.

This argument implicitly acknowledges some of the counter-objections raised against the individual arguments, by not *guaranteeing* that participatory democracy will be better for the climate. It claims that participatory democracy is a good precondition for dealing with the ecological crisis, and increases the likelihood that we can mitigate climate change. What remains is to present evidence that substantiates these claims, and to discuss how a participatory democracy could work. Notwithstanding, I think this is the strongest reply that can be given to the main question of this article.

We also have to admit that participatory democracy is not the *one* solution to the climate crisis, but part of a larger effort to provide concrete answers for refining and consuming energy sustainably. It is also important to remember that participatory democracy does not hinge on its ability to solve the climate crisis. Even if it would not make it easier to mitigate climate change, there are many other good arguments for participatory democracy, such as providing equal opportunities, preventing human exploitation, and showing respect to everyone's needs.

THE RETURN OF
CAPITALISM'S INTERNAL
CONTRADICTIONS

MAT LITTLE

One of the animating beliefs of twentieth century social ecology was that capitalism had tamed its dangerous contradictions. "The unprecedented fact remains that capitalism has been free of a 'chronic crisis' for a half-century," wrote Murray Bookchin in his 1989 essay, *Radical Politics in an Era of Advanced Capitalism*. "Nor are there signs that we are faced in the foreseeable future with a crisis comparable to that of the Great Depression," he went on. "Far from having an internal source of long-term economic breakdown that will presumably create a general interest for a new society, capitalism has been more successful in crisis management in the last fifty years than it was in the previous century and a half."[1]

Indeed, a robust, incessantly growing capitalism, shorn of past weaknesses and instabilities, was precisely the nub of the problem. With the help of the state and Keynesian economic innovations, capitalism had subdued its internal contradictions. But this success left in place a "new, perhaps paramount" *external* contradiction: the "clash," as Bookchin put it, "between an economy based on unending growth and the desiccation of the natural environment."[2]

It is true that social ecology did not exclude the possibility that capitalism could relapse into a chronic stagnation nor believe that the system's contradictions had somehow vanished. Bookchin regarded capitalism as "one of the most unstable economies in history" and inherently unpredictable. But the "traditional radical notion" that periodic or chronic crises would unfailingly occur was "uncertain," he averred, and the prospect of capitalism sinking into a "major chronic crisis" remained unexpected.[3]

Today the unexpected has happened. The economic events of the last few years have demonstrated that, in the advanced capitalist countries, rumors of the death of capitalism's contradictions have been greatly exaggerated. We now need to face the fact that both the internal and external contradictions of capitalism have come to the fore. The crisis that has emerged cannot be mistaken for a periodic downturn; it is unmistakably chronic in character. This has important implications for how a post-capitalist, ecological movement relates to masses of people whose material underpinnings are declining and unstable.

But it is equally important to recognize that, contrary to the hopes of leftists in previous eras, crisis and stagnation does not mean that capitalism is about to self-destruct. Nor are there legions of class-conscious proletarians ready to, in Marx's famous words, "expropriate the expropriators." What makes this crisis unique is that it has emerged after capitalism has vanquished all meaningful opposition, borrowed deeply into society, and expanded across the globe.

We should proceed from an agreement as to what capitalism is. Social ecology recognizes that capitalism is primarily a system in which money is invested to make more money, and so on ad infinitum. This creates an insatiable necessity for growth. Zero-growth capitalism is a contradiction in terms. "To keep to a satisfactory growth rate right now would mean finding profitable opportunities for an extra $2 trillion compared to the 'mere' $6 billion that was needed in 1970," says Marxian geographer David Harvey. "By the time 2030 rolls around, when estimates suggest the global economy should be worth more than $96 trillion, profitable investment opportunities of close to $3 trillion will be needed."[4]

But in the core, advanced capitalist countries—the US, Western Europe and Japan—the growth rate, though still positive, has not been satisfactory for some time. Between 2001 and 2011, the rate of economic growth in the US was 63% below that of the 1960s.[5] In Japan, growth between 1973 and 2008 was just one quarter of the level it reached between 1950 and 1973. In Western Europe, it has contracted by more than half.[6] In the UK, the rate of GDP growth was 2.7% in the 1980s, 2.2% in the 1990s, 1.8% between 2000 and 2010 and 1.3% between 2010 and 2014.[7] In the core countries, decline is in evidence virtually everywhere.

There are differing theories as to what lies at the root of this stagnating growth. One culprit that looms large in many explanations is a drop in the purchasing power of the mass of people. A 2011 report from the UK Resolution Foundation describes an extreme "decoupling" of average incomes from the rate of economic growth.[8] Since the 1970s, the report says, median pay has grown at less than half the rate of economic output in the US, Canada and Australia. In Britain, France and Germany, median pay tracked economic growth for a long period but in the past decade has increased by less than half the growth rate. Only in Scandinavia and Japan has the divergence between economic growth and average pay been "mild" the report concludes. In recent years, this contraction of wealth has been intensified. According to the US Russell Sage Foundation, the net wealth of the typical American household declined by a staggering 36% between 2003 and 2013.[9] In the UK, real wages, the value of wages when you factor in the effect of inflation, have dropped by 8.5% since 2009, the largest fall since the 19th century.[10] Four out of ten of the new jobs "created" in Britain since 2010 are self-employed and well-paid managerial posts are being replaced by more "elementary" jobs such as cleaning.[11]

So we are left with a standoff between two intractable features of the economy. On the one side, there exists a "wall of money," as English economist Harry Shutt puts it, demanding more and more profit-generating opportunities and, on the other, the declining purchasing power of the majority of people. This is not a recipe for economic health. The unavoidable consequences are, in the absence of productive investment for which demand is lacking, an increase in speculation (the buying of assets, currency futures or collateralized debt obligations for example, in the hope their value will rise), and spiralling household debt. These are the prime underlying causes of the 2007-09 economic crisis, and revealingly, nothing that has happened subsequently has done anything to ameliorate them. It can be argued that privatization, which began in the 1980s, was another way to utilize all this "surplus capital." But state-owned services and assets are obviously a finite resource. And despite the best efforts of governments like that of the UK, the gravy train cannot go on forever.

It is very hard to escape from this situation. To do so would require reversing the war on organized labor that has occurred since the 1970s, and I can sense no appetite among employers to do this, or placing restrictions on credit and raising interest rates which, though they may reduce household debt, would have the unfortunate side effect of sinking the economy.

Given this, the official government reaction has been to put the economy on life support through the printing of enormous sums of money (officially known as Quantitative Easing), pioneered by Japan and now part of the economic toolkit of the US, UK and most recently the European Central Bank. This is done in conjunction with near zero interest rates, which makes the borrowing of money incredibly cheap. Meanwhile, the political and economic authorities feel they have no option but to reboot and reinstall the casino economy.

But if nothing is done to change the underlying conditions that brought forth economic crisis, merely a smoothing over of the cracks, then the extreme likelihood is that further crises will erupt in the near future. In fact, the current crisis has yet to play itself out fully, as the economic torpor in the Eurozone aptly demonstrates. Not for nothing is this called "the Great Recession." The economic engine of capitalism is clearly sputtering, despite huge government action and financial rescues. The successful "crisis management" that at the end of the 1980s Bookchin credited capitalism with has been transformed into a series of desperate measures. Capitalism's contradictions, thought to have been banished to the history books, have re-emerged.

However, there are important caveats to be made before we become engrossed in making comparisons with the last great crisis of capitalism, the Great Depression of the 1930s. The first concerns poverty. The inhabitants of the wealthy core capitalist countries are clearly getting poorer but, in the main, they cannot be classed as poor. Contrary to the predictions of Marxism, the working class in these countries enjoyed burgeoning wealth throughout most of the twentieth century, particularly in the decades after the Second World War. According to the economist Thomas Piketty, whose book *Capital in the Twenty-First Century* predicts growing inequality in the coming decades, the emergence of what he terms a "patrimonial middle class" in the 20th century should not be underestimated. Tens of millions of individuals in Europe or 40% of the population, says Piketty, "individually own property worth hundreds of thousands of euros and collectively lay claim to one-quarter to one-third of national wealth: this is a change of some moment."[12] These people are not destitute and "do not like to be treated as poor," Piketty asserts. Despite the fact that the 1%, and especially the 0.1%, seem to inhabit a different universe both materially and spiritually to the rest of us, we haven't suddenly jumped in a time machine and travelled back a hundred years to an era when the top 10% owned virtually everything and the bottom 90% nothing. So Bookchin was not being blinkered when he noted in 2002 that "almost 50% of American households own stocks and bonds, while a huge number are proprietors of one kind or another, possessing their own homes, gardens and rural summer retreats."[13] It is just that many millions of people in the wealthy countries are now going, in the words of one recent book, "down the up escalator."[14]

The second qualification is that low growth and recurrent economic crises are malaises that seem peculiar to the wealthy capitalist countries. Yes, China was affected by the global financial crisis and economic growth slowed there but it still reached over 7% in 2012. China, with its chronic air pollution reducing life expectancy, is contending with problems generated by a vigorous capitalism, not a faltering one. Likewise, the Turkish economy expanded by 8.5% in 2011. So-called "emerging markets" have the advantage of increasing populations and a rising middle class. Economically speaking, they are more sustainable.

But the most important caveat to understand is that a dysfunctional capitalism displaying contradictions that are harder and harder to hide is not simply going to disappear. Bookchin's departure from the Marxist orthodoxy of the early twentieth century stemmed from an exasperation with the idea that, because of its internal development, capitalism would inevitably collapse and give way to socialism. This old leftist conviction was entwined with a resolute faith that a class-conscious working class would be ready and willing to take over when capitalism faltered and guide society to a communist future. "For generations," Bookchin wrote in his 1989 book, *Remaking Society,* "radical theorists opined about the 'inner limits' of the capitalist system, the 'internal' mechanisms within its operations as an economy that would yield its self-destruction. Marx gained the plaudits of endless writers for advancing the possibility that capitalism would be destroyed and replaced by socialism because it would enter a chronic crisis of diminishing profits, economic stagnation and class war with an ever-impoverished proletariat."[15]

What makes the current period of economic stagnation and chronic capitalist crisis unique in historical terms is that, in the palpable absence of a revolutionary alternative, capitalism shows no signs of self-destructing or meekly conceding to "socialism." It was, ironically, Lenin who remarked that there were no absolutely hopeless situations for capitalism. And the present situation is far from hopeless. Capitalism will, despite its attendant shocks and contradictions, and despite growing evidence in its heartlands of stagnation and decline, inexorably go on. There is no such thing as a *last stage* of capitalism while capitalism still exists. The last stage can only be identified retrospectively when and *if* it is replaced by another economic system. The system will not jump, it has to be pushed. And today, nobody is pushing.

The fact is that the overwhelming majority of people, even in the wealthy countries, are wage and capital dependent. They need jobs and money and a functional economy. This means that they have a clear interest in re-installing the economic system whenever it breaks down. "So long as the basic institutions of capitalism remain in place, it is in rational self-interest of almost everyone to keep the capitalists happy," wrote American mathematician David Schweickart in his 2002 book, *After Capitalism*.[16] "Economic growth is in the immediate interest of virtually every sector of society—growth in the straight-forwards sense as measured by GDP."

This truth holds in spite of low growth and recurrent recessions or crises. Consider the clamor to do "whatever it takes" to restore business as usual after the 2008 crash when the system really did threaten to break down and there was the immediate danger of ATM machines not dispensing cash and companies not being able to pay their workforce. With no alternative on the horizon, political elites were always going to intervene with trillions of dollars of "taxpayers" money. That is why it's presumptuous to describe any of capitalism's increasingly visible contradictions as fatal. The aforementioned David Harvey lists seventeen contradictions of capital in his latest book but maintains that only one of them is "potentially fatal." But it will turn out to be fatal, he elaborates, "only if a revolutionary movement arises to change the evolutionary path that the endless accumulation of capital dictates. Whether or not a revolutionary spirit crystallises out to force radical changes in the way in which we live is not given in the stars. It depends entirely on human volition."[17]

So is there any value in being aware of capitalism's resurgent contradictions if they are probably not fatal, and even if they result in economic breakdown simply produce a clamor on the part of the public as well as the elites to restore the system to, if not health, at least basic functionality? The point, I would suggest, is that there is a crying need for a post-capitalist, ecological movement to articulate an alternative to a capitalism that is seriously not delivering for millions of people and not delivering in a way that hasn't been true since before the Second World War. I was brought up with the idea that although capitalism may have terrible side effects it delivered the goods in terms of rising wealth and consumerist distractions. From where I am sitting that is simply not the case anymore. Whereas, not so long ago, politicians promised a better future, however much those promises were empty public relations flannel, now their message is conspicuously negative. Politics has become nasty and vicious (and in its treatment of the unemployed and the disabled verging on the sadistic) and all about adapting to the demands of a creaking economy. Forget the sunlit uplands, the future comprises differing gradations of pain.

I believe a social ecology and assembly democracy movement that wishes to thrive and become a genuine rival to capitalism has to respond to this new situation and mood. If I were to crudely summarise the message of social ecology up to this point it is along the lines of: capitalism incessantly grows, creating soulless and energy draining urbanization and megacities, and at the same time as it destroys and pollutes the natural environment, the market economy steadily remakes society in its own image, commodifying more and more aspects of life and imposing a buyer-seller relationship. But explicit within the concept of "post-scarcity" was the assumption that the material foundations of people in wealthy capitalist countries were assured. The period after the Second World War, Bookchin wrote, was infused with "a buoyant sense of promise" and this feeling of optimism was "clearly materialistic." A radical ethic developed, he asserted in *Remaking Society*, possessed of "the reasonable certainty that the abolition of oppression in any form—of the senses as well as of the body and mind—could be achieved even on the *bourgeois* grounds of economic instrumentalism."[18] The trouble with the capitalist machine, as well as its potential, was not its internal contradictions but that it had become remarkably stable and successful. I am not arguing that capitalist growth is no longer a problem. Even during the "crisis years" of 2008 to 2012, the advanced capitalist countries grew by around 1% a year, which is high by long-term historical standards. Economic stagnation in Japan has been accompanied by a rise, not a fall, in carbon emissions. And commodification has, if anything, intensified after the crash as the rich countries try to resuscitate growth. However, what cannot be ignored is that capitalism is no longer the machine of prosperity for millions of people in the rich countries. A growth in absolute poverty, mass unemployment, under-employment, low-paying self-employment, declining incomes, housing precarity and evictions, and a disavowal of responsibility to vulnerable people dependent on vanishing state welfare benefits, are all features of this new landscape. The buoyant sense of promise Bookchin discerned in the spirit of the 1960s has been transformed into virtually its polar opposite—an atmosphere of dread and fatalism.

What this signifies is that if social ecology wishes to really make headway as a movement for ecological transformation, it needs to invigorate its social dimension. It is revealing that, Kurdistan aside, the outbreaks of assembly democracy that have occurred in recent years have all taken place in countries suffering from economic breakdown and trauma, namely Argentina, Greece and Spain. In addition to assemblies of indignados, co-operative economic alternatives—in energy, food and housing, for example—have flourished in Spain after the crash, partly for the prosaic reason that the dominant capitalist economy has simply ceased to be a reliable presence in people's lives. If capitalism fails, alternatives will happen, that is an absolute guarantee. The question that remains is what will be the relationship of the economic alternatives to the popular assemblies that also spring up. As a theory, libertarian municipalism, the political dimension of social ecology, is clear on how political power can be reclaimed from the state, but less so about how it can be wrested from capital.[19] There is little doubt that representative democracy has failed. It has exposed itself as simply a component in the economic and political oligarchy that rules Western societies. But to take on that oligarchy requires an assembly democracy to, for example, provide oversight of and control over a new public system of credit and banking. And even if it is agreed that the nation state is the crux of the oligarchy, the issue remains that millions of people are dependent on state services and benefits. To merely leave them to the wolves in an existential rejection of the state and its entire works, is not an option. A post-capitalist movement must be defensive as well as creative.

Despite the proliferation of sages, nobody really knows what will happen to capitalism in the wealthy countries in the coming decades. The only certainty is that we are in a period of uncertainty. "The validity of a theory and a movement will depend profoundly on how clearly it can see what lies just ahead," Bookchin said in 2002.[20] Yet what lies just ahead is far from clear. It is quite possible that a new and overwhelming financial crisis will occur, leaving the state unable to bail out financial institutions and other corporations and thus precipitating a wave of bankruptcies and a destruction of capital value comparable to the Great Depression of the 1930s. This will leave some form of state capitalism as the only possible option and create millions more "superfluous" people—superfluous in capitalist terms. Capitalism is no longer capable of playing the role assigned to it by social ecology in the past: that of a well-tuned, efficient machine that spews out endless change in all directions, from compound growth to urbanization, from work to climate change, from ethics to popular culture, while itself remaining free of volatility and disequilibrium. The machine itself is now malfunctioning. This changes everything.

NOTES:

1. Murray Bookchin, *Social Ecology and Communalism* (San Francisco: AK Press: 2007), 55.

2. Ibid., 85.

3. Murray Bookchin, *Free Cities: Communalism and the Left*, edited by Eirik Eiglad (Unpublished manuscript, 2008: available at The International Institute of Social History, Amsterdam), 63–64.

4. David Harvey, *Seventeen Contradictions and the End of Capitalism* (Oxford: Oxford University Press, 2014), 228.

5. See John Bellamy Foster and Robert McChesney, *The Endless Crisis: How Monopoly-Finance Capital Produces Stagnation and Upheaval from the USA to China* (New York: Monthly Review Press, 2012), 4.

6. For the decline of both Japanese and Western European economic growth, see Andrew Kliman, *The Failure of Capitalist Production: Underlying Causes of the Great Recession* (London: Pluto, 2011), 53.

7. These figures come from the UK's Office for National Statistics: See "Living Standards and Economic Growth: The Depressing Tango," *We are not the beautiful*, 3 February 2014. (Available at idealoblog.blogspot.co.uk).

8. Jess Bailey, Joe Coward, and Matthew Whittaker, *Painful Separation: An*

International Study of the Weakening Relationship Between Economic Growth and the Pay of Ordinary Workers (London: Resolution Foundation, October 2011).

9. Anna Bernasek, *New York Times*, 26 July 2014.

10. See the UK's Office for National Statistics, "Real Wages Down by 8.5% Since 2009," 5 April 2013 (Available at ons.gov.uk).

11. Laura Gardiner and Matthew Whittaker, *Why 2014 Hasn't Been the Year of the Pay Rise* (London: Resolution Foundation, November 2014).

12. Thomas Piketty, *Capital in the Twenty-First Century*, translated by Arthur Goldhammer (Harvard: Belknap Press, 2014), 262.

13. Bookchin, *Social Ecology and Communalism*, 83.

14. Barbara Garson, *Down the Up Escalator: How the 99% Live in the Great Recession* (New York: Doubleday, 2013).

15. Murray Bookchin, *Remaking Society: Pathways to a Green Future* (Montréal: Black Rose Books, 1989), 94.

16. David Schweickart, *After Capitalism* (Plymouth: Rowman & Littlefield, 2002), 110, 122.

17. Harvey, *Seventeen Contradictions*, 221.

18. Bookchin, *Remaking Society*, 141, 143.

19. Janet Biehl, *The Politics of Social Ecology: Libertarian Municipalism* (Montréal: Black Rose Books, 1997).

20. Bookchin, *Free Cities*, 70.

TOWARD AN ECONOMY OF REPAIR

ADAM KRAUSE

We see ourselves acting upon the world. There is subject and object. Action upon. Separation. We do things to things. But this view obscures the active role of the non-human. The world also acts. And the boundary between that active world and human beings is porous and fluid.

In some ways this is obvious. We inhale and exhale. We eat things and they become us. We excrete what we cannot use, and it rejoins the world. There are also hundreds of microbial species in our stomachs that help us digest our food. We could not do it without them, yet they are not us. Or are they? Are we a single organism or many?

And our skin, the apparent boundary between us and the world, is similarly teeming with microorganisms, many of which are essential to our health. The normally benign *Staphylococcus epidermidis* makes fatty acids and glycerol out of the lipids our sebaceous glands release. This is an important process. And this same species helps produce anti-microbial peptides, antibiotic-like substances that prevent pathogens from colonizing our flesh.[1]

Essential elements of our existence are performed by separate organisms. Our boundaries are ambiguous. We are not discrete beings navigating an environment. We are assemblages operating along the border of self and other. There is not organism *and* environment. There is no *and*. A human is like a house with no roof, walls, or floor. We are but the barest of structures, interpenetrating whatever environments we inhabit. We realize we are just a few planks of wood, a series of thoughts, and a lot of empty space. A bird flies through.

These assemblages we call our selves were composed from materials we did not choose, through a process we were not there to control. For example, cyanobacteria evolved about 2.5 billion years ago. These organisms were the first to perform oxygenic photosynthesis, and now, thanks to the process they introduced, our planet has the most oxygen-rich atmosphere in the known Universe. About a billion years later, massive movements of Earth's tectonic plates washed minerals like calcium carbonate into the oceans. Some organisms assimilated these minerals to make exoskeletons and endoskeletons, putting Earth's inhabitants on the path to possessing bones.

We emerged from earth, water, sun, and air. But the journey from soil to cyanobacteria to cities started very slowly and eventually accelerated. The Earth formed about 4.6 billion years ago. Photosynthesis emerged 2.5 billion years ago. But it was not until about 550 million years ago that the first fish appeared. Mammals showed up about 300 million years after that. Anatomically modern humans evolved roughly 200,000 years ago, and it was a mere 5000 years ago that the Mesopotamians developed the first written language.

The bulk of history, as well as human history, has been spent developing the physically grounded part of animal systems—the part that perceives and navigates the world. Linguistic and symbolic representations of reality are a relatively recent acquisition. As we perform our daily movements, as we yawn and we stretch, we don't make symbols to represent what we're doing. We dig much deeper into our evolutionary past, and employ functions developed by our most ancient ancestors. For most activities, the world is its own best map. We just perceive it and deal with it.

But it is an unpredictable map in perpetual motion. We are surrounded and filled with materials that transcend our wills and the roles we assign them. The outside world, wherever that begins, is not a mere mechanical automaton, but a swirling sea of things, each with a vitality of its own. And this is not just true of other organisms. There is the chaos of water and weather, and electricity that can reverse directions and ignore the path humans put it on. Electricity seeks its own balance and always finds it. Downed lines have caused sudden power reversals, leading to overloads and outages that no human foresaw.[2]

We are coextensive with a world we cannot completely command. This is nothing new. But there is an update. We are coextensive with a world we cannot completely command that is falling apart. There are now more than 400 dead zones in the oceans.[3] Ninety percent of the large predator fish are gone.[4] In May 2014, the collapse of the western Antarctic ice sheet began.[5] It cannot be halted. Between 2010 and 2014, the Antarctic ice-melt rate doubled.[6] Things are looking increasingly cataclysmic, and the more sudden and dramatic the changes, the less likely it will be that plants and animals will be able to adapt. The world is crumbling, and the biology of our being is connected to it. We are consuming, discarding, and destroying the basis of our being.

Our expanding populations and increasing consumption levels are driving this destruction. Following centuries of fairly steady populations and economies, we discovered fossil fuels, free markets, and imperialism. That's when things really took off. In 1820, there were about 1 billion people on the planet with a combined annual economic output of roughly $690 billion. By 2000, there were more than 6 billion people and economic output was a staggering $40 trillion. Since just 1960, the world economy has doubled its annual output.[7] In the United States, where bigger is always better and the biggest is undoubtedly the best, the size of the average home has nearly doubled since 1970. At the same time, population increased by 100 million. There are more people, and they apparently need more space than anyone did before. But it's still not enough space for all their things. The first storage facilities—extra space people can rent to store all their extra stuff—appeared in Texas in the 1960s. There are now nearly 2 billion square feet of storage space all across the United States.[8]

Human insecurities fuel competitive consumption, which yields more insecurities and more consumption. The stagnant or falling real wages of the last several decades have not slowed our purchases, but merely increased our debts. We spend money we never had to buy things no one should have made. We are eating the Earth alive in the process.

And we really are destroying the world to make things we simply do not need. The ancient Egyptians believed gold was "the skin of the gods," in particular, the sun god Ra. And although this belief is no longer widely held, gold has somehow retained its popularity. Keeping new gold on the market to meet its demand involves bulldozing rainforests, removing the soil, then sifting through that soil to find a bit of gold, while filling the surrounding rivers with mercury, cyanide, and other pollutants.

Gold dust bonds to mercury, and its use in mining dates back at least to the Romans, who even banned it for a while, due to its obvious environmental impacts. But cyanide works even better, since it can amalgamate even microscopic gold particles into usable chunks, and the modern miner much prefers cyanide to mercury. Each gram of successfully extracted gold requires the use of about one and a half tons of pollutants. So any piece of the planet can become our private property, no matter how small and hard to locate it might be. We may need to ruin a river or two in the process, but at least the market survives.[9]

And we do love our market. Economic growth, the quest for wealth, and the glories of owning have become the central tenets in a secular religion that revolves around consumption, with economic growth as *the* central tenet in this belief system. It is frequently presented as a cure for all sorts of ills. How's the economy doing? Good? Then we should be fine. Not much stops a piece of legislation as quickly as the claim that it might slow the economy. Economic growth is monitored to the decimal point and endlessly analyzed in the news. When a business stops growing, that is, if it fails to sell more and more products every quarter, investors panic and flee. We get worried when growth slows. We forget that our ancestors managed to eat.

Adam Smith, one of the earliest theorists of capitalism, saw "the propensity to truck, barter, and exchange one thing for another," and "the uniform, constant, and uninterrupted effort of every man to better his condition," as *the* defining human characteristics.[10] But Smith failed to recognize that these supposedly natural characteristics arose in a very specific historical milieu. The drive for never-ending economic growth arose along with the changed circumstances that made capitalism possible. It is a relatively recent historical development. And in the early decades of capitalism's ascendance, there was resistance to the new values and practices it was introducing. Its global dominance was never assured. Our current propensity toward gathering more, more, more, and then a little bit more after that, is not human nature, but a social circumstance made possible by the rise of the market economy.

Wrapped in these social circumstances, we lose sight of the physical and biological contingencies that sustain our activities. Yet no matter how disconnected we appear to be, we remain attached to our planet. Even while driving down a road, trading stocks on a cell phone, we remain firmly embedded in the physics and biology of Earth. Rubber tires, once made from trees, now made from petroleum, spin along a mixture of crushed limestone, sand, and gravel. Electricity moves through mined copper, bearing bad news about the state of the stock market. Meanwhile, photosynthesized oxygen travels the bloodstream, bones of ancient rock keep hands on the wheel, and microorganisms ride along in the stomach and on the flesh. The line between the human and non-human cannot be drawn. And as we subsume and consume these surroundings, we remove the very basis for our being.

Why do we do this? Why do we continue to sacrifice the world at the altar of the market? The world is real, but we invented the market. We dote upon our human contrivances, but forget about the planet that was fertile enough to allow for their creation in the first place.

Although our economies are socially fabricated, and our money is made up, these things are still based on the movements of actual goods and services. And all those goods and services are created and performed by utilizing bits and pieces of the planet. And it seems the bout of economic turmoil we are currently encountering is based on the very real destruction of the Earth. Our made up money is doing poorly because our very real planet is doing worse. We are asking the impossible of it. It would take six to eight Earths to give everyone on just this one a North American level of consumption.

According to the laws of thermodynamics, matter and energy cannot be created or destroyed, just used and dissipated. There is thus an inverse relationship between a system's sustainability and the volume of matter and energy it utilizes. Just based on physics, our current trajectory is ascending toward collapse. Entropy is a law of nature. We cannot just ignore it and hope it will go away.

We may be meeting the limits of growth. An economic recovery for our current system may no longer be possible. The planet is nearly plundered. Affordable and accessible resources for industrial production are diminishing. Copper, zinc, iron, and other metals are growing harder to find and extract. Gathering them requires increasingly massive amounts of energy—energy that almost invariably comes from fossil fuels collected from deeper and deeper sea beds, or by hydraulically fracturing rocks. The world's supply of enriched uranium has, much like oil, passed its peak. Solar and wind power may produce electricity, but industrial capitalism requires vast supplies of stored and transportable energy. Fossil fuels come conveniently pre-packaged as stored energy, and their use helped make our industrial expansion possible in the first place. But existing methods for storing solar and wind power as liquid hydrogen are so energy intensive that the whole process yields a net loss. Our current methods of living cannot last long. We won't have the energy or the resources.

Of course, the collapse of capitalism has been declared imminent for about as long as it's been an "ism," and that collapse has been watched for with a fervor rivaled only by the Second Coming of Christ. Yet the collapse has not come. Why is this? There are many reasons, including the fact that the market economy is incredibly mutable and adaptive. Business practices have been revolutionized generation after generation. And it is also a complex and deeply embedded social system that actually manages to supply basic needs for enough people that only a small minority ever hit the streets. And the truly destitute rarely get organized. Just surviving requires too much time and effort.

So while the collapse of capitalism may seem increasingly imminent, it may not be imminent enough to prevent the pillage of our planet. There is still a lot of money to be made. We will cut the tops off mountains to find minerals, pump water into rocks to release every drop of oil and gas, drill deeper into the oceans, chop down all the trees, and eat all the fish, just to keep economic growth where the economists say it ought to be.

We cannot go on like this, but many of our fellow humans seem determined to go on exactly like this. And those with the most interest in perpetuating our present patterns are those with the most power to do the perpetuating. The preservation of our planet will require total determination and stubborn perseverance in the presence of such entrenched power.

We need truly radical solutions. And I mean "radical" in the radical sense of the word—tracing its etymology back to the Latin *radix*, meaning "root." And also radish, or the foot of a hill, or a base, foundation, or origin. We should remember and remain aware of the physical and biological roots of our being. We came from Earth and live on Earth. We're not so different from radishes, really. We need good soil and clean water to stay alive. If we want to ever have those things again, we will need to radically rethink everything we do. We should put our roots back down.

We currently produce, consume, and discard more than the world can handle. Obsolescence is built into many of the things we buy. And producers of consumer goods don't want to create objects with longer lifespans. Goods need to be used up, become outmoded, or fall out of fashion. If objects were made to last, their producers would quickly put themselves out of business. And we are not encouraged to repair our broken things. We can often acquire new items more cheaply and easily than we can fix old ones. We consume and discard and consume again. We feel proud of our purchasing power as we confidently send one item to a landfill and buy another to replace it.

Does this mean we are too materialistic? If materialism is used in its ordinary sense to mean valuing wealth, possessions, and their acquisition over other values, then we are way too materialistic. But materialism has another meaning—the belief that everything that exists is matter, or dependent on matter for its existence. Taken to its logical conclusion, this latter type of materialism would discourage treating every piece of the planet as a resource for the taking, and would encourage handling the physical world and other organisms as fellow travelers on Earth— essential companions instead of guilty indulgences.

The reality of our being should inform our modes of being. We could create an economy of repair—one based on respect for the world and its materials. We should have what we need and fix what we have. Durability and quality ought to replace fashion and newness as the most appealing elements of any object. Learning to create and maintain long lasting items would be the most important skills one could have. Carefully crafting, repairing, and maintaining these things could become the basis of our economies. There would be far less production, consumption, and waste if we bought better, bought less, and made it last.

It should be apparent that this new materialism would not require an ascetic renunciation of the pleasures of living, but rather, a re-enchantment of the world, and a rediscovery of the child's eyes that see wonders everywhere. We would find ourselves a new kind of unhappy if we replaced over-consumption with austerity. It would be like abstinence education for teenagers. Self-denial sells poorly without a more appealing alternative. Luckily, this redefined materialism would encourage living with our minds and senses more fully engaged. A move in this direction would actually enhance happiness and well-being.

Knowing how things work attaches us to the things we have. Careful craftsmanship requires time and attention to detail. This care becomes embodied and perceived in the finished product. The maker and the user feel closer to the materials involved. Just think about our relationship to food. The more we understand the process that brought it there, the more we appreciate what's on our plates.

We have lost much of our manual competence and our connection to our things. Most of us are incapable of knowledgeably dealing with the materials of our world beyond the simple acts of buying them and plugging them in. Shop classes have largely been removed from schools, and students in the first world are primarily steered toward a high-tech, virtual future. Computer literacy is certainly important, but as our educations and livelihoods become increasingly virtual, we lose our connection to the physical world—a physical world that further suffers from our virtual lives as inhabitants of the third world melt our discarded devices to get the lithium, mercury, and copper back on the market.

All this is more than a request that we support our local cobblers, carpenters, and tailors, although we can and should. So much more is required. We need a complete paradigm shift. Everything we do should be reassessed. We must live in new ways, and create possibilities for others to do the same. Ignore and avoid the economy of consumption. Create and encourage the economy of repair.

With the breakdown of capitalism spotted on every horizon for well over a century, the question that almost inevitably follows each declaration of this supposedly imminent event is, so what could we do after capitalism? How would we survive? We have at least part of an answer. To put it quite simply, we could tend to the world and its materials. We could take care of things. We could base our economies around maintaining what we have. There would be plenty of work to do.

What I am proposing here will require a complete reversal in how we perceive and behave toward the world. We currently construct our egos and define ourselves largely through the things we buy. So to change our relationship to the world, we not only need to dismantle our socially constructed selves, but actually change the way we construct those selves. Our minds have been so conditioned by capitalism that this may seem to fall somewhere between daunting and impossible. But the market economy molded and shifted our values. Why couldn't the rise of the repair economy do the same? So here's to hoping we can change our minds. Death to materialism. Long live materialism.

NOTES:

1. Richard L. Gallo and Teruaki Nakatsuji, "Microbial Symbiosis with the Immune Defense System of the Skin," *Journal of Investigative Dermatology*, 131 (2011): 1974-1980.

2. James Ganz, "The Nation: A Nation Unplugged; Its Coils Tighten, and the Grid Bites Back," *The New York Times*, August 17, 2003.

3. David Perlman, "Scientists alarmed by ocean dead-zone growth," *SF Gate*, August 15, 2008.

4. Boris Worm et al, "Global patterns of predatory diversity in the open oceans," *Science* 309 (2005): 1365-1369.

5. Hannah Hickey, "Western Antarctic Ice Sheet collapse is under way," *University of Washington*, May 12, 2014.

6. Malcolm McMillan et al, "Increased ice losses from Antarctic detected by CryoSat-2," *Geophysical Research Letters* 41 (June 2014): 3904.

7. James Gustave Speth, *The Bridge at the Edge of the World* (New Haven: Yale University Press, 2008), 4.

8. Tom Vanderbilt, "Self-Storage Nation," *Slate*, July 18, 2005.

9. For an in-depth account of gold extraction, see R.T. Naylor, Crass Struggle: *Greed, Glitz, and Gluttony in the Wanna-Have World* (Montreal: McGill-Queen's University Press, 2011), 23-51.

10. Adam Smith, *The Wealth of Nations* (1776: New York: Bantam Classics, 2003), 22, 438.

CAPITALISM, COMMUNALISM, AND CITIZENSHIP

MARCO ROSAIRE ROSSI

There are many differences between the natural sciences and the social sciences, but the one of greatest importance is the issue of identity and change. In the natural sciences, how people view aspects of the nonsocial world does not inherently change the nature of those things. This, however, is precisely what happens when humans attempt to understand themselves in their own societies. How humans view themselves inevitably determines how they interact with their political and social environment. No social science can therefore be a detached science in the same way that the natural sciences are. The social sciences are always active forms of inquiry that change the world as much as they seek to understand it.

The significance in pointing out this truism is in the realization that a revolutionary transformation of society requires a revolutionary transformation of human identity and self-perception. How people see themselves—and the past that they draw from—plays a critical role in defining how they will make their own futures. This does not mean that humans are always the victims of their own identities; only that people cannot take an active role in creating their own histories unless their conception of who they are and where they have come from supports and encourages such activity.

For these reasons, we need to rethink our concepts of revolutionary agency and identity. Throughout much of the history of the Left, the revolutionary agent was primarily identified as the "worker," or in the case of Marxism, the "industrial proletariat," who is supposed to change all over society through the overthrow capitalism, or, in the case of anarchism, capitalism and the state. This has been highly problematic. The "worker" is a limited identity that fails to include entire sections of the population, and clinging to it as the most significant revolutionary identity ties radical theory to antiquated notions of economic determinism. Most important though, is that the concept of the "worker," preoccupied with matters of production and consumption, is a poor starting place to form an ecological consciousness. Environmental destruction is not a product of alienated labor, but the results of an irrationally planned economy. Sustainability is not only about how things are produced and consumed, but also about how new technologies and ecological systems alter our overall production and consumption patterns.

Communalists emphasize that human beings are essentially "political animals" and insist on the need to create a radically democratic public sphere. We believe that the appropriate revolutionary identity for exciting social change is the *citizen*. It is citizens—people who participate in the public sphere for the sake of creating a good life— that can institute the most comprehensive changes in society. Here, I will flesh out communalism's idea of citizenship by revealing the shortcomings of the notion of the revolutionary worker in the struggle for socialism, and how we can work toward a cooperative and ecological economy by fostering a civic consciousness within the working class. It is the civic nature of socialism, I will argue, as opposed to the strictly economic, that has the greatest potential for producing an ecologically sustainable world.

The exact role of the worker as a revolutionary agent was a question that preoccupied what is now referred to as the Old Left. Early socialists, having their roots in the European Enlightenment, were of course interested in fundamental questions of human nature. However, what separated the political ideals of the mid-eighteenth century and that of the mid-nineteenth century was not merely that one was "bourgeois" and the other was "proletarian," but that one saw revolutionary agency as a matter of belief and the other saw it a matter of consciousness formed because of one's social position. In the eighteenth and early nineteenth centuries the revolutionary identity was understood to be the patriot, defined as how a person *felt* about one's country, and specifically how one felt in relations to a monarchical regime. In contrast, in the mid-nineteenth and early twentieth centuries the revolutionary identity was recognized as the class-conscious worker. It was an identity formed through the intersection between how one *felt* about society and *where* one was actually positioned in the capitalist mode of production. The importance of socialist theory in this regard was in contextualizing political consciousness to its social conditions. Human subjectivity, and, by extension, personal freedom could only be understood in the context of objective factors determined by technological, geographical, and institutional limits.

Marxist theory produced the most theoretically advanced understanding of this contextualization of human emancipation; yet, at the same time, it was also the most dogmatic one. For Marxists, the revolutionary identity was not just the worker, but specifically the industrial proletariat, understood in the terms of its economic capacity. A major problem in Marxism has always been in determining how much agency this revolutionary identity actually had in relation to the supposed laws of historical and economic development. Marx's own views of the matter were contradictory. In his preface to *A Contribution to the Critique of Political Economy*, Marx noted, "the mode of production of material life conditions the social, political and intellectual life process in general. It is not the consciousness of men that determines their being, but, on the contrary, their social being that determines their consciousness."[1]

This view, that the "social production of existence" is "indispensable and independent of... will,"[2] sharply contrasts with Marx's famous proclamation that "the philosophers have only *interpreted* the world, in various ways; the point, however, is to change it."[3] The later proclamation implies a moral burden to use intellectual resources to change society for the better, thus calling on people to exercise a will independent of relations that determine the social reproduction of existence.

To what degree consciousness and social position influence each other were never definitely answered within the Old Left. And, often times the tension between the two was sidestepped completely, in favor of a crude historical materialism. For all the hopes and cheering on the revolutionary potential of the working class, in the end, the worker was elevated to such messianic heights because the role it played within the capitalist system. Its revolutionary potential was dependent of its strategic ability to expropriate production and its material—rather than ethical—interest in eliminating capitalism.

Both in Marx's time and immediately after, the belief in the revolutionary identity of the worker was challenged by both libertarian and authoritarian arguments. Marx's anarchist rival Michael Bakunin had no patience for the development of such historical forces, and he cared little for the strategic importance of the industrial proletariat in abolishing capitalism. Unlike Marx's emphasis on historical laws, Bakunin, though still holding on to a loose version of historical materialism, believed that the pursuit of socialism was determined by humanity's innate "instinct for freedom." As he explained, humans were "endowed in a higher degree than the animals of any other species with two precious faculties—*the power to think and the desire to rebel.*"[4]

Bakunin emphasis on the instinctual nature of human freedom was the first, though partial, challenge to the hegemony of the worker in the creation of socialism. Since freedom was a matter of instinct, the drive for freedom and the creation of a free society was a universal characteristic. Creating a socialist society was a matter of tapping into the masses' innate capacity for anti-political spontaneous social action. Bakunin, though not a Luddite, was critical of the sociological features of urban industrialized life. He believed that the rigidity of factory life robbed the masses of their potential for spontaneity and thus started a process of "*embourgeoisment*" of the working class. Instead of a social revolution being led by the industrial proletariat, Bakunin believed that it would be fostered through a mixture of social classes including the *lumpenproletariat* of urban bohemians and vagabonds, rural peasants and farmers, and young *déclassé* intellectuals, as well as industrial proletarians.

Bakunin's more eclectic approach to revolutionary transformation had the effect of making the socialist revolution a social rather than a purely economic affair, and his prognosis on the participation of a variety of social classes and identities in formatting revolution was more prescient. None of the great revolutions of the Old Left happened in advanced industrialized nations, where the industrial proletariat could constitute a possible majority. Far from always existing on the revolutionary vanguard, the revolutionary potential of the industrial proletariat has waxed and waned over the years, and at times this proletariat even adopted an openly reactionary politics.

However, Bakunin's anarchist emphasis on an "instinct for freedom" has its own problems. If freedom was simply a matter of tapping into "instinct," then it is curious why anyone would have to fight for it all? If there is an instinct for freedom, then there must also be an instinct for domination and submission. In which case institutions and history become essential elements in ensuring that humanity's instinct for freedom triumphs over other, possibly even more demanding, instincts. This means that anarchism's anti-political focus of the spontaneous action on the masses, separate from institution building, becomes a poor strategy for winning or maintaining a free society.

Along authoritarian lines the preoccupation with the worker as a revolutionary identity was challenged by Lenin. More so than any other socialist theorist, Lenin understood the inherent contradiction in believing that that the worker, as an *economic* agent, was supposed to formulate a *political* revolution. In the name of Marxism, Lenin sought to relegate the role of class-consciousness in fomenting the socialist revolution to political consciousness.[5] For Lenin, workers, absent the influence of a political party, were only able to develop an economic consciousness that demanded day-to-day reforms within capitalism. It was only through the agitation of a Marxist political party that workers could become educated enough to see the necessity for overthrowing capitalism completely.

Lenin's transfer of the revolutionary identity from the worker to the vanguard party was an elitist molestation of socialist doctrine, but there is a point within Lenin's argument that has significance. Fixating on workers as economic agents alienates them from the very revolution they are supposed to create. Entering into the political sphere, even one of a highly elitist nature where workers are reduced to mere party members, creates a type of consciousness in workers that allows them to comprehend the totality of capitalist oppression.

After the Second World War, the age of worker socialism ended. The experiments in economical social revolutions, though with inspiring successes, failed to create the societies their advocates were aiming for. In addition, the world was remade in dramatic ways that the Old Left failed to anticipate. Developed nations were shaken by demographic changes. An entire youth subculture had formed that was violently at odds with assumed cultural and aesthetic rigidity of the post-World War II era. Meanwhile, developing nations experienced a series of national revolutions that upturned the global order and ended up redefining the meaning of sovereignty.

However, the biggest change unforeseen by the Old Left was the growth of an ecological consciousness, which called into question certain economic assumptions of material prosperity and progress that dominated Old Left thinking. As Ted Nordhaus and Michael Shellenberg have pointed out, the post-War prosperity brought new leisure opportunities for millions of people.[6] What they decided to fill this leisure time with was a newfound appreciation for the natural world. It was not that environmental destruction had become more intense; it clearly had not. Air and water quality, along with sanitation, had improved, and many environmental issues, both caused by and prior to industrialization, were finding solutions. However, these improvements were not undertaken for environmental reasons, because, at the time, none of these issues was considered an *environmental* problem. It was only through new leisure opportunities, along with greater public education, and a general anxiety about the future, that a mass ecological consciousness was born. After this, certain social issues were seen in environmental terms, and the state of the environment became interwoven with questions of production and consumption.

These factors greatly influenced the development of the New Left. The New Left embraced a revolutionary consciousness that went beyond capitalism and the state and recognized the multiple ways in which oppression operated. Under its influence, the revolutionary identity was not transformed from the worker to some other specific group, but fractured to include women, youth, gays and lesbians, even nature itself, along with many others. This had the effect of expanding the cause of socialism beyond its economic boundaries. The struggle for equality became as much a cultural struggle as it was an economic one.

Fracturing the worker as a revolutionary identity has made revolutionary politics more inclusive, but also more desultory. Currently, the need for a revolutionary identity has been so muddled by the growth of identity politics, conflicting hierarchies of oppression, and the influence of postmodernism's extreme relativism that barely any leftists today consider it an issue. At the same time, it remains one of the most important issues for actually transforming *society*. Fundamental questions, such as what does it mean to be a member of a free society, what are the duties that individuals have in such a society, and how can each and all of us—despite our social, sexual, cultural, and geographical differences—equally participate in this society, have not only gone unanswered; they are barely ever asked.

The major problem within leftist theory is that it has not matured beyond the world described by its founders. The industrial revolution shocked the senses of European society, and the economic determinism that it inspired has had a slow death. It has always been assumed that socialism, being an economic system, could only be established through embracing an economic identity. Socialism was to be realized by *workers*—once workers became conscious of themselves *as workers*—that is, conscious of themselves as a *class*, and aware of their economic standing within capitalism. There is no doubt that workers as workers have made great strides in peeling away some of the harshest elements within capitalism, but they have only been able to negotiate better terms within an economic system because their ability to negotiate in the first place was already won politically. As much as it may begrudge leftwing libertarians to acknowledge it, Lenin was correct on this point, and his correctness explains much of the appeal of Leninism among Marxists. Workers are only able to make great strides within capitalism because they see themselves not only in the terms of their *class* consciousness but also in the terms of their *civic* consciousness, and they are willing to engaged *politically* in the struggle against capitalism as *citizens* and not simply as workers. In this manner, socialism is not necessarily realized through the embracing of an economic identity but rather through the embracing of a political identity.

Unfortunately, the civic character of socialism has been downplayed throughout the history of the Left. The greatest threat to capitalism has been the wholesale removal of certain economic activities away from hierarchical and market relations. The attempt to codify certain economic rights has been far more successful in creating a more cooperative and egalitarian society than most people, including many leftists, have realized. When voting rights were tied to the ownership of property, participation in elections was considered an economic right. Once suffrage was open to all people regardless of property, it was understood as a political right, even though the struggle for universal suffrage was specifically fought along class lines. The same is true in varying degrees of the right to an attorney, to a jury of one's peers, to freedom of association, to freedom of the speech, and to public education. There is no reason to think that current "economic" rights will not go through a similar "politicizing" process if the civic character of socialism is embraced more fully.

The most important aspect of emphasizing the civic character of socialism, however, is that it orientates our attention away from economic production and toward economic planning. The belief that a socialist economy can be established through workers seizing the means of production, either through a workers' state or more directly through a labor syndicate, assumes that there is nothing inherently flawed with the overall means of production. This view is not tenable within the context of climate change. The current climate crisis is driven by the manner in which energy, the essential commodity for the running of any economy, is produced. Because of this, the crisis of climate change cannot me ameliorated by simply seizing the means of production. Workers' control of coal power plants, no matter how egalitarian, will still produce ghastly amounts of carbon dioxide. Moreover, nor can it mean that *not* seizing the means of production, even an energy source as dangerous as coal, is an option. Without control of an economy's energy sources, and for many areas of the world that is still coal, the means of production in the economy have not actually been seized. It is only through conscious planning—both the intentional mitigating of the deleterious effects within an industry and the utilizing and developing of new technologies for the creation of new industries—that economies will be able to de-carbonize. In this manner, it is not enough to simply control the means of production. People must also learn how to plan their economies in such a way that the wealth of each industry is used to displace that industry. Economies should not just expand, but evolve. This intentional evolving of the economy is only possible with a society that has a vibrant civic sphere where people behave *as citizens*, because it is only in this realm that the evolution of the economy can be considered as a whole and not in its parts as individual rival industries.

The main objection to embracing the identity of a revolutionary citizen instead of revolutionary worker is that the notion of "citizen" is thought to be a bourgeois concept connected to the nation-state. In the hopes that the abolishment of capitalism will also lead to the destruction of the nation-state, there is a reluctance to adopt such a conceptual framework. Citizen, however, is anything but a bourgeois concept. For communalists, the citizen exists not just separate from the nation-state, but as an idea that is in radical opposition to it.

The power of the state is derived from two sources. The first is an exclusionary power that is able to declare those outside its borders as aliens, and the second is a repressive power that is able to transform those within its borders into subjects. Opposition to the nation-state means a breakdown of the concept of nationhood through a localist force that emphasizes municipal democracy and a globalist force that emphasizes world government. For communalists, the idea of citizenship combines the concepts of communal democracy with that of cosmopolitan confederalism to represent a dual threat to the nation-state, and indeed any state, for both its hierarchy and its parochialism. This dual approach is a product of looking into the ancient past at more democratic forms of government while at the same time looking forward into the near future at a world that is far more interconnected.

In the terms of ancient past, the idea of a revolutionary civic identity draws upon ancient Athenian notions of governance that understood citizenship as a form of direct democratic engagement with one's community. In ancient Athens politics was seen as a means through which the highest form of ethical life could be obtained. The more citizens engaged in politics, the more generous and self-aware they were to become.

This unique and positive aspect of Athenian democracy does not mean that the ancient Athenian institutions can, or even should, be reproduced. Ancient Athenian democracy was intensely xenophobic and imperialistic. After Athens helped liberate Greek city-states from Persian rule, it engaged in a brutal subjection of its weaker neighbors. This imperialist project brought Athens into armed conflict with its rival Sparta, which eventually resulted in the demise of the Athenian empire and the dismantling of Athenian democracy.

The failures of Athenian democracy point us toward the future. Capitalism has become genuinely international with the globalization of the nation-state system. International socialism still lags behind. Considering the ecological consequences of the "anarchy in production," rational planning remains a pillar of a communalist economy, and a global system of government is a prerequisite for transforming global capitalism. Indeed, the failure to deal with climate change has been the failure of an international system that respects each nation-state's sovereignty over its own carbon emissions. International treaties, even ones with bold emission reductions, still are voluntary instruments that give elites in each country considerable latitude over environmental objectives. Such *voluntary* measures are unlikely to focus the global economy away from dependency on fossil fuels, especially when compared to a *mandatory* system that require reductions as a matter of global law. In this sense, sovereignty must be extracted from each nation-state, and placed in the hands of the world as a whole. To ensure that this extraction of sovereignty does not lead to a world-state, it is necessary that this global government constitutes itself as a confederation founded on municipal democracy.

Major existential threats to the planet, such as nuclear war and global warming, require that our world become more local, in the sense that everyday people must have more control over their lives, and, more global, in the sense that we recognize the common humanity in each person and the greater good of the planet.

The creation of a communalist economy would be an important step forward in assuaging these existential threats, but, unfortunately, socialist theory has not weighed the importance of this convergence between the local and the global. Instead, it has been too preoccupied with the nation-state and the economic capacity of people as workers. The belief that workers will seize the state or abolish the state through local uprisings alone is becoming a confused and almost anachronistic cry in a world polarized between international institutions and tribal warlords. For countries such as Libya, Somalia, and the Democratic Republic of the Congo, among others, the whole question of a traditional nation-state is trapped between the violence of highly decentralized militias and terrorist organizations and highly centralized international financial institutions and bureaucracies. Currently, none of these countries has a stable and conventional nation-state to either seize or abolish, and yet the dire situations in all these countries means that they are the ones in most need of the type of transformation for which radical socialists have advocated.

Countries in Africa and the Middle East are the extreme examples, but the world as a whole is experiencing this process of polarization. Far from mitigating these existential threats, this polarization is aggravating them. In a world where our technological capacity to destroy ourselves has become so grand, where the survival of species and other complex forms of life are at stake, such risks should not be taken lightly. A new vision of us as humans is required. Communalism proposes that this new vision is that of the citizen who is invested in a civic form of socialism. This new identity will not be a panacea for the entire world's problem, but it will be an essential step in creating a free, sustainable, and harmonious world.

NOTES:

1. Karl Marx, "A Contribution to the Critique of Political Economy," in Robert C. Tucker, ed., *The Marx-Engels Reader*, 2nd Edition, (New York: W.W. Norton 1978), 4.

2. ibid.

3. Karl Marx, "Theses on Feuerbach," in Tucker, ed., *The Marx-Engels Reader*, 145.

4. Michael Bakunin, *God and the State* (New York: Dover, 1970), 9, emphasis in original.

5. See Vladimir Lenin, "What Is to Be Done?" In Robert Tucker, ed., *The Lenin Anthology* (New York: W.W. Norton & Company 1975).

6. See Ted Nordhaus and Michael Shellenberger, *Breakthrough: From the Death of Environmentalism to the Politics of Possibility* (New York: Houghton Mifflin, 2007).

SOLIDARITY THROUGH CITIZENSHIP IN SOCIAL ECOLOGY

JOHN NIGHTINGALE

A truly ecological society, argues Murray Bookchin in *The Ecology of Freedom*, is necessarily founded on "a communion of humanity and nature that patently [expresses] the communion of humans with each other; a solidarity of the community with the world of life that [articulates] an intense solidarity within the community itself."[1] According to Bookchin's theory of social ecology, solidarity within human society is absolutely fundamental for the creation of an ecological society. For Bookchin, a crucial ingredient for achieving such a solidarity, and thus an ecological society, is the "exercise of authentic citizenship," which in turn requires a "redefinition of politics as the management of the community or *polis* by means of direct face-to-face assemblies of the people in the formulation of public policy and based on an ethics of complementarity and solidarity."[2]

What is, more specifically, the relationship between solidarity and citizenship in Bookchin's thought? Ultimately, Bookchin's political project aims to achieve solidarity *through* citizenship and we need to emphasize the importance of this idea for understanding the theoretical assumptions of social ecology as well as for its practical political implications. Since social solidarity is a prerequisite for an ecological society, we need to explore Bookchin's prescriptions for fostering such a solidarity through a radical redefinition of politics and citizenship. The relationship between solidarity and citizenship in Bookchin's work is central to his theory of social ecology, and thus merits significant attention both from scholars attempting to interpret and refine the theory of social ecology and from activists, groups and communities who are continually striving to create and enact ecologically sustainable forms of living.

On the very first page of *The Ecology of Freedom*, Bookchin explains the principal thesis of social ecology: "the very notion of the domination of nature by man stems from the very real domination of human by human."[3] In the most general terms, then, social ecology insists upon the social origin of environmental degradation, and that there is a direct link between hierarchical relations within human society and the ecologically catastrophic dislocation of humanity from nature. The assertion that anti-ecological outcomes are rooted in the hierarchical organization of social life implies that ecological problems are in fact *social* problems and therefore require radical social solutions. For Bookchin, the first cause of ecological degradation is not human alienation from nature, but the inevitable tendency of society to project the logic of its own internal associations onto its interaction with the natural world, thus reproducing a relationship with nature that reflects those within society itself. When hierarchy and domination characterize our internal social relations, the relationship between human society and non-human nature is bound to reflect that. According to this view, the creation of an ecological society necessitates a profound social transformation, whereby hierarchical forms of organization are replaced by a new politics that nurtures social solidarity and subsequently produces a more harmonious relation between humanity and non-human nature.

Bookchin's anthropological account associates the development of civilization with the inevitable decline of the parochial solidarities that had prevailed in so-called "organic societies"—the preliterate and essentially egalitarian human communities that preceded the emergence of hierarchy and were characterized, Bookchin claims, by "their intense solidarity internally and with the natural world"—and the emergence of a need for new forms of social organization that would allow the individual to function in an "increasingly atomized" social world.[4] The intense sense of collective purpose that had characterized organic society, says Bookchin, was replaced by the development of a "resourceful, comparatively self-sufficient, and self-reliant ego that could readily adapt itself to ... a society that was losing its human scale and developing more complex political institutions and commercial ties."[5] On Bookchin's reading, classical antiquity was marked by unprecedented levels of social, economic, and political development that rendered previous modes of association simply unworkable. He sees the shift from intense, parochial forms of group solidarity to more outward-looking, self-assertive individuals as both a symptom and a cause of these developments, with the result that social networks based primarily on kinship, marriage and tribal ties became incompatible with the emerging modes of technology, distribution, and association. The increasingly sophisticated political realm—and indeed society generally—witnessed a steady transformation of the notion of individuality. Ultimately, the rise of civilization signaled the departure from the parochial solidarities that characterized organic society, and oversaw the development of "autonomous egos ... free to undertake the varied functions of citizenship."[6] However, the type of individuality whose emergence occurred alongside civilization's development was very different to the unfettered individuality (or, more properly, individual*ism*) we might associate with classical liberalism. Its function was not to disconnect individuals from one another and from the social body, but rather to prepare them for the role of citizenship that would prove so essential both for the administration of public life and for reinforcing the solidarity of the whole.

For Bookchin, *citizenship* refers to the exercise of civic virtue by means of active political participation, and is essential for the genuine expression of collective freedom and the realization of group solidarity. As such, the erosion of solidarity brought about by capitalist development and urbanization was (and is) manifest partly in civic estrangement, as Bookchin expresses it in his 1987 work on "the decline of citizenship."[7] Today, he argues, we are no longer "citizens" in any meaningful sense, or at least not according to the original meaning of the word, whose etymology is rooted in the Latin *civitas*, meaning a cohesive social body united by a series of rights and responsibilities. It is clear that the modern notion of citizenship differs quite dramatically from this ancient ideal: today, we are more commonly thought of as "the electorate," "taxpayers," and "constituents"—a terminology that reflects the more distant relationship we now have to public life and politics.[8] This decline of citizenship results from the "rise of urbanization," whereby city life— initially characterized by a thriving civic culture—has been absorbed by the commodification of urban space and institutional centralization.[9] The antidote, insists Bookchin, is to redefine and reshape "the citizen" as an active agent in a political community, to reclaim "politics" from the discipline of "statecraft," and to reinvigorate the public sphere ("the city") as an "ethical union, a humanly scaled form of personal empowerment, a participatory, even ecological system of decision making, and a distinctive source of civic culture."[10] As Damian White puts it, Bookchin's scheme necessitates a retrieval and reevaluation of the "classic conceptions of politics, citizenship and the city."[11] These conceptions have been manifest with varying degrees of durability in fleeting moments throughout history, but by far the most sustained and authentic exercise in participatory democracy and civic virtue was embodied in the classical Athenian *polis*.[12] Despite the fact that the citizenry of ancient Athens represented an elite minority in comparison to the population of women, slaves, artisans, manual laborers, and disenfranchised resident aliens, Bookchin insists that this system of governance was distinctly and "consciously amateur" and lacked a "professionalized bureaucracy of social control."[13] In other words, the Athenian *polis* resembled the very antithesis of a state as such; its administration relied entirely upon the direct participation of citizens.

The significance of this in terms of the relationship between Bookchin's concepts of solidarity and citizenship lies in his reading of Aristotle, the eminent theorist of the Hellenic *polis*. For Aristotle, Bookchin tells us, our self-fulfillment as political animals is dependent on the existence of institutions substantiated by a "body of ethics" and a "civic center" offering a plethora of "social activities" that serve to "nourish interactions and discourse" and "foster the growth of ethical and intellectual insight."[14] Crucially, Aristotle's necessary means for human self-fulfillment are, Bookchin tells us, grounded in a notion of "human solidarity or *philia*."[15] Ordinarily translated as "friendship," Bookchin insists that *philia* is in fact a much more far-reaching notion that "implies an expansive degree of sociality that is a civic attribute of the *polis* and the political life involved in its administration."[16] In Bookchin's account, *philia* transcends that which pertains merely to the intimate associations implied by "friendship." Rather, it concerns the more pervasive social interactions that take place beyond immediate circles of solidarity and that are necessary for genuine human fulfilment. That the workings of the *polis* were necessarily underpinned by *philia* is thus reflective of the latter's generality, since the term patently refers to a much broader range of associations than those that are played out in our immediate social circles. Indeed, the prevalence of *philia* suggests an extension of solidarity by members of a collective to those with whom they have no immediate personal relationship. As Bookchin puts it, "Aristotle's notion of *philia* or solidarity as a crucial precondition for a political life expressed the unique identity politics possessed as a form of governance, one that transcended mere kinship obligations."[17] Further, the pervasive nature of association implied by Aristotle's concept serves to enrich the idea of citizenship. The civic commitment implied by *philia* imbues the concept of citizenship with a profound sense of ethical responsibility toward fellow citizens and the larger political community. As such, *philia* represents a meaningful and genuine social bond—manifest in "civic ties" and "ethical precepts" as opposed to "blood ties" or "tribal custom"—that embodies a set of relations between individuals and their communities that may properly be referred to as solidarity.[18]

While the direct-democratic tradition has flowered in sporadic bursts since the time of the Athenian *polis*—most notably in the medieval city-states and the town meetings and sectional assemblies that arose briefly during the American and French revolutions respectively—it was ultimately usurped by the centralizing tendencies of emerging nation states which had more in common with the Roman model than the Athenian. Despite this, for Bookchin, the legacy bequeathed to modernity by the Hellenic experiment is considerable and the Athenian ideals of citizenship and politics demand close inspection if we are to wrest politics away from professional bureaucrats and reinstate ourselves as political agents; as active, empowered citizens within a thriving public sphere.[19]

An important aspect of Bookchin's project involves making a clear distinction between the political and the social areas of life. For Bookchin, politics emerge when the activities involved in human beings' social interactions become organized into institutions, when we establish working practices and norms for decision making by the community.[20] Accordingly, politics is a distinctly human activity, since other social animals do not have institutions and have not developed ways of ordering their communities that are "continually subject to historical change."[21] For Bookchin, professionalized "politics"—statecraft—is a relatively recent development in human history and has "no authentic basis in community life." Indeed, "by assigning political functions and prerogatives to 'politicians' ... we have lost our sense of what it means to be political."[22] A genuine politics, argues Bookchin, must be firmly rooted in social life; it emerges from human beings natural tendency for sociability and is expressed in the development of practices which function to reinforce a sense of community and collective endeavor. Accordingly, the modern conception of politics is a deception, since statecraft is, by definition, detached from the social life of the community. Politics as an activity is no longer something in which the whole community participates; it has become the preserve of a distant elite of professional bureaucrats and administrators. The result, says Bookchin, is that "we have lost our sense of what it means to be a citizen."[23]

To rediscover a meaningful notion of citizenship, argues Bookchin, we must embark upon a program of decentralization that places political power back in the hands of communities and individuals.[24]

The very activity of doing politics must be physically and geographically relocated from the centralized state to a new public sphere and center of civic engagement: the municipality. Importantly, argues Bookchin, the reclamation of politics and a renewal of citizenship might well constitute a practical strategy for tackling the ecological crisis, for they represent antidotes to the "new individualism" that has driven the commodification of the natural world and the consequent over-consumption that has led to its degradation.[25] As such, Bookchin's notion of citizenship is crucial to both the theory and practice of social ecology. In his attempt to reshape citizenship according to the classical idea of civic virtue, Bookchin seeks to nurture an inclusive, participatory politics that sharply departs from the representative models that have dominated modern conceptions of the political. According to Bookchin, politics is necessarily a community activity, and it depends on the development of an active and empowered citizenry. Further, citizenship fulfills an important function for social solidarity; the exercise of civic virtue through political participation is both an expression of solidarity and a supportive frame on which solidarity can be built. It is therefore integral to creating and regenerating a solidaristic and ecological society.

It is not difficult to grasp how the notion of citizenship constitutes a workable basis for solidarity. Indeed, the idea that a reinvigorated and re-empowered local politics can foster group unity and cooperation is very straightforward. However, the task of reclaiming a participatory politics from statecraft and revitalizing a genuine citizenry from the current mass of disconnected individuals that comprise modern society is more problematic. Indeed, the question remains: how are we to free our selves and our politics from the auspices of the market and centralized authority so as to avert both social and ecological degradation? Bookchin proposes a program of "libertarian municipalism," which involves an explicit reconceptualization of "politics" according to the word's classical meaning, and aims for fully participatory and democratic decision-making processes to manage community affairs.

Fundamental to Bookchin's vision is his notion of the municipality—an "association of people reinforced by its own economic power, its own institutionalization of the grass roots, and the confederal support of nearby communities organized into a territorial network on a local and regional scale."[26] He proposes a radical dissolution of hierarchical relations through removing politics from the nation-state and relocating it in the municipality. Bookchin accepts that "cast in strictly structural and administrative forms" a project of decentralization on this scale amounts to a formidable problem, since many contemporary urban conurbations simply and literally have no way of "assembling" if they attempt to emulate ancient Athens, whose citizenry was relatively small.[27] Quite aside from the probability of state resistance to any such attempt at radical democratization, it is logistically impossible for all of the citizens of London or New York or Beijing, for instance, to physically assemble in one place. But Bookchin's notion of "the city" does not equate to the megalopolises that dominate contemporary urban space. Indeed, what is required, says Bookchin, is a shift *from urbanization*—a socially moribund, anti-ecological phenomenon—*to citification*, the recreation of genuine cities, understood as centers of civic engagement and social exchange. Furthermore, Bookchin reminds us, even the vastest of today's urban conurbations are themselves made up of neighborhoods— "organic communities that have a certain measure of identity"—which actually render large cities quite amenable to political decentralization. For *political* decentralization is a foundational principle of libertarian municipalism and, claims Bookchin, "No city ... is so large that it cannot be networked by popular assemblies for political purposes."[28] It is true that the *administration* of municipal projects would likely require expert coordination; we would for example need architects and engineers to design and construct buildings and infrastructure; doctors and nurses to provide healthcare; and farmers and agricultural specialists to manage cultivation and food production. But the *politics* of the municipality—that is to say, the processes of decision making—are, according to Bookchin, eminently open to participation by non-experts. The *formulation* of public policy is entirely different from its *execution* and *administration*; while the latter activities will inevitably require some level of specialist expertise, the former is one in which amateurism is both feasible and desirable.

However, Bookchin insists, libertarian municipalism is absolutely not a politics of the referendum. Under such a model, he argues, the individual in his or her capacity as a voter "becomes a seemingly asocial being whose very freedom is denuded of vital traits that provide the necessary flesh and blood for genuine individuality."[29] For Bookchin, the referendum represents the privatization, quantification and consequently the subversion of democracy. In reducing "views into mere preferences" and "ideals into mere taste," and an "overall comprehension into quantification," such a system does not allow for the full expression of our political wills and convictions.[30] Referendum politics do not encourage a genuine or meaningful form of citizenship, since the individual is not politically grounded in his or her community. In conducting politics in the privacy of the voting booth, the individual becomes separated from society rather than a part of it. Further, says Bookchin, the so-called "independence" afforded the individual by this form of politics is often "confused with independent thinking and autonomy of behavior," and "has been so marbled by pure bourgeois egoism that we tend to forget that our freedom as individuals depends heavily on community support systems and solidarity."[31] Accordingly, when citizenship is divorced from the community and we defer our roles as political animals, we achieve neither individuality nor community in any real sense. To reiterate: "it is interdependence within an institutionally rich and rounded community that fleshes out the individual with the rationality, solidarity, sense of justice, and, ultimately, the reality of freedom that makes for a creative and caring citizen."[32] Not only does our development as individuals depend on social solidarity, but solidarity in turn requires a network of relations and institutions that provide the intimacy and interaction without which it suffocates.

This is why the municipality is given such prominence in Bookchin's political program. For Bookchin, the municipality constitutes the fundamental unit of political life and provides the arena in which citizens engage in intimate and genuinely political discourse, and that is what makes it a physical, necessary condition for solidarity. Indeed, it enables the very activity of "communizing, of the on-going intercourse of many levels of life that makes for solidarity, not only the 'neighborliness,' so indispensable for truly organic interpersonal relationships."[33] As such, collective decision-making must amount to much more than merely registering the sum of individual preferences via the ballot; it necessarily involves face-to-face experiences. Further, the communal setting of the municipality encourages the Athenian notion of personal development or education (*paideia*) that helps shape individuals as citizens. "True citizenship and politics," Bookchin insists, "entail the on-going formulation of personality, education, a growing sense of public responsibility and commitment that render communing and an active body politic meaningful."[34] The notion of *paideia*, Bookchin tells us, is an important bulwark for solidarity, since it encourages a sense of communal loyalty through a political education rooted in participation. This is markedly different to an "institutional obedience" or patriotism, which implies a "mindless, indeed, infantile relationship to the state."[35] Indeed, Bookchin explicitly states that "solidarity is the ultimate result of the educational and self-formative process that *paideia* was meant to achieve."[36] This is something which, for Bookchin, is painfully absent from modern conceptions of politics, where political engagement and participation are gauged according to turnout at elections and membership of parliamentary political parties.

The idea that social solidarity can only be achieved through a radical remodeling of citizenship allows for the practical application of Bookchin's philosophy in his political project of libertarian municipalism. It is impossible to fully grasp Bookchin's municipalist vision without understanding the way in which its prescriptions are inextricably and interdependently linked to the central idea of solidarity. Indeed, the reinvigoration of citizenship and the reclamation of politics are explicitly expressed as phenomena that are simultaneously fundamental to the realization of solidarity and themselves strengthened by solidaristic social bonds. An active notion of citizenship requires a certain level of social solidarity, but communities also achieve greater levels of solidarity through the very practice of citizenship. If we accept

Bookchin's assertion that an ecological society is necessarily founded on human solidarity, then the notion of the realization of *solidarity through citizenship* is one that warrants the attention of the broader ecology movement. I hope that social ecologists—theorists and activists alike—will continue to explore the ways in which we may help institute that renewal of citizenship, forge genuine forms of social solidarity, and discover ways of life that help us create an ecological future.

NOTES:

1. Murray Bookchin, *The Ecology of Freedom* (Edinburgh: AK Press, 2005), p. 129.

2. Murray Bookchin, "Libertarian Municipalism: An Overview," *Green Perspectives*, 24 (1991), 4.

3. Bookchin, *Ecology of Freedom*, 65; see also 129, 147-150. And Bookchin does mean *man*, tracing, as he does, the emergence of social hierarchy and the consequent domination of nature partly to the gradual shift away from "matricentrism" (a term he borrows from Erich Fromm) in organic society towards increasingly patriarchal institutions.

4. Ibid., 110, 229.

5. Ibid.

6. Ibid., 231.

7. Murray Bookchin, *The Rise of Urbanization and the Decline of Citizenship* (San Francisco, CA: Sierra Club Books, 1987).

8. Ibid., 11.

9. Ibid., 3.

10. Ibid., 57, 54.

11. Damian F. White, *Bookchin: A Critical Appraisal* (London: Pluto Press, 2008), 183.

12. Bookchin, *Rise of Urbanization*, 3, 35.

13. Ibid., 35.

14. Ibid., 37.

15. Ibid.

16. Ibid., 38.

17. Ibid., 52.

18. Ibid., 52-53.

19. Ibid.

20. Ibid., 226.

21. Ibid.

22. Ibid., 226, 227.

23. Ibid., 227.

24. Ibid., 228.

25. Ibid.

26. Ibid., 245.

27. Ibid., 246.

28. Ibid., 247.

29. Ibid., 248.

30. Ibid., 250.

31. Ibid., 249.

32. Ibid.

33. Ibid., 250.

34. Ibid.

35. Ibid.

36. Ibid., 251.

THE AMERICAN BUILT ENVIRONMENT AS AN ECOLOGICAL CHALLENGE

JANET BIEHL

I n 2012 fossil-fuel-based transportation generated 28 percent of all greenhouse gas emissions in the United States. That year motor vehicles—passenger cars and light-duty trucks—spewed 18 percent more CO2 and other greenhouse gases than they had in 1990, traveling 35 percent more miles. Far too much of the country's built environment is auto-dependent: more than half the population live in sprawling suburbs, a landscape that requires every adult living in every household to have a car in order to function.

This sprawl was built by conscious design. Starting in the 1930s, during the Great Depression, the federal government promoted it with housing policies, specifically through the program of mortgage guarantees of the Federal Housing Administration. The FHA encouraged the construction of new homes over the repair of old ones; it supported the construction of single-family homes instead of multifamily buildings, apartment buildings, or even rowhouses. It encouraged such construction on the urban periphery, on greenfields, rather than in urban cores. It discouraged mixed-use buildings, like ones where a family might live on the second floor above a shop. It specified a uniform ethnicity, as African Americans were barred from obtaining FHA-guaranteed mortgages. It even specified uniform heights, widths, and setbacks for these new single-family homes.

The culture at large for decades hailed the design of sprawling suburbia as embodying the ideal of the American dream, dovetailing with the American ideology of the independent individual. Given the tiny or nonexistent down payment required on the new house and the long term of the mortgage loans, the choice was simple, as the historian Kenneth Jackson puts it: "quite simply, it often became cheaper to buy than to rent."[1] The FHA insured mortgages for millions of new homes. Middle-class white Americans flocked to the suburbs, which grew by leaps and bounds over the second half of the twentieth century. The number of suburban dwellers grew from 31 percent in 1960 to 51 percent in 2010, meaning about 158 million Americans.[2]

The character of suburbia was further shaped by zoning, at all levels of government. Before the Second World War, downtowns were, to use a retronym, mixed use: that is, residential, commercial, workplace, and recreational areas nestled more or less alongside one another, people could live in apartments above shops, for example, and walk to work. But the new zoning separated out these functions, consigning them to separate districts. The result of this separate-use zoning was an array of car-dependent pods: residential enclaves, also known as housing subdivisions; shopping enclaves, also known as strip malls; and workplace enclaves, also known as office parks. Since these various enclaves are separated by distance, people had to drive to get from one to the other.

The federal government further promoted automobile use with the 1956 Federal-Aid Highway Act, which authorized the construction of the interstate highway system, which eventually totaled 41,000 miles (66,000 km) of high-speed traffic arteries and multilane limited-access roadways. The federal Highway Trust Fund, with revenues coming from taxes on gasoline, vehicles, and tires, paid for 90 percent of the construction.

In these and many other ways, government policy gave priority to car travel. By contrast, it underfunded mass transit. Streetcars, once prevalent in cities including Chicago and Los Angeles, languished and then died, largely due to a campaign organized by General Motors.[3] Wide streets and plenty of parking have been the twin goals of much of "city planning" since World War II. The planning and layout of cities was essentially handed over to traffic engineers and technicians, whose primary goal was and still is to expedite the continuous, uncongested flow of traffic.

The social and ecological problems generated by sprawl are well known. Above all, suburban lifestyles are environmentally unsustainable: they spew higher emissions than urban ones, due to their dependency on the automobile for every trip outside the home. The single-family homes lack the energy efficiency of multiple unit buildings. And low-density settlement pattern renders suburbia unable to support public transit.

The long distances between destinations, and inadequate sidewalks, disqualify walking as a mode of transportation. Pedestrians who wish to cross an intersection on an arterial connecting enclaves risk their lives, darting across a yawning chasm in brief pauses in traffic. Schools are no longer an easily walk from home: back in 1969, about half (49 percent) of grade-school children walked or bicycled to school, but only 13 percent did in 2009. Parents now routinely drive children to play dates instead of letting them walk. In some suburbs children aren't allowed to play on sidewalks. The result has been an epidemic of obesity—children today have a one in three chance of getting diabetes.[4]

Governmental, cultural, and economic policy all preferred sprawling suburbia over older cities, whose street layouts dated to the pre-automobile age. But that preference resulted in neglect of those cities. Like any form of human settlement, city neighborhoods have to be maintained by programs of repair. But the FHA did not provide for reasonable loans for the renovation or upgrade of existing urban homes—such loans were small and of short duration, conducive only to minor repairs.[5] The result was that old houses, buildings, and entire neighborhoods fell into neglect, then decay and deterioration.

Other urban cores were all but suffocated with pavement and

concrete. Eager to lure auto-dependent suburbanites to come downtown, officials and their consultants welcomes even interstate highways into the urban core. They narrowed sidewalks and widened city streets and made them one way. They chopped down street trees, on the assumption that they were "fixed hazardous objects." They demolished graceful historic buildings and on their sites built massive parking lots. "Between one third and one half of urban America's land is typically dedicated to the driving and parking of vehicles," reads one antisprawl manifesto. "In Los Angeles it's two-thirds."[6]

In other places, public officials and private developers created new automobile-dependent cities that gave priority to cars and parking. Phoenix, Arizona, for example, lacks an urban core altogether—it has no pedestrian-scale downtown. In this classic Sun Belt city, "civic life has almost ceased to exist."[7]

Finally sprawling suburbia has had a negative impact on American democracy. By destroying public and civic spaces, it destroys community and sociability. In a traditional compact urban neighborhood, people stroll on sidewalks and in streets, they encounter their neighbors and pause to talk. Frequent street interactions gave rise to familiarity and friendliness and the attachments that are crucial for civic trust and civic engagement. "Lowly, unpurposeful, and random as they may appear," wrote the great urban critic Jane Jacobs, "sidewalk contacts are the small change from which a city's wealth of public life may grow." Moreover, compact mixed-use neighborhoods have gathering places within walking distance of people's homes and workplaces, like the local tavern or the corner store, where they can meet and talk on a regular basis.[8]

But in sprawling suburbia these walkable public spaces are minimized or absent. And cars have the opposite effect: they cut us off from others, making us less sociable. As a person spends ever more time alone behind the wheel of car, he or she becomes "a self-sufficient nation of one," observes one critic. The car "is everything a city is not." As Jeff Speck and his coauthors observe, "As a motorist, you cannot get to know your neighbor, because the prevailing relationship is competitive. You are competing for asphalt. ... The social contract is voided."[9]

Spending more time behind the wheel, people volunteer less, join clubs less, and participate in community projects less. According to the sociologist Robert Putnam, "Each ten additional minutes in daily commute time cuts involvement in community affairs by 10 percent— fewer public meetings attended, fewer committees chaired, fewer petitions signed, fewer church services attended, and so on."[10]

The result is the destruction of the public realm. People retreat to their private home, where they interact with the rest of the world via television and computer. They are losing the ability to get along face to face, and even civil conversation is becoming rarer, a specialized art.

Auto-dependent sprawl was built by conscious design; fortunately, it can be unbuilt by conscious design as well. In the past twenty years a new generation of urban planners has emerged, who studied the advantages of the urban built environment over that of suburban sprawl. They are reviving traditional town planning methods and the kind of urban design that was common before the Second World War: an easily identifiable town center; a main street featuring densely mixed commercial and residential buildings—stores, workplaces, and housing; narrow (and hence pedestrian safer) streets lined with trees; a mixture of housing types, including townhouses, rowhouses, and single-family homes; sidewalks and parks; and robust public transit. These planners consider themselves pupils of Jane Jacobs, who enunciated the need for walkable urbanism in the 1960s.

But their ideas date back as well to a radical tradition that sought an integration of town and country at the local level, for the sake of local self-management, the health and well being of all, and advancing a humanly scaled civilization. Beginning with Kropotkin, the tradition evolved through Ebenezer Howard, Lewis Mumford, and Murray Bookchin, among others. Another source is the traditional European city, with its dense core. Léon Krier, a Luxembourgian architect, urban planner, and architectural theorist, has been influential in calling for an "architecture of community" based on a renovation of the European city model.[11]

The Congress for a New Urbanism, founded in 1993, is a group of about 2,500 architects, planners, designers, developers, policymakers, journalists, and others who promote the design and building of small-scale neighborhoods as an antidote to sprawl. Its founders were the architects Andrés Duany and Elizabeth Plater-Zyberk, based in Miami; and also the California-based urbanist and architect Peter Calthorpe, a pioneer of urban villages, or transit-oriented, walkable development. The CNU's charter defines it as standing "for the restoration of existing urban centers and towns within coherent metropolitan regions, the reconfiguration of sprawling suburbs into communities of real neighborhoods and diverse districts, the conservation of natural environments, and the preservation of our built legacy."[12]

At almost the same time, at the 1992 Rio summit, the term *smart growth* came into use. The ten smart growth principles, as defined by the U.S. Environmental Protection Agency, resemble those of the new urbanists: (1) mix land uses; (2) take advantage of compact business design; (3) create a range of housing opportunities and choices; (4) create walkable neighborhoods; (5) create distinctive, attractive communities; (6) preserve open space, farmland, natural beauty, and critical environmental areas; (7) strengthen and direct development towards existing communities; (8) provide a variety of transportation choices; (9); make development decisions predictable, fair, and cost effective; and (10) encourage community and stakeholder collaboration in development decisions.[13]

These and other groups share a commitment to several general principles by which we may shape our built environment—in urban neighborhoods, in small or large towns, and even in sprawling suburbia itself—so that it will enhance community and sustainability rather than vitiate them.

First, a sustainable community is dense. Considered on a per-capita basis, compact, dense places—cities—are inherently greener than low-density suburbs. In fact, the average urban dweller has one-third the carbon footprint of the average suburban dweller. For one thing, energy efficiencies are built into the urban infrastructure: in apartment buildings, units share adjoining walls and heat escapes into the units above, so that less energy is wasted than in single-family homes. For another, cities, unlike suburbia, have density sufficient to support public transit.[14]

Second, a sustainable community is walkable. In cities, the places where people want and need to go are closer together: destinations are within walking distance. And walkability, as we have seen, has excellent social, ecological, community, and health effects.[15]

Third, a sustainable community is mixed use. The new urban planners are discarding separate-use zoning. Using traditional town planning methods, they are bringing houses, stores, offices, civic buildings, and streets into closer proximity. They create easily identifiable town centers with plazas, and other common spaces that welcome pedestrians rather than threatening them with car dominance. Their closely woven, small-scale neighborhoods mix shops and offices with a variety of home types including rowhouses, narrow and tree-lined streets, sidewalks, and parks.

Fourth, a sustainable community is humanly scaled. In the name of density, some planners and architects are building high rises. But others recognize that districts with smaller buildings—humanly scaled buildings—have more vitality. Jan Gehl, the Danish urban theorist who mentored the new generation of planners and architects, studied how humans behave in different urban environments and concluded that the most comfortable building height for urban pedestrians is 12.5 to 25 meters, or about three to six stories.[16]

Moreover, the benefits of density are found mostly at the lower end of the density spectrum; increasing density to 20 homes per acre (50 per hectare) produces environmental gains. But achieving densities above about 60 homes per acre (150 per hectare) brings little additional benefit.[17] Hence humanly scaled buildings, as Gehl defined them, bring the benefits of density without the problems brought about by dense high-rises.

Over the past twenty years, the new urbanists, the smart growth movement, and others equipped with these ideas have begun to transform the American approach to urban planning. Their efforts have taken several forms.

Some have created compact, walkable places by going out into open green areas and constructing them anew, like suburbs. The new urbanists' Norton Commons was built on bluegrass outside Louisville, Kentucky;

and Kentlands, in Gaithersburg, Maryland, rose from 350 acres (140 hectares) of former farmland. Such projects have been criticized as "new suburbanism" and tend to be unaffordable. Moreover, building on green space or farmlands is the least desirable approach. Far more desirable, as the smart growth principles advise, is the transformation of existing places.

Another approach is to revitalize pre-automobile urban centers and towns, which fell into neglect and decay in the age of the automobile, or were paved over. They already have density and compactness, a mixed-use infrastructure, corner stores, and hangouts. The bones of their urban cores are scaled to the pedestrian; they have walkable narrow streets, short blocks, and multiple-unit dwellings. Now that we understand the value of traditional neighborhoods, they can and are being rebuilt and renovated. One city that has revitalized along smart growth lines is Minneapolis. The National Trust for Historic Preservation provides information, technical assistance, and advocacy on downtown revitalization in urban neighborhoods, rural towns, and small and mid-sized cities. The list of successes includes Saratoga Springs, New York; Chippewa Falls, Wisconsin; Natchitoches, Louisiana; Encinitas, California; Greenville, South Carolina; and many more.[18]

Another approach is to transform automobile-oriented cities by giving them urban centers. Some of the most sprawled-out American cities are reurbanizing in this way. A notable example is Stapleton, Colorado, a massive project designed by Peter Calthorpe on the site of the former Stapleton International Airport. Phoenix, Arizona, the epitome of a low-density, car-dependent city, has adopted a program called Reinvent PHX to create more walkable centers and connect them by public light rail. Smart growth principles are being accepted even in Texas: the city of El Paso now requires that architects working in city projects have accreditation in the new urbanism. And the Texas department of transportation's new rulebook actually recommends new-urbanist street design.[19]

The presence of already-existing good public transportation has been an important force for generating smart growth, in what is called transit-oriented development. Arlington, Virginia, home to five Metro stations, has become a dense, mixed-use development. Fruitvale Village in Oakland, a mixed-use, mixed-income community, was built near a Bay Area Rapid Transit (BART) station, on former BART parking lots. Its buildings are three to four stories tall, with varying dimensions so that pedestrians enjoy a variety of facades and sight distances. "The pedestrian street and plaza also serve as a major community-gathering place," writes one reviewer. Bethesda Row in suburban Maryland is another mixed-use, walkable, transit-accessible development predicated on the existence of a metro station three blocks away. Constructed on the Capital Crescent Trail, a popular biking and walking route, it has building heights range from two to six stories. As the Washington, D.C., metro system expands further, other places near stations, like Rockville and Tysons Corner, Maryland, are recreating themselves with smart growth and new urbanist principles in mind.[20]

The greatest and most important challenge, however, is to retrofit suburban sprawl itself—to urbanize the suburbs, making them more sociable and sustainable.[21] The new urban planners, or at least those who have successfully obtained waivers from separate-use zoning codes, are reconfiguring sprawl into neighborhoods with communities.

At present, about two-thirds of the existing twelve-hundred-odd indoor shopping malls in the United States are struggling to survive, due to Internet shopping and changes in people's choices around residence and shopping. Some malls have gone out of business, and when they do die, their huge concrete shells have been put to new uses: as civic centers, medical centers, schools, offices, art spaces, nursing homes, even universities.[22] About forty shopping malls have been razed altogether; in their place have risen city halls and parks and even entire downtown cores. Dead big box stores have been converted to schools, churches, and libraries—purposes that enhance community.

For example, in Lakewood, Colorado, one hundred acres (40 hectares) that were once the site of a large regional mall are now dedicated to a development called Belmar: 22 blocks of walkable streets, lined with multiuse buildings and a range of housing types with households. The buildings have photovoltaic arrays and wind turbines on the roofs. Eight bus lines serve this community, which also has two parks. Belmar is the downtown that Lakewood never had. Now eight of the thirteen remaining regional malls in Denver have said they plan to retrofit.[23]

Many parking lots that were built in the early years of sprawl are currently underused, as newer sprawl construction has leapfrogged over them. They now have a relatively central location, and since they so often lie empty, they are in many cases being dug up and repurposed for downtowns for centerless suburbs. The earliest such retrofit, Mashpee Commons, in Massachusetts, was created this way, on top of an old parking lot. Incrementally, the result has been a compact, mixed-use New England village.

Still another aspect of retrofitting is to focus on the corridors. Commercial roadways in sprawl can be retrofitted as complete streets with mixed-use buildings. In Cathedral City, California, a commercial strip corridor has been transformed into a boulevard that became the main street of the town. In sprawling Atlanta, an old rail corridor was retrofitted into a multi-use trail and connected park system, which opened up affordable housing options in forty-five city neighborhoods.[24]

The final option is to regreen. In some places smart growth principles don't work—for example, a subdivision is just too far from transit, or people have chosen not to live there anymore. They can be returned to green areas or suburban farms. When a shopping mall in Phalen Village, outside Minneapolis, went out of business, the city tore it up and restored the wetland that had been there before. Elsewhere, as in Seattle, creeks and wetlands are being daylighted.

For much of the 2000s, population growth in the outer suburbs continued to be the engine of U.S. residential growth. But recently Americans have started to move in the other direction. From 2010 to 2011, according to census data, outer suburban population growth nearly ceased, increasing by just 0.4 percent. For the first time in twenty years, cities grew faster than suburbs. And for the first time in one hundred years—for the first time since the invention of the automobile—the largest cities grew faster than suburbs. According to land-use strategist Christopher Leinberger, "The pendulum is swinging back toward building walkable urbanism."[25]

One reason is a demographic shift. A large share of today's millennial generation (the 80 million Americans born between 1977 and 1995) is rejecting the car-dependent lifeways of their parents. Back in 1980, 66 percent of all seventeen-year-olds had their driver's license, but in 2010 the figure was down to 47 percent. Moreover, millennials drive less. They are the first generation since the internal combustion engine was invented to be less enthusiastic about cars and driving than the previous generation. Moreover, having grown up in the suburbs, 77 percent of millennials say they prefer to live in places with walkable neighborhoods, transit, biking facilities, and a lively pulse. That could mean an urban core or an urbanized small town or suburb, but one thing it does not mean is a conventional suburb.[26]

The baby boomers (about 77 million strong) are retiring or soon to retire; as they do; they may find compact communities with convenient transit to be highly desirable.[27] Their choice is unclear, but whatever they decide, a rejection of classic suburbia is under way. American urban form is no longer reflexively being dictated by the automobile, and planners are discarding the old land-use codes that catered to it. In my view, these efforts are among the most promising developments under way in mitigating our carbon footprint.

This essay has focused on the United States, but worldwide, cities now account for most of the world's population. In 2009 the percentage of human beings living in urbanized areas surpassed the percentage living in rural areas. Today 54 percent of people live in cities. In Europe and North America, which industrialized long ago, urban density leads to energy efficiency; but elsewhere city dwellers have higher emissions per capita, simply because they are wealthier than rural dwellers and have greater access to electricity and the conveniences it brings. As a result, in 2013, despite their possible per-capita energy savings, cities geographically accounted for around 70 percent of greenhouse gas emissions and 80 percent of the increase in emissions last year.[28]

Still urban dwellers are freer to do something about their emissions because their cities are "not beholden to rural, fossil-fuel-dependent constituencies."[29] Cities can reduce emissions by adopting rigorous green building codes, expanding mass transit, switching to electric public vehicles and buses, and adopting smart growth to reduce driving. To do so, they have formed alliances, like the C40 Cities Climate Leadership Group, and the Mayors National Climate Action Agenda. Fifteen of C40's seventy-five member countries have made public commitments to reduce their emissions by 80 percent by the year 2050.[30]

The goal of urban design should be about more than reducing sprawl, lowering emissions, and achieving sustainability, as important as those goals are. Good urban design should also strengthen our social bonds and foster community. A dense, compact, human-scale built environment can be the infrastructure for community. By enhancing encounters and interactions among people on foot, walkability knits communities together and nourishes the public realm. Good urban design also promotes diversity, so that rich and poor, whites and nonwhites, elderly and young can live near one another and meet in the street. People need opportunities to meet and interact so that they don't become afraid of one another and can learn to talk together. As Duany and colleagues point out in *Suburban Nation*, "A society is healthier when its diverse members are in daily contact with one another."[31] Walkability strengthens both sustainability and the civic sphere that underpins a robust democracy.

NOTES:

1. Kenneth T. Jackson, *Crabgrass Frontier: The Suburbanization of the United States* (New York: Oxford University Press, 1985), 205-8.
2. Leigh Gallager, *The End of the Suburbs* (New York: Viking Penguin, 2013), 9.
3. Jackson, *Crabgrass Frontier,* chapter 9.
4. K.M.V. Narayan et al., "Lifetime Risk for Diabetes Mellitus in the United States," *Journal of the American Medical Association* 290, no. 14 (2003): 1884-90.
5. Richard Moe and Carter Wilkie, *Changing Places: Rebuilding Community in*

the Age of Sprawl (New York: Henry Holt, 1987), 50.

6. Andres Duany, Elizabeth Plater-Zyberk, and Jeff Speck, *Suburban Nation: The Rise of Sprawl and the Decline of the American Dream,* 10th anniversary ed. (New York: North Point Press, 2010), 158-59.

7. Ibid., 137-38.

8. Jane Jacobs, *The Death and Life of Great American Cities* (New York: Random House, 1961), 72; Ray Oldenburg, *The Great Good Place: Cafés, Coffee Shops, Community Centers, Beauty Parlors, General Stores, Bars, Hangouts, and How They Got You Through the Day* (New York: Paragon House, 1989).

9. David Owen, *Green Metropolis: Why Living Smaller, Living Closer, and Driving Less are the Keys to Sustainability* (New York: Penguin/Riverhead 2009), 115; Duany, Plater-Zyberk, and Speck, *Suburban Nation,* 61.

10. Robert Putnam, *Bowling Alone: The Collapse and Revival of American Community* (New York: Simon & Schuster, 2000), 213.

11. Peter Kropotkin, *Fields, Factories and Workshops* (1898); Ebenezer Howard, *Garden Cities of To-Morrow* (1902); Lewis Mumford, *The City in History* (1962); Murray Bookchin, *Our Synthetic Environment* (1962); Léon Krier, *The Architecture of Community* (Washington, D.C.: Island Press, 2009).

12. Peter Calthorpe, *Urbanism in the Age of Climate Change* (Washington, D.C.: Island Press, 2013); Charter of the New Urbanism (2001; available at cnu.org/charter.)

13. "Smart Growth Principles," U.S. Environmental Protection Agency.

14. Owen, *Green Metropolis.*

15. On walkability generally, see Jeff Speck, *Walkable City: How Downtown Can Save America, One Step at a Time* (New York: North Point Press, 2012).

16. Jan Gehl, *Cities for People* (Washington, D.C.: Island Press, 2010).

17. Speck, *Walkable City,* 60-61.

18. "National Award for Smart Growth Achievement 2003 Winners," U.S. Environmental Protection Agency; "Great American Main Street Awards," National Trust for Historic Preservation.

19. Reinvent PHX, "El Paso Teaches New Urbanism to Architects, Engineers," *Governing the States and Localities,* October 2, 2013.

20. Arlington County, Virginia, National Award for Smart Growth Achievement, 2002; Kaid Benfield, "The Remarkable Story of Oakland's Fruitvale Transit Village," *NRDC Switchboard,* February 17, 2011; Benfield, "The

Country's Best Suburban Retrofit: Bethesda Row Reaches Maturity," *NRDC Switchboard,* January 28, 2010; Benfield, "Do Go Back to Rock-vil-ille . . ." *NRDC Switchboard,* December 12, 2008; and Benfield, "Retrofitting Suburbia for the 21st Century," *NRDC Switchboard,* October 7, 2008.

21. Ellen Dunham-Jones and June Williamson, *Retrofitting Suburbia: Urban Design Solutions for Redesigning Suburbs* (Hoboken, NJ: John Wiley, 2011).

22. Amanda Erickson, "7 Uses for Failing Shopping Malls," *Atlantic CityLab,* January 8, 2013; Ellen Dunham-Jones, "Here's What's Become of America's Dead Shopping Malls," National Public Radio, September 10, 2014.

23. Dunham-Jones, *Retrofitting Suburbia.*

24. Ibid., fig. 4-21; "Overall Excellence in Smart Growth: Atlanta BeltLine Eastside Trail and Historic Fourth Ward," U.S. Environmental Protection Agency, 2013. See also Kaid Benfield, "The Country's Most Ambitious Smart Growth Project," *Atlantic,* July 26, 2011.

25. William H. Frey, "Population Growth in Metro America Since 1980: Putting the 2000s in Perspective," *Brookings,* March 20, 2012; Yonah Freemark, "In New Census Data, an Improved Outlook for Core Counties," *TransportPolitic,* April 8, 2012. Leinberg is quoted in Jim Jaquish, "New Study: Walkable Urban Communities Having Huge Impact on Growth," Atlanta Regional Commission, October 4, 2013. See also Christopher B. Leinberger, *The Option of Urbanism: Investing in a New American Dream* (Island Press, 2009), 96-98.

26. John Schwartz, "Young Americans Lead Trend to Less Driving," *New York Times,* May 13, 2013; Gallagher, *End of Suburbs,* 20.

27. Tara Bahrampour, "The Kids Gone, Aging Baby Boomers Opt for City Life," *Washington Post,* August 9, 2013.

28. Ben Adler, "Cities are Lapping Countries on Climate Action," *Grist,* September 29, 2014.

29. Ibid. See also "Ten Features of a Resilient City," *Sustainable Cities Collective,* October 2, 2014.

30. C40 Cities, "Advancing Climate Ambition: Cities as Partners in Global Climate Action" (September 2014), p. 4

31. Duany et al., *Suburban Nation,* 47.

ARE WE INVENTORS
OR REPAIRMEN?

ARNOŠT NOVÁK

cological activists aim for a society that no longer plunders, pollutes, damages, and exploits nature and people. But many ecological idealists have become professional lobbyists, loyal bureaucrats, and pragmatic politicians, and they no longer seek to create an ecological society. I believe that the story of Czech environmentalism shows how political moderation and a strict focus on legal forms of action proves to be a dangerous impasse for new movements that seek to change society and create an ecological future.

To be sure, the genealogy of the Czech environmental movement differs from Western ones. During the period of "real socialism," environmentalism represented very moderate, apolitical and tolerated dissent within the bounds of law. It did not challenge the establishment. In the early 1990s, however, new ecological organizations and groups emerged, with fresh ideas and an unconventional protest repertoire. They were inventors of new thoughts, concepts, and visions. But after short period of enthusiasm and openness to radical ideas and activism, even these Czech environmental organizations became professionalized and politically moderate: they ceased to challenge the status quo and its growth economy. Rather than seeking to create an ecological society, they focused on repairing the existing system.

Since the 1970s environmental movements have been influential in the West. This movement, however, has never been a single, unified movement; it is rather a loose term that refers to highly differentiated sets of opinions, ideology, and actions, ranging from liberal environmentalists to radical ecologists. The most radical currents came up with new repertoires of direct action and protests as well with new utopian, ecological cosmologies. They did—at least potentially—fundamentally challenge the existing capitalist system.[1]

Moderate and pragmatic forms of environmentalism have undergone a thorough "institutionalization," both in terms of how they have professionalized their activities and in terms of how they have regularized their access to policy-makers. In a highly symbolic way this mainstream movement was coopted at the 1992 Earth Summit in Rio de Janeiro, when the establishment responded to the green critique with its own concepts of "sustainable development" and "ecological modernization."[2]

Yet, while this "institutionalization" of environmentalism took place, there emerged new, more confrontational grassroots mobilizations. During the 1990s, the UK saw a dramatic increase in green radicalism.[3] Radical ecologists from Reclaim the Streets and British Earth First! launched the idea of a Global Day of Actions and promoted anticapitalist perspectives in the framework of the newly emerging alter-globalization movement.[4] This green radicalism often used imaginative and novel tactics of resistance and protests, such as street parties, protest camps, sabotage of machinery or GMO fields, or the occupation of offices and factories.[5]

These protest actions were not simply a strategy to get media attention. The London-based group Reclaim the Streets explained their approach: "Direct action is not just a tactic; it is individuals asserting their identity to control their own lives and to participate in social life without the need for mediation or control by bureaucrats or professional politicians. Direct action places moral commitment above positive law.

Direct action is not a last resort when other methods have failed, but the preferred way of doing things."[6]

For environmental organizations as Greenpeace or Friends of the Earth, direct action constituted an instrument of the last resort. For radical ecologists, however, direct action was the only justified means of political activism. Michael Duckett distinguishes a liberal form of direct action, which considers it primarily as a tool, from an anarchist concept of direct action, which emphasizes the unity of ideals and practice. All forms of direct action, it seems, exist in the tension between practical achievements that change our everyday lives and ecological visions that promise to transcend the status quo.[7]

In Western countries, it has been first and foremost the radical strands of the ecology movement—for example Rising Tide, Earth First! and Reclaim the Streets—that have used the more anarchistic concept of direct action. In the UK, this ecological direct action movement consists of "a series of overlapping and biodegradable networks that continuously change and adapt," and which "seek to transgress political norms, to advance an ethic which is at odds with that reflected in dominant institutions and to try to bring the future into the present by creating alternative communities and through confrontational action."[8] Such movements, it is argued, have the potential to challenge the basic rules of the game and give rise to creative social and political change.[9]

According to sociologist Brian Doherty, this radical branch of the ecology movement has four characteristics: it is based on a conscious collective identity; it acts, at least partly, outside political institutions and uses protest as a common form of action; it is characterized by non-institutionalized networks of interaction; and it rejects dominant forms of power.[10] The ecology movement has the potential to engender a new society, but to do so, it must be willing to go beyond the instrumentalist mindset that prevails today: a new political approach will partly be shaped by our ability "to break free of mental constraints and think differently."[11] Some forms of ecological direct action are glimpses of other possible worlds; they radically expand our imagination. They are perhaps most significant when they constitute ruptures in everyday life of capitalist society.

The Czech environmental movement differs from its counterparts in Western Europe in several important respects. Above all, it has no roots in the tradition of New Left and the new social movements. The Czech movement developed out of an officially recognized conservationism, in virtual isolation from Western ecological thought, and even from the embryonic array of moderate dissident activists that opposed the "communist" regime in the late 1980s.[12] Therefore, in marked contrast to its Western counterparts, Czech environmentalists did not identify any structural features of capitalism as causing ecological problems; rather, ecological damage was perceived as consequence of the centrally planned socialist system. Indeed, Czech environmentalists saw capitalist society and the market economy as their hope and the solution to the ecological problems of their country.[13] Their actions and ideology were based on moderate criticism, dialogue with the establishment, expert knowledge, and latent anti-communist sentiments. Because they viewed ecological problems primarily through lens of science and technology, and also because they wanted to enter into a dialogue with the authorities, they had to emphasize scientific, "apolitical," and "value-free" arguments. The solution to environmental problems, they argued, was to be found in better scientific understanding and the application of less damaging technologies. The Czech environmentalism of the late 1980s was a peculiar blend of an officially sanctioned current of technocratic and scientific thinking and a strong romantic undercurrent extolling the virtues of pristine nature and individual freedom.[14] This, together with the fear of repression and a latent anti-leftism, gave rise to a particular type of environmentalist: a cautious person upholding the ideals of tolerance and liberal democracy.[15] This psychologically prepared the way for a liberal environmentalism in the 1990s.

After 1989, the "post-revolutionary" era was one of open opportunities and explorations of new ideas, identities, and social relations. Some more politicized organizations were founded in Prague and Brno and groups as Děti Země (Children of the Earth) or Hnutí Duha (Rainbow Movement) emerged as alternatives to the moderate Czech environmental movement. In particular, Hnutí Duha was critical of Western industrial and consumerist society. It did not aim to change society through the political party system, but rather through unconventional protests or blockades. The experiences of the Velvet Revolution played an important role: they allowed for a new repertoire of action, more confrontational and unconventional. The successful regime change and their experiences from strikes, mobilizations, and protests, imbued in young people a feeling that it was indeed possible to change society.

At first, the newly emerging ecology movement was quite confrontational. In the first half of the 1990's, there was a series of important direct actions, demonstrations, and blockades: against the construction of a nuclear power plant, against the demolition of the village of Libkovice because of mining, as well as against the felling of trees in the Šumava National Park. Although both Děti Země and Hnutí Duha used direct action throughout the first half of the 1990s, they were under the influence of environmental organizations such as Greenpeace or Friends of the Earth. These organizations always considered direct action as a last resort, only to be used when all other means had been exhausted; it was instrumentalized as an inferior part of their long-term campaigns. During the blockade of the Temelín nuclear power plant, Hnutí Duha released a handbook entitled "The Legal Guide for Direct Action," which clearly defines its understanding of direct action: it "is essentially effectuated in public and its organizers bear political and legal responsibility for its course and consequences ... it must not be anonymous," the handbook says. "Direct action is an extreme method used when all legal means have been exhausted."[16]

During the first half of the 1990s, radical environmental organizations and groups underwent a gradual process of professionalization and institutionalization, and most of them eventually became the very opposite of their former ideals. Notably, the Czech Republic saw the arrival of new type of "transactional activism," spurred by international backing.[17] "Instead of direct participation and membership, this form of activism is based to a significant extent upon the existence of (often small) non-membership advocacy groups and is characterized by its dependence on external resources as well as by its accentuation of inter-organizational interaction/transaction."[18] This new transactional activism became typical for NGOs such as Hnutí Duha and Děti Země. They were not able to mobilize a large number of followers, and did not primarily focus on confrontational, protesting strategies, but gradually preferred systematic lobbying and exerting political pressure.[19]

After the initial radicalization in the early 1990s, the Czech environmental movement gave up on direct actions and vocal criticisms of the system in favor of lobbying and direct dialogues with the political authorities. During the second half of the 1990s, although the environmental organizations were moderate, they still questioned the dominant social paradigm of the transitional period: economic growth and the desire to catch up with Western countries in terms of levels of consumption.[20]

During the 1990s, there were three crucial events that defined the trajectory of Czech environmentalism. The first came in 1992, when Václav Klaus and his right-wing coalition won the general election, a victory that resulted in four years of marginalization of the ecology movement. Klaus had a vision of "Catching up with Europe" and the prosperity of Western countries. The enthusiasm of openness ended abruptly, and the environmental movement now faced a political elite whose expressed aim was to deregulate the economy and society. The environmentalists, which opposed unregulated growth, were branded as communist relics.

In January 1995, the antipathy towards the environmentalists reached a second critical point when environmental organizations like Greenpeace, Děti Země, and Hnutí Duha were placed on the national list of "extremist organizations," together with anarchists and right-wing fascists. After former president Václav Havel and a number of prominent figures of Czech society intervened, the environmental organizations were eventually removed from this list, but no apology was ever issued and the label "dangerous extremist" has stuck. To cope with this situation, Czech environmental organizations disciplined themselves to be acceptable for an increasingly conservative Czech society.

The third crucial event came in 1996. The new election weakened Klaus' government and the climate of outright hostility to environmental organizations was replaced by period of tentative cooperation. The end of Klaus' government in 1998 brought a new era for the movement. New and again more open political opportunities came to restructure the focus and interests of the environmental organizations themselves. Once seemingly radical groups as Hnutí Duha and Děti Země gradually gave up any strategy of direct action and civil disobedience and transformed themselves in professional lobbyists that sought to influence national policy. The more radical critiques of parliamentarism and the party system—or even the tentative glimpses of more radical deep and social ecologies—were all but expunged from their agenda. They now focused entirely on lobbying the Parliament, offering specific recommendations to achieve limited improvements, steps they hoped would ensure future sustainability without alienating any investors. They were eager to prove that they were politically moderate and to demonstrate a professionalism that was acceptable to public officials and politicians. This strategy of gaining acceptability as a professional organization meant that they eventually got their chairs around the negotiation table. But any alternatives to representative democracy and globalized capitalism definitely disappeared from their imagination.

This trend of organizational professionalization and political moderation was consolidated during the next decade. Already in 2000, when Prague saw broad mobilizations against the IMF and World Bank Summit, the major Czech environmental organizations didn't even participate. During the first decade of the new millennium, these organizations, which once advanced bold ecological visions had definitely given up on radical activism; their strategies were lobbying, commenting on laws, and participating in administrative proceedings.

There are several common explanations for this de-radicalization, professionalization and loss of imagination. First, we should recognize that Czech environmentalism stems from a different tradition to its Western counterpart. In the West, environmentalism originated as a protest movement influenced by student radicalism and above all by the New Left and the counterculture. This movement had, from its inception, potential to challenge the dominant economic system in the West, capitalism. The Czech environmental movement, by contrast, originated in an authoritarian regime of "real socialism," as officially tolerated associations, and through dissidents who repaid this tolerance by political prudence and moderation. Unlike in the West, the origins of the Czech movement were not framed by the antagonistic social conflicts and criticisms of the establishment, but more by a "dialogue with power."[21]

Second, we must recognize how the whole culture and structure of political opportunity has changed the Czech republic. As a result of living under an authoritarian regime for forty years, the Czech public is markedly conservative, and not accustomed to unconventional protest strategies such as demonstrations, blockades, or countercultural lifestyles.[22] Until 1989, Czech society was strongly conformist and everything was aimed to preserve the status quo. Two years of enthusiasm, when society was opened to new ideas and initiatives, was effectively ended in 1992, when Václav Klaus won the national election and a new politics of "normalization" began to marginalize alternative, critical, and radical perspectives: in this process, environmental organizations were branded as enemies of European integration.

These commonly stated reasons are important to understand the peculiar Czech situation, But I must emphasize that these shifts were also driven by internal dynamics within the ecology movement. The Czech environmental organizations were not only victims of political ostracism and marginalization: they themselves made a series of decisions about their activities and their organizational forms, which influenced their political trajectories. Hnutí Duha, for instance, was the organization that used direct action most extensively as a tactic in the 1990s, but it was also a very hierarchical and undemocratic organization. Its leadership was not elected: it was managed by a "board of elders," composed of the organization's founders and select people they considered trustworthy. In 1994, Hnutí Duha stated that it was not a democratic but a trust-based organization.[23] This internal structure was supposedly a defensive mechanism to protect Hnutí Duha against the influence of new members who did not share the founders' opinions. Their internal structure was not antihierarchical—like many radical ecology groups in the West—but it had more in common with traditionalism and tribal councils of elders.

Jakub Patočka, one of the founders of Hnutí Duha, was a charismatic person who introduced an intellectually isolated Czech audience to many ideas from Western radical green thought. Above all, these were the ideas of deep ecology, traditionalism, and the "resurgence of natural relationships."[24] They did not include any typical leftwing issues of Western radical ecologists, such as womens' rights, participatory democracy, animal rights, and anticapitalism, as this did not fit well into their cosmology. And yet, even before the environmental organizations were placed on lists of extremist organizations in 1995, charismatic leader Jakub Patočka warned against any collaboration with anarchists and the punk subculture. Beginning in 1993, he took a sharp stand against any kind of cooperation with the anarchists; he refused their ideas, their alternative culture, and their "ambiguous relation to violence."[25] Still, he also had practical reasons for rejecting anarchist influences. If the more numerous anarchists would consider Duha to be their movement's environmental flagship, they would certainly have succeeded in making it so. To maintain control, it was probably necessary to express public misgivings and emphasize political differences.[26] When environmental organizations were labelled extremists, this tendency was strengthened, and the organizations disassociated themselves from all anarchists and from whatever could appear as radical and, from a mainstream point of view, extremist.

On the other hand, the anarchist movement also underwent a certain evolution, and what once were overlapping milieus took different trajectories. The long-standing tensions between lifestyle anarchists and social anarchists led to a breakup of the movement in 1997, where some tendencies, such as the Federation of Social Anarchists (FSA) were hostile to any cooperation with environmental and other nongovernmental organizations; these were designated as "collaborators"—and so too were any of those anarchists who chose to cooperate with them.[27] As a result, many sympathizers got discouraged and left anarchist activism altogether and the scene gradually disintegrated.

The environmental and anarchist milieus took different trajectories, and this did not allow an overlapping between them that could prove mutually enriching, one that could encourage the development of direct action as the preferred way of ecological activism, and allow for visionary alternatives of ecological utopianism to help challenge the status quo. On the contrary, both milieus had strong core groups and charismatic personalities, with a clear vision and full of vigor—such as Jakub Patočka, the head of Hnutí Duha, or, in a way, also Petr Wolmuth from the Federation of Social Anarchists—and these dynamics fuelled the separatist discourses within their respective spheres of influence. Toward the end of the 1990s, the environmentalists and the anarchists were on markedly different political paths. By then, the environmentalists chose institutionalization and professionalization, and came to accept ecological modernization as a core concept. In the process, they abandoned all unconventional forms of activism.[28] The unfortunate consequence was that "environmentalism was not allowed to develop as a social and political critique of, or as a visionary alternative to, the existing social order."[29] The anarchist movement, on the other hand, purged all "collaborators" and "lifestyle anarchists" from its ranks: They lost potential activists and supporters amongst young people from subcultures, while also failing to achieve broader popular support and to appeal to the working class.

I n 2011, after a ten-year hiatus, activists from Hnutí Duha again used direct action and civil disobedience to defend trees at the Šumava National Park. This, unfortunately, does not disprove that the movement has lost its radicalism and its imagination. These acts of civil disobedience were completely framed as a justified defense of the law against the illegal action of the authorities. In the conservative Czech political culture, it was perhaps an unconventional action, but it did nothing to challenge the profit and accumulation of capital, or the more fundamental growth imperatives that threaten nature and society alike. Contemporary Czech environmentalism remains allured by the chimera of ecological modernization. Their organizations only point out when authorities and corporations break the laws and suggest minor adjustment of laws and regulations. But they no longer strive for social change.

Twenty-five years ago, the Czech environmentalists tried to invent alternatives to "real socialism" and the incoming "real capitalism," however cautious, but they gradually became repairmen, and now, they no longer seek to invent any new kinds of politics. But the ecology movement cannot afford to lose our visions of a genuinely ecological future: we strive for a society that no longer plunders, pollutes, damages and exploits nature and people. The only way to get out of this impasse, I think, is to stop believing that we can repair a fundamentally unsustainable economic system. Instead we should radicalize our ecological visions, expand our repertoire of actions, and create a broad, popular movement. As social ecologists, we must continually ask ourselves whether we are inventors of a new society, or repairmen of the old.

NOTES:

1. Brian Doherty, *Ideas and Actions in the Green Movement* (London: Routledge, 2002); Kevin Bradley and Johan Hedrén, *Green Utopianism: Perspectives, Politics and Micro-Practices* (London: Routledge, 2014).

2. Phil Macnaghten and John Urry, *Contested Natures* (London: SAGE Publications, 1998).

3. Benjamin Seel and Alex Plows, "Coming live and direct: strategies of the Earth First!" in Benjamin Seel, Matthew Paterson, and Brian Doherty, eds., *Direct Action in British Environmentalism* (London: Routledge, 2000); Derek Wall, *Earth First! and the Anti-Roads Movement* (London: Routledge, 1999).

4. Giorel Curran, *21st Century Dissent: Anarchism, Anti-Globalism And Environmentalism* (London: Palgrave, 2007).

5. Seel, Paterson, and Doherty, eds., *Direct Action in British Environmentalism*; Raphael Schlembach, "How do radical climate movements negotiate their environmental and their social agenda? A study of debates within the Camp for Climate Action (UK)," in *Critical Social Policy*, 31 (2011), 194-215.

6. Brian Doherty, Alexandra Plows, and Derek Wall, "The Preferred Way of Doing Things: The British Direct Action Movement," *Parliamentary Affairs* 56 (2003), 670.

7. Michael Duckett, "Ecological Direct Action and the Nature of Anarchism: Explorations from 1992 to 2005" (PhD diss., Newcastle University, 2006), 154.

8. Seel and Plows, "Coming live and direct," 113,

9. Doherty, Plows, and Wall, "The Preferred Way of Doing Things," 684.

10. Doherty, *Ideas and Actions*, 7.

11. Lucy Sargisson, *Utopian Bodies and the Politics of Transgression* (London: Routledge, 2000), 3.

12. Adam Fagan, *Environment and Democracy in the Czech Republic: The Environmental Movement in the Transition* (London: Edward Elgar, 2004); and Petr Jehlička, "The New Subversives: Czech Environmentalism after 1989," in Helen Flam, ed., *Pink, Purple, Green. Women's, Religious, Environmental and Gay/Lesbian Movements in Central Europe Today* (New York: Columbia University Press, 2001).

13. Petr Jehlička, Philip Sarre, and Juraj Podoba, "The Czech Environmental Movement's Knowledge Interest in the 1990s: Compatability of Western Influences with pre-1989 Perspectives," *Environmental Politics* 14:1 (2005), 64-82.

14. Ibid., 75.

15. Miroslav Vaněk, "Zelené mládí," in Miroslav Vaněk, ed., *Ostrůvky svobody: kulturní a občanské aktivity mladé generace v 80. letech v Československu* (Praha: Votobia, 2002), 250.

16. Martin Prokop, *Právní rádce do přímé akce* (Praha: Ekologický právní servis, 1997), 7.

17. Ondřej Císař, *Politický aktivismus v České republice. Sociální hnutí a občanská společnost v období transformace a evropeizace* (Brno: CDK, 2008).

18. Ondřej Císař, Jiří Navrátil and Kateřina Vráblíková, "Staří, noví, radikální: politický aktivismus v České republice očima teorie sociálních hnutí," in *Sociologický časopis* 47:1 (2011), 141.

19. Císař, *Politický aktivismus*; Císař, Navrátil, and Vráblíková, "Staří, noví, radikální," 137-167.

20. Jehlička, Sarre, and Podoba, "The Czech Environmental Movement's Knowledge Interest."

21. For more on the trajectory of Czech environmentalism in the 1990s, see Fagan, *Environment and Democracy*.

22. Ladislav Holý, *The Little Czech and the Great Czech Nation: National Identity and Post-Communist Social Transformation* (Cambridge: Cambridge University Press, 1996).

23. Bohuslav Binka, *Zelený extremismus* (Brno: Masarykova univerzita, 2008), 129.

24. "The resurgence of natural relationships" was used as the subtitle of Hnutí Duha's magazine *Poslední generace* (The Last generation).

25. Jakub Patočka, "Anarchisté a Hnutí Duha," in *Autonomie* 16 (1993), 12.

26. Jakub Patočka, "Duha deset let na cestě: lidé a křižovatky," *Sedmá generace*, 8:10 (1999), 20.

27. "The assignment," said FSA, "is to first and foremost sever our ties with democratic 'green' collaborators because it is these organizations and their connection to 'anarchists' which drag our movement down a slippery slope." Martin Bastl, *Radikální levice v České republice: Devadesátá léta dvacátého století* (Brno: Masarykova univerzita, 2001). And: "Let's not confuse the social anarchism movement with some 'alternative-autonomous-eco-anarcho-antitechnological-humanistist-pacifist' scene. We may subvert the scene but we solidify the movement. ... The way out runs through a clear rejection of all 'autonomism,' radical ecology, punkish lifestyle, HC and music subcultures in general." PW "Anarchismus: nutně sociální, nutně revoluční, nutně kolektivistický a racionalistický," *Svobodná práce* 12 (1998), 3.

28. Jehlička, Sarre, and Podoba, "The Czech Environmental Movement's Knowledge Interest."

29. Ibid., 72.

TOWARD A ZERO MARGINAL COST MUNICIPALITY

JONATHAN KORSÁR

Zero marginal cost occurs when it costs nothing, or next to nothing, to produce one or thousands of additional goods or services once the necessary productive equipment and organizational framework exists. Zero marginal cost arises in many sectors of the economy today, in a time increasingly characterized by "extreme productivity."

According to Jeremy Rifkin in *The Zero Marginal Cost Society: The Internet of Things, the Collaborative Commons and the Eclipse of Capitalism*, in most cases of extreme productivity, capitalism is incapable of managing the situation in a collectively beneficial way, as it is not fit to deal with the technologies and systems currently under rapid development and proliferation. We need new systems of interaction between new technologies, and new social organizations that can meet and manage the demands of increased productivity from these new technologies.

Rifkin suggests cooperative management and commons arrangements, along with patience to allow these systems to come into their own. New technology, cooperatives, and commons structures can create a foundation for an altogether new society—a zero marginal cost society—marked by "extreme productivity," resource sharing, and production controlled by the people, in place of property rights, mass production, and concentrated capital. In Rifkin's view, commons make resources available for everyone who needs them, while cooperatives allow for horizontally integrated and democratic management as an alternative to the vertical, hierarchical management structures of capitalism.

Although Rifkin's book confronts a range of issues that municipal politics needs to address in order to progress toward an ecological society, he doesn't actually emphasize the role of municipalities. Municipalities, I argue, must play a central role in creating a zero marginal cost society. In sharp contrast to narrowly defined ideas about "municipal competence"—as something limited, rigid, and almost ahistorically defined—it is fitting to adopt a new understanding of the role of municipalities in relation to emerging technological, social, and economic opportunities in various fields.

In the last decades, the "harvesting power" and use of wind and solar has grown exponentially. Millions are employed in these sectors, and as Rifkin notes, industry analysts forecast that within 20 years, the harvesting technology for solar and small wind power will be as cheap as cell phones and laptops. And we have yet to adequately explore biomass, wave, hydro and geothermal power, whose efficiency is only increasing.

Moreover, the development of more efficient solar panels and other renewable energy harvesters will not halt as the demand for alternatives over increasingly expensive fossil fuels rises. In 2011, the cost of generating electricity with solar panels became lower than the cost of generating electricity with diesel generators, setting the scene for a radical new era in energy generation, affecting developing countries like India and Nigeria in particular. And this trend of lowered costs and increased deployment of renewable energy is set to continue. Of course, there are substantial initial costs, but once the systems are established, the marginal costs are small in comparison to fossil fuels.

The transition to renewable energy will follow not only from deployment of new harvesting technologies, but through a range of new practices throughout society. Different estimates show that substantial energy cuts are possible in industry and the built environment by making use of better technology in the form of pumps, insulation, and better windows, among other things. Potentially bigger cuts could result from new forms of management in the economic life of communities, as a consequence of a wide sharing of resources, labor and other social innovations.

The link between new energy and municipalities arises from the scale and nature of the resources that will be used. Solar, wind, and most other forms of renewable energy are best distributed locally as energy that is "laterally empowering," to quote Rifkin. Rather than promoting centralized powers that have long benefited from highly concentrated forms of fossil fuel energy, renewable technologies have the ability to empower local people, neighborhoods, and municipalities. Energy efficiency measures are also "laterally empowering" as they encourage municipalities to do more with less resources.

The trend towards locally controlled renewable energy is facilitated by new information and communication technology that allows not only people, but things, to "speak" with each other. This enables new means of oversight, control, and intelligent coordination of different processes. This creates more possibilities to increase thermodynamic efficiencies, and strengthens our ability to do more with the same amount of energy—a necessary skill for the creation of an ecological society.

These information and communication technologies are already in use at both city, regional, and in some cases, national levels. In Germany, millions of citizens have gone from being only users, or "consumers" of energy services, to becoming "prosumers," that is, both users and managers of the energy system. Small scale energy generation technologies capable of "harvesting" energy, including solar panels, wind power, and bioenergy plants, have been connected in smart regional grids. In those grids, the intermittent renewable energy of the sun and wind is shared and used where it is needed. Electricity must be used or distributed where there is an energy need or the possibility of storage. It is possible to control and manage energy in relation to its availability. There are already many applications for this that are working very well. For example, there are washing machines as well as factories that rest when there is less energy available on the grid, only to put on "full steam" when more energy is available.

What these examples show is how the material world, in this case energy generation technologies and things that use energy, have been integrated into what is now being called an "Internet of Things," where the internet, as well as other similar networks manage how things are set in motion and used for maximum benefit. The promise of the Internet of Things is immense, and its development and construction seems poised to be one of the central challenges and sources of conflict in the decades ahead. Besides the generation and distribution of energy, the Internet of Things opens up possibilities for big changes in how we use energy throughout society more generally. This includes forms of management in the economic life of communities, wider sharing of resources, labor and wealth, intelligent and radical reforms in our logistics and transport systems, environmental monitoring, as well as more efficient and intelligently integrated production systems utilizing local resources.

The construction of a comprehensive Internet of Things would benefit enormously if an actor concerned primarily with people's well-being could take the lead in building it. Fully utilizing its potential is dependent upon managing it without selling out to the commercial interests that seek to profit by collecting data on everyone and everything. It is also dependent upon our collective ability of making today's often segregated subdivisions of society to collaborate much more extensively. It is here that municipalities have a very important role to play. Municipalities must take over the networks that will enable efficient and democratic control, as well as aggressively promote the wide sharing of resources, labor, and wealth.

The era of dirty, concentrated energy has been a logistical frenzy. As a consequence of the low price of dirty, highly concentrated forms of energy, production facilities have been built with no consideration of minimizing transport. Transport and logistics companies are making amazing profits while the environment and the climate are being severely degraded.

Municipalities today are the locus of considerable volumes of transport work. They also depend on massive amounts of global transport work shuffling goods from one corner of the earth to the other. The system as a whole is not very efficient, and this inefficiency is harming both the global climate and local environments. Efforts to make it more efficient often come from within the system itself. For example, there has been a widespread deployment of computing and automation to make loading and coordinating trucks and ships more efficient. Still, the actors involved are not coordinated, and there is a lack of common protocols. But even more importantly, the actors involved may have an interest in making their own logistics chains more efficient, but that does not mean they have an interest in making the whole system more lean and productive within ecological boundaries.

In *The Zero Marginal Cost Society*, Jeremy Rifkin quotes several studies that highlight that trucks and ships often are traveling less than half full. This is a problem both globally and in our municipalities. In Sweden, for example, most cars go less than half full every day, and stand unused in parking lots most of the day. Yet more than 50% of Swedish cities are dedicated to roads.

It is quite obvious that there is a huge potential to make the system radically leaner and increase its thermodynamic efficiency. Many enlightened industrialists as well as transport planners propose a combination of shared standards and regulations, combined with the deployment of information and communication technology that can make the smaller parts in the system do more to serve the whole, rather than operating according to the demands of bits and pieces of the overall system. Globally and regionally, the goal would be to cut the waste of going with less than full ships, planes, trains, and trucks.

Within municipalities, there are even more bold proposals. It is worth mentioning self-directed cars—cars driven by robots, a system that would allow most cars to serve as taxis going around the city "on demand," thus minimizing the time cars travel less than full or just stand idle in parking lots. Utilizing this technology to the fullest would involve essentially banning the private car, and radically cutting the numbers of cars needed to serve any city. Of course, beginning by doing more with local resources and producing better quality goods are strategies that would substantially lessen the load on the logistics system as a whole.

Another proposed system that could radically increase efficiency includes complementing high speed trams with electric bike taxi schemes. This system, similar to a system employing robot-operated taxis in combination with buses or trams, would not only cut energy needed for logistics, but would radically reduce the area required for roads from about 50% to less than 25%.

Whatever the specific lean logistics solutions, we must confront a number of questions: Who can take on the work of radically cutting the waste in today's logistics sector? Who could take the overarching local and regional perspective necessary for implementing energy efficient logistics at multiple scales? Who can radically cut the need for transport work carried out by global actors who depend upon dirty fossil fuels by systematically strengthening the local and regional actors? Who can manage the logistics system locally and regionally as a commons that could benefit everyone? In a world where cities and towns are hubs of the economy, municipalities seem to be the political organizations destined to take on those tasks. In general, other actors are too immersed in processes and operations at other scales to succeed in such an undertaking.

In manufacturing, the nearly workerless factory is on its way to becoming the norm, in both highly industrialized and developing countries. A few examples may illustrate what is happening. Rifkin takes many of his examples from the US, but what happens there hints at developments on the way elsewhere. Between 1982 and 2002, steel production in the US increased from 75 million tons to 120 tons a year. At the same time, the sector went from employing 289,000 to 74,000 workers. In other words, output increased 30%, even though the employed workforce decreased to one quarter its original volume. This means that output per worker increased tenfold from 160 tons per person to 1600. Nor is this trend limited to steel production. Between 1995 and 2002, a total of 22 million manufacturing jobs disappeared, but overall production still rose 30%.

An increased use of robotics is one explanation for these changes. In 2011 alone, the sales of robots increased 40% in the EU and US. And robots were deployed in operations of every scale. Rifkin quotes experts in the field who believe that the 163 million manufacturing jobs that still existed in the US in 2003 will have decreased to just a few million in 2040. In manufacturing, as in energy, the upfront costs of getting rid of the need for labor are still big, but the marginal costs of operating production without workers is very low, or "close to zero."

3D printing is another important trend in manufacturing. This technology promises to find an ever increasing array of applications in the coming decades. For many, it promises to be the lever that enables local production of everything from organs, to houses, to medical aids, to spare parts.

"Extreme productivity" in manufacturing means that less working hours are needed to produce the goods we need. Combining this with a more efficient and collaborative use of resources, raises a series of interesting and challenging issues. Can we continue with the present model for distributing and managing labor? What other alternatives are there? How should we make people who are not needed, according to the old market-based way of distributing labor and wages, into participants in a collaborative economy? These are pressing challenges, and they become very non-abstract issues at the regional and local level.

Of course, municipalities may not look like the obvious winners in a world of "extreme productivity." Rising productivity within a capitalist framework rarely strengthens local communities. Still, could municipalities reevaluate and change their role in manufacturing? Regions and communities could take a proactive role. Local self-reliance might arise as the new ideal, and alliances of municipalities and other local economic actors capable of working together may make the economy able to serve local and regional needs.

Huge changes in mining, agriculture, forestry, and fishing shaped the outlook of the 20th Century. New technology in these fields—for better and for worse—caused people to leave those trades long before "extreme productivity" made jobs begin to disappear from the manufacturing and service sectors. The countryside was left with fewer people and mounting difficulties in sustaining itself and its inhabitants.

Considering the coming changes in the energy sector mentioned earlier, it's clear that the countryside has a new role to play as a provider of essential energy services to cities. Still, this will probably not be enough to invigorate the countryside. It will probably only be the movement toward more local production, and an increasing dependence of cities on their surrounding hinterland for materials, food, and strengthened ecosystem services that will suffice.

Innovation is needed on many fronts in the economy, with environmental issues in general, and the climate issues in particular, driving the discussion. There is already plenty of activity on the margins of the economy. There is a large interest in open source programming, open source hardware, reuse and recycling, agroecology and "farm hacking," carbon agriculture to deal with excess CO2, the "maker" movement, and a widely felt desire to be more self-reliant. On the other hand, there are ongoing innovations and developments inside more conventional businesses. The municipality could, if managed intelligently, make all this come together in a massive popular movement focused on producing the most creative and high quality culture possible.

Car and bike sharing schemes. Land sharing schemes in the cities. Health oriented commons initiatives. Buying clubs. Couch surfing and other forms of sharing and utilizing space more efficiently. The sharing of cultural wealth in the form of music, literature, theater, or movies. MOOCS, or free online high quality education. The sharing of radio bandwidth and network resources locally and globally. Sharing tools, work spaces, and other means of production. The list could go on. This explosion of sharing promises to provide an affordable, or even better, an *accessible* way to make life decent for everyone in the world, as well as a very potent means for cutting thermodynamic waste, thus increasing the capacity of society to operate within ecological boundaries.

It is here that the municipality holds the most promise. Can it expand the principles of the public library, and free—or at least close to free— public education and health care to the other areas of the economy? Can it take on responsibility for fundamentally transforming our transport, manufacturing and energy systems? As was already discussed, we approach zero marginal cost in different sectors of our economy as new ways of producing, using and sharing are developed. Utilizing information and communication technology to do this on a new level is possible now.

Today, many call for a "big push" and large investments to make universal well-being and an ecological society possible. Looking at some of these emerging technologies, and how to approach them best, makes it clear that the main challenges associated with creating a zero marginal cost society are indeed municipal challenges. Zero marginal cost production of goods and services depends on creating and promoting new forms of sharing. Municipalities are the most sensible locus for developing these new forms of sharing, and as such, could become the basis of a new economy and an ecological society.

RADICAL APPROACHES TO TRANSPORT PLANNING

ERSILIA VERLINGHIERI

There is something utterly absurd about our everyday urban environments. Think about your experience of walking—or trying to walk—around in our cities, congested by traffic. And then sum up the overwhelming data on traffic-related air pollution, land consumption, injuries, risks, and health problems. During the last century, infrastructure and transportation planning developed a car-based system that heavily contributes to the social and ecological catastrophes we face today.

In response, an agenda for sustainable transportation is emerging: the goal of transport policies now increasingly aims to protect our environment, and shift our societies to low-speed mobility, based primarily on walking and cycling. But this approach is slow to assume a clear operative form and to implement the necessary changes. And it is even slower to challenge the current patterns of car-dependency and to radically change the way we move about—or not—in our cities. Moreover, this agenda still fundamentally directed towards top-down implementation of enlightened policies, or on encouraging individual solutions, and it is still excessively focused at reducing emissions, while it does not really take any critical approach to the underlying transport planning. It does not consider the fundamental question of "what are we going to do with a city free from exhaust gas, if the city remains occupied and congested by masses of cars?"[1]

But there are alternatives. Recently we have seen the emergence of social movements that present genuinely radical approaches to transport planning. I would like us to consider some of the social movements and grassroots groups in Rio de Janeiro, a city with one of the most disastrous traffic jams in the world, which practice a grassroots approach to transport planning. Their experiences reveal to us the real problems we are facing today, concerning how transportation is currently planned and how we can build viable alternative. I believe the time has come for urban planners to learn from the practices, projects, and needs of social movements, and support them in their struggles to construct a genuinely ecological society.

I would like to provide a brief exposition of some of the key elements that are missing from transport planning before I go on to explore some approaches that could address these gaps, taking inspiration from the programs and practices developed in Rio de Janeiro. I will bring attention to some key concepts that I believe can be useful to ground critical approaches to transport planning, concepts that not only seek to find possible ways out of the current environmental and social crises, but can also pathways to find better living conditions for us all.

There is now a global acknowledgement of the threat of climate change and in the decades that followed the Brundtland Commission's 1987 report, *Our Common Future*, sustainability has become one of the core concepts behind contemporary planning practices. This is certainly true for transport planning, which is becoming increasingly concerned about environmental impacts and emission reduction. Sustainability has become the desired outcome of planning and policymaking. The dominant paradigm is what geographer Marcelo Lopez de Souza calls "ecological planning." This is a paradigm based on the "binomial of modernization with ecological sustainability of the city," a profound belief in economic development as a winning choice and technocratic approach.[2] Focus is therefore mostly on the economic and environmental aspects of sustainability and broader ecological challenges are mainly addressed by an intrinsically positivist approach that hesitates to initiate new forms of radical planning.[3] The cross-spatial nature of transport and its presumed technicality creates the feeling that participatory planning practices for transport are difficult to realize, missing also the opportunity to learn from important radical developments in urban planning theory. Within the current paradigm, transportation essentially remains an engineering problem, which can only be solved by developing new technologies and infrastructures.

An alternative is proposed within new qualitative research approaches that try to understand patterns of personal behavior and influence our modal choices. This "behavioral turn," however, replicates the epistemic problem of reducing mobility needs to an individualized choice of different travel patterns, an individualization that already contributed to the disastrous advent of the automobile, under the clear assumption that "public and private transport are outstanding symbols of collectivism and individualism."[4]

On the other hand, these paradigmatic problems of transport planning seem to be clear to a range of new social movements, which instead propose that transportation is crucial to understand the development of cities, that it represents a key area to see the connection between environmental and social crises, and they use it to challenge the prevailing paradigm of mobility.

In Latin America, the Brazilian city of Rio de Janeiro represents a fascinating case of coordinated globalized development and social inequalities. Trapped in a fast "tourism urbanization" with a view to the 2014 FIFA World Cup and the 2016 Olympics, the city is changing at an incredible speed. But this rapid economic development sustains Rio's exceptional levels of inequalities and injustice. The western demand for easy investments drives a huge amount of privatization and renewal projects, while the situation for poor people concerning the right to education and health care—or, more appropriately, their right to the city—have not improved.[5]

In the urban development of Rio, transportation plays a crucial role. The city's transport system suffers from endemic problems of congestion and its public transports are relatively inaccessible, of low quality, and poor capacity. While the western romantization of private car mobility dramatically fuels the world's famous traffic jams, the right to mobility is far from guaranteed for all.

This is obvious when we look at some of the recent investments for mobility: in preparation for the mega events, the city is redesigning all its transport infrastructures, implementing a new metro line (Line 4) together with several Bus Rapid Transit lines and the highly contested construction of cableways in the favelas. A full 50,37% of the investments for the World Cup was devoted to urban mobility and even more is coming from the Olympics, but these huge investments are not only incapable of answering the crucial needs of the city's population, but have also necessitated an exponential number of evictions and removals.[6] A public transport infrastructure, when privatized and focused on cars and roads, is and probably will remain a service dramatically incapable of meeting the population's demands.

In light of this, it not surprising that increased bus ticket price became the "straw that broke the camel's back," when the city experienced a broad social uprising in June 2013. This uprising demanded access to a better public transportation, health and education system; and it demanded an end to privatizations and evictions, indeed, for a universal right to the city. The population did not limit their demands to a normalization of the situation; they sought to expand their traditions of grassroots planning for transport which started years earlier. Indeed, the June 2013 explosion is intimately connected to the work done by several groups in Brazil, such as the famous Movimento Passe Livre, MPL, the "movement for free fares" that has existed at the national level since 2005 and whose objective is a "genuinely public transport service, free for the population and not privatized."[7]

In the Rio area, several radical social movements have been working on or have born out of the struggles over transportation issues, such as the Fórum de Luta contra o Aumento da Passagem (Forum for the Struggle Against the Increase of Bus Fare), Operação Para o Aumento (Operation Stop the Increase) and the Frente Independente Popular (The Independent Popular Front). Their campaigns practice radical contestation in the streets, but they are not limited to that: these movements have study groups to explore the issues and propose new alternatives, and are doing an important work to theorize the problem of accessibility and transport justice, and for recognizing public transportation as a fundamental right. For example, at the national level, Movimento Passe Livre has been able to produce important studies on the possibility of implementing the Free Fare for public transport (Tarifa Zero), a policy that is has been already implemented in other Brazilian cities. Together with these social movements, other groups are also acting at the city level, such as O Metrô Que o Rio Precisa, MQRP (The Tube that Rio needs) and Quero Metrô, QM (I want Metro), which are proposing a counter-plan for the Line 4 of the Metro.

MQRP is a network of 30 Neighborhood Associations that are located in the areas that are to be served by the planned new Metro, and they are supported by other groups, individuals, and politicians. This organization developed a clear manifesto claiming that a new plan for the metro should be in the public interest of people in Rio, putting together the request of "1.5 million residents—increasingly concerned with the harmful legacy of a subway route that will serve principally the two or three weeks of the Olympic Games, but which will not serve the need for rapid and comfortable transport in the years after 2016."[8] They advanced, with the support of technicians and experts, a series of precise guidelines for a new metro line, the Line 4. They took inspiration from a never implemented public plan from the 1990's and took legal action to promote their agenda. Thanks to their political pressure, based on active monitoring, public debates, protests, and rallies, some modification on the new Metro line have been implemented.

The other group, Quero Metrô, was also born out work on issues regarding the new metro system: two university students started reflecting on possible solutions, supported by a blog. The project rapidly extended to include all available means of public transport and today it is a comprehensive alternative mobility plan for the whole city, based on the 12 metro lines, the rationalization and strengthening of the existing underdeveloped local trains, and strong cross-modal integration. The whole plan has been eagerly debated on the web and it has had great repercussions in local media and even for the local authorities.

Both these groups are close to the Fórum de Mobilidade (Mobility Forum), where representatives of Residents' Associations and Federations, Professional Councils and Service Clubs, Unions, various institutions, NGOs, and citizens, meet weekly to discuss mobility issues within the city. Here, technicians and non-specialists come together to discuss current issues and the future of their city. Initiated by the local Professional Association of Engineers, one of its aims is to provide information and research instruments to community groups, social movements—and disadvantaged groups more generally—in understanding mobility issues and help them in their struggles for a better transport system. For example, they collaborate closely with the inhabitants of the favela Rochinha in criticizing the new cableway construction.

These groups interpret the role of the technician in an innovative and horizontal way, breaking away from some of the classical planning problems I mentioned earlier: they confirm the necessity of a planner that act as advocate in support of the community struggles, the ability to support disadvantaged groups, and the need for a methodology and language that could be horizontal and not esoteric and unavailable for the general public.[9] Moreover, the ability of producing an alternative plan as well as providing people with highly detailed information material, the ability to engage lay people in technical debates, and their horizontal approach are all exemplifying an uncommon planning practice, but it helps them stay focused on their ultimate goal: making transport equity real.

The demands made by these social movements to solve the condition of the public transport system in Rio de Janeiro are a good place to start reflecting on the possibilities of alternative approaches to transport planning and urban mobility. I believe there are several lessons we can learn from their practice.

First, it is crucial that we look at the social dimension of transportation, at how questions of urban space are connected to social justice. The phenomena of urban segregation, peripherization of the poor, the creation of favelas and forced removals, are all phenomena connected to social struggles over mobility. The current car-based transportation system makes the poor poorer and more segregated.[10]

Second, transportation and mobility have a political dimension: decisions about transportation are crucially related to the politics of our cities. The struggle for mobility is transversal to the entire urban question and challenges the whole development project of the capitalist city.[11] In Rio de Janeiro, the building of new transport infrastructures are evidently part of a broader strategy of marketing the city: in the project of reshaping the city to host mega-events, the investments are entirely tailored to support increased capitalist accumulation.

Third, the transport system itself determines the physical space of the city impacts the lives of all citizens and shapes the possible futures of the city itself: for these reasons it is crucially important to democratize how decisions about transport are made. Social movements and grassroots groups propose new governance structures, tools and insights that can strengthen such processes.

As I mentioned earlier, the concept of sustainability—or, more precisely, sustainable development—has played a crucial role in defining the goals of transport planning in the last decades, building upon classical rational planning practices. However, the lack of holistic approach embedded in the accepted definition of sustainability, and the consequent separation of environmental and social issues, has permitted that transport studies by necessity has focused exclusively on the environmental damages caused by the prevailing car-based model of development, without a due analysis of the *social* aspects of this model.

The ineffectiveness of this approach to transport planning has been clear to the social movements I have discussed here: they work in a context where there is a glaring contradiction "between the romanticized discourse of social justice and environmental sustainability promoted by the authorities, and the hidden reality lived by citizens, one that is violent and segregating."[12] Even as sustainability has been proposed as the overarching goal of the strategic planning for the city, the reality of social inequality and suffering perpetuated within this model is evident, something which is obvious even from official documents published by the city council.[13]

Furthermore, the nature of the discipline called transport planning has associated it strongly to quantitative analysis and engineering solutions, and it has always been focused on the adoption of technical fixes, green technologies, and top-down strategies.

In sharp opposition to all this, the grassroots groups who approach transport planning in Rio recognize the need for a profound analysis of living conditions for the whole population, the crucial role of transportation in shaping cities, and its intimate connection to political issues of social equality. For example, the campaign Tarifa Zero built by the Movimento Passe Livre in Brazil urges us to understand the struggle for free public transport in a broader social context. "The struggle for the Zero-Fare is fundamental to guarantee access to public transport for people," they say, but "more than that, however, it is crucial because access to transport means better access to all other rights: to school, to hospital, to theatre. It unites therefore the set of social struggles."[14] Transportation and mobility, then, is intimately connected with the concept of right to the city. This is the right to participate at the political life of the city: transportation should not only be functional to capital accumulation, guaranteeing cheap labour force to be on time at the production place and then at the places of consumption, but should allow everyone to have access to the urban space of culture, leisure and political life.

For all these reasons, it is vitally important that we consider, both from a theoretical and from a practical perspective, the sum total of all the environmental and economic consequences of our choices in transport planning, and how our use of various technologies impacts our societies. Most of these analyses are excluded from the everyday transport choices and practices: what lacks is a radical stand and ideas of more fundamental social change as a possible solution to crises of transportation, an approach which would obviously challenge the status of contemporary transport planners. Moreover, it fails to recognize the deep connection between social and environmental crises: here, it is clear that Murray Bookchin's social ecological analysis of the concept of domination and the role of technology is still relevant and could contribute to changing the perspectives of transport studies.

There is one main thing that needs to be said about "the sustainability approach" and thus to the whole paradigm that governs current transport planning choices. "The focus on 'sustainable' development, as it emerges on the world stage," says Dan Chodorkoff, is primarily about "finding a means to sustain the expansion of capitalism."[15] This is something that these social movements in Rio are acutely aware of: sustainability is not about ecology, it is a concept inextricable linked to the neoliberal agenda and is incapable of going beyond sustaining the current socio-political model.

The analyses produced by social movements can lead more transformative perspectives, recognizing the necessity and possibility to solve mobility issues through new typologies and levels of interventions, which are not limited to the classic rigid dichotomy that traps transport planning between a top-down conditioning of behavioral changes or heavy infrastructural interventions. To begin with they identify transportation as a public good and a fundamental right to be guaranteed for all. Therefore, they claim, transportation should not be under the control of private companies. This is in sharp contrast to the general western trend of privatizations, which is now spreading worldwide on the English model. To support their point, these organizations have produced several critical studies on the damaging effects privatization have for public transport, as well as concrete proposals for how transportation can be managed differently.[16]

These social movements also produced extensive critiques of the construction of new transport infrastructures and the consequent processes of gentrification and violent evictions, which were seen as part of a more general critique of the capitalistic models that undergird the planning strategies for our cities. Today, it remains clear that the "political lobby of the people who produce and distribute cars, lorries, oil and petrol, concrete, asphalt and rubber" are the main responsible for the implementation of certain transport policies.[17] Their profit is far more important than guaranteeing better living conditions for all.

Following these points it is clear that, if mobility is a collective issue, it is also a collective struggle, and indeed a *political* struggle. Can we, after all, "blame working people for using car when the logistics of American society were deliberately structured by General Motors and the energy industry around highways?"[18] Several campaigns exemplify this, such as "Ocupa Onibus" (Occupy the Bus) in Rio de Janeiro, whose name explicitly refers to the global Occupy movement. For them the non-space of transport becomes a new space of contestation, and through visual interventions such as stickers and graffiti the struggle over the bus fares enters the very same buses. This is also reflected in the practices of the Swedish movement Planka.nu—which has been highly influential for the Brazilian MPL—aiming for free public transport as they cooperate on freeriding insurance funds.[19]

Could participatory democracy address also the issues of transportation and mobility? On the face of it, it seems that the nature of transportation, extending across communities, demands planning on a higher level and even needs to be heavily regulated by government[20]. Is it possible to build alternative grassroots planning groups that consider also transportation issues?

Yes, I believe that the practices of the Brazilian groups, with their alternative planning processes and struggles for a better public transport system, show that democratizing the whole planning process is in fact currently possible and can have a great impact, but that it requires great efforts and long-term grassroots work. Indeed, I believe that these practices are crucial for both developing ecological consciousness and for allowing planning to focus on what is good for society as a whole.

First, their work in disclosing information plays an important role in building a real ecological consciousness: they share data and show the reality of inequalities, the effects of a car-centered society, or the evictions caused by elitist transport infrastructures. This focus on providing critical information pursue a radical form of education that encourages people "to look critically not just at the impacts of individual decisions as consumers, not just at how they pollute, but rather how the dominant culture produces the conditions that make pollution inevitable."[21] Secondly, their alternative planning practices and concrete proposals have been able to influence future decisions about transportation. They are grounded in the community and show how forceful utopian thinking can be in framing new transport planning procedures. Indeed, "if transport planning is considered to be an activity in which groups and individuals see themselves as having the potential for influencing the future, irrespective of whether they have 'top-down authorization' to do so, then utopian thinking is likely to be highly potent."[22] These are utopias not of authoritarian determination, or single-man visions as in a pure rationalist planning approach, but they are horizontally produced projects, which support the struggles of the poor and the excluded. Their collective discussions challenge the current patterns of domination. It is a form of utopian thinking that stems from the necessity of restating core values at the very bases of the planning processes. They create their plans through participatory processes, demonstrating how people's willingness to participate goes well beyond the existing formal spaces for consultations and reveal people's ability to look at the complexity of transport issues in profound and meaningful way, and that they have the collective capacity to develop valid and accountable proposals. In Rio de Janeiro today, there is a woeful lack of institutional spaces for participation, but these social movements are able to open new participatory spaces. As broad forms of grassroots organization they prove that extensive participatory practices are possible in transport planning. The spaces they create show forms of political transformation and self-government that could be used as a basis for even broader implementation of alternative forms of participatory planning.

Their practices, moreover, convey another critical lesson for those who are currently planning our cities: working together with social movements, supporting their struggles, proposals, and projects, opens up a space for urban planners, researchers, engineers, and academics, and makes it possible for them to work concretely for real social change, and contribute to building a better world and an ecological future.

To sum up, I would say that there are two main lessons we can learn from the social movements in Rio de Janeiro I have presented here. The first is a plea for transport planners and academics to disconnect their practices from business-centered research and start looking at how they can work concretely to build transport equity paths, analyzing the possibilities that lie outside the range of the current economic and political system. Recognizing their responsibility and the important role they can play, they can become powerful allies of social movements, supporting their processes of questioning and developing proposals. The second lesson is for social ecology movements across the globe to recognize the importance of transportation and mobility in their struggle. We need to fight for a more egalitarian transport system that guarantee for all the right to move around freely with little or no environmental impact. There exists a series of examples that illustrate how we can develop radical approaches to transport planning, ranging from information disclosure to producing alternative development plans. These approaches can help us deconstruct the still predominant image of freedom as car-ownership. At the same time, they can help us reclaim the right to public space, the right to the city, and also the right to mobility.[23] Most importantly, however, is that they emphasize the collective dimension of ecological struggles and the transformative power that lies in the common construction of new ecological utopias.

NOTES:

1. Franco La Cecla, "Per Un'antropologia Dell'automobile," foreword to Colin Ward, *Dopo l'Automobile* (Milan: Elèuthera, 1997), 7–13, 12.

2. Marcelo Lopes de Souza, *Mudar a Cidade: Uma Introdução Crítica Ao Planejamento E À Gestão Urbanos* (Rio de Janeiro: Bertrand Brasil, 2001), 146.

3. See, for example, the work of Tim Schwanen, David Banister, and Jillian Anable, "Scientific Research about Climate Change Mitigation in Transport: A Critical Review," *Transportation Research Part A: Policy and Practice*, 45:10 (December 2011), 993–1006.

4. Colin Ward, *Freedom To Go: After the Motor Age* (London: Freedom Press, 1991), 13.

5. For detailed data on the national and regional level, see Chico Alencar, *A Rua, a Nação E O Sonho: Uma Reflexão Para as Novas Gerações, 2013* (Rio de Janeiro: Mardeideias, 2013); and the report from Universidade Federal do Rio de Janeiro (UFRJ) and Instituto de Pesquisa e Planejamento Urbano e Regional (IPPUR), *Projeto Metropolização E Megaeventos: Os Impactos Da Copa Do Mundo 2014 E Das Olimpíadas 2016 Relatório Parcial Nacional, April 2012* (available at observatoriodasmetropoles.net).

6. On the social impacts of new Olympic transport infrastructures, see, for example, Jean Legroux, "Mega-Events in Rio de Janeiro... And the Winners Are? Perceptions of the Impacts of Transport Policies on Socio-Spatial Justice to Reveal Mega-Events Contradictions," *13th WCTR*, July 2013 (Rio de Janeiro, 2013).

7. Tarifa Zero, "Sao Paulo Sem Catracas: Cartilha Da Campanha Tarifa Zero," 2011; available at tarifazerosp.net.

8. O metrô que o Rio precisa, "Manifesto Pelo Melhor Traçado Da Linha 4 Do Metrô Rio," 2011 (available at metrolinha4queoriorecisa.com.br).

9. This approach builds on Davidoff's term "advocacy planning," as explained in classical essay: Paul Davidoff, "Advocacy and Pluralism in Planning," *Journal of the American Institute of Planners*, 31:4 (1965), 331–338.

10. See Milton Santos, *A urbanização brasileira* (São Paulo: Edusp, 2002).

11. Ermìnia Maricato, "É a questão urbana, estúpido!" in the Passe Livre publication, *Cidades rebeldes: passe livre e as manifestações que tomaram as*

ruas do Brasil (São Paulo: Carta Maior, 2013), 19-26.

12. Mathieu Labrie, "International Competition Launched for 2016 Rio Olympic Park," *RioOnWatch*, 2011 (available at rioonwatch.org).

13. See Rio Prefeitura, *Plano Estrategico Da Prefeitura Do Rio de Janeiro 2013-2016, 2013* (available at rio.rj.gov.br).

14. Tarifa Zero, "Sao Paulo Sem Catracas."

15. Dan Chodorkoff, *The Anthropology of Utopia: Essays on Social Ecology and Community Development* (Porsgrunn: New Compass Press, 2014), 42.

16. See, for example, the material produced by Movimento Passe Livre or Ocupa Camara.

17. Ward, *Freedom To Go*, 28.

18. Murray Bookchin, *Toward an Ecological Society* (Montréal: Black Rose Books, 1980), 39.

19. For more about freeriding insurance funds, see Planka.nu/eng; and the international campaigns for free public transportation, see freepublictransport.com.

20. Ward, *Freedom To Go*, 7.

21. Chodorkoff, *Anthropology of Utopia*, 167.

22. Paul Timms, Miles Tight, and David Watling, "Imagineering Mobility: Constructing Utopias for Future Urban Transport," *Environment and Planning A*, 46:1 (2014), 90.

23. Or to "immotility," as suggested by Antonio Ferreira, Luca Bertolini, Petter Naess and Greg Marsden, "Immotility as Resilience," forthcoming in *Environment and Planning A*. If high mobility is increasingly required to allow capital accumulation, then refusing to move could be a form of resistance.

MOBILIZING COMMUNITIES AGAINST ORGANIZED CRIME

MONICA CAGGIANO
& SALVATORE PAOLO DE ROSA

The Land of Fires is a plain located between Caserta and Naples in the Campania region of southern Italy, infamous for the risks of contamination caused by more than twenty years of urban waste mismanagement and illegal dumping and burning of toxic waste. Organized criminal networks are responsible for this crisis, and the situation for the local population in Campania is difficult and dangerous. But there are sparks of hope. The recent collaboration between ecological activists and social cooperatives, working on farmlands confiscated from the Mafia, is pointing to an alternative economy organized from the ground up. Besides strengthening the political struggle for a safe environment, these new grassroots initiatives challenge Mafia culture and increase the self-organization and self-confidence of local communities.

Today, Campania is held in tight grip by a highly organized criminal network, namely the Camorra. The Camorra is an armed organization whose main goal is to maintain power by controlling territory. It does so by providing services, using political patronage, committing violent acts, and supporting specific cultural values. The criminal economy it creates in Campania can be seen as an extension or an extreme form of capitalist accumulation, sharing practices intended to boost economic performance, cut costs, and decrease social unrest.

In the last two decades, the mismanagement of waste disposal has become a major issue in Campania. The urban waste cycle has been managed by a special government agency and it was carried out by private firms, operating under the legal framework of an unending "urban waste emergency." Also, along the mismanagement of urban waste, hazardous wastes have been illegally dumped and burned in unsuitable landfills. The perpetrators are a complex network of entrepreneurs, state officials, industry managers, landowners, and organized crime groups; their actions blur the demarcation between legal and illegal practices. Their common factor is the profit-driven logic of "accumulation by contamination": the conversion of waste into a commodity to gain profits by appropriating socio-ecological space and socializing costs.[1]

Meanwhile, throughout the Land of Fires, air, water and soil have become contaminated, endangering residents' health. Higher rates of cancer among the local population have been connected to the presence of pollutants from hazardous waste.[2] Local agriculture suffers because consumers reject produce from this area, even when scientific evidence certifies its safety. Many small-scale, family-owned farms are at risk of failing.

From the toxic fields of Campania has emerged a complex constellation of grassroots movements. This social mobilization is striking for its heterogeneity, uniting people from economically deprived areas, the middle class, and the scientific community. These citizens rarely call themselves environmentalists: far more than any supposed wish to "protect nature," they cite personal reasons for their activism, such as health concerns.[3] They also cite unsettling changes in their everyday environment as a reason to investigate the causes and effects of waste flows. By combining their sensory perceptions with scientific expertise, they have generated autonomous environmental knowledge. The focus on the workings of unequal power relations in rearranging the landscape led to the politicization of their struggle.

In 2000 Campania's popular environmental mobilizations began with the "waste wars." Initially the State planned to dispose of urban trash through incineration and commodification. This plan encountered steady opposition from local communities, where grassroots committees objected to an "authoritarian and unjust governance of waste." They presented alternative means of disposal, including waste reduction and recycling of materials, which became the most powerful instrument in their critique.

The State's response, however, was mostly physical repression to crush the resistance: it imposed the companies' plan using police batons. Besides exercising violence, the State attempted to delegitimize activists in the national media by stereotyping these southern Italians as "mafia associates" and "uncivil."[4] News reports blamed Campanians' lifestyles for their rising cancer rates. Meanwhile, organized crime and corrupt officials continued to illegally dump toxic waste.

After eleven years of "waste wars," the local movement began to broaden its political scope. In the fall of 2013, grassroots committees came together to form a common regional coalition called Fiume in Piena (Raging River), which denounced the multifaceted mechanisms of socio-ecological exploitation. Through its activism, the coalition succeeded in bringing the environmental problems and health risks of the Land of Fires to the national political agenda. However, government institutions that drafted countermeasures only marginally involved activists. So the coalition went further as well, calling for real democracy as the basis for addressing all inequities.

Today Campanian activists, while still engaging in the defensive struggle against toxic wastes and unwanted land uses, are also attempting to reappropriate knowledge and space in order to improve self-organization. They are starting to reclaim their environments for community use, shifting their eco-political performance to physically and symbolically reappropriating territories. In Campania, this territorial reappropriation intersects with community self-organization, and activists have started a range of social cooperatives on land confiscated to mafia. Their collaboration produces a new economic model, grounded in democratic and ecological principles.

In Italy, social cooperatives are the most common type of social enterprise that provides social services. Italian law recognizes social cooperatives as private non-profit enterprises aiming at "the human promotion and social integration of citizens." In 2012 four social cooperatives that share common principles and visions—Al di là dei sogni, Eureka, Agropoli, and Millepiedi—came together to form the New Organized Cooperation. At this writing, a fifth cooperative, Resistenza, is well on its way to joining them.

The cooperative consortium deliberately and ironically appropriated the acronym used by the New Organized Camorra (Nuova Camorra Organizzata; the Italian acronym for both is NCO, which we will use here). This powerful mafia organization was founded in the late 1970s by Raffaele Cutolo to renew the old rural Camorra and reconstitute it as a business organization. The vision of the cooperative consortium, by contrast, is to organize and build networks to fight the Mafia and at the same time to contest prejudices against disabled or other disadvantaged people, as we will see.

The social cooperatives arose in the context of the "Basaglian revolution" in the treatment of mental illness. In the 1970s the movement for antipsychiatry or Democratic Psychiatry culminated in the passage, in 1978, of the Basaglia Law, which reconfigured psychiatry by initiating a gradual shutdown of psychiatric hospitals and reassigning prevention, care, and rehabilitation in mental health to new community-based services.

The Basaglian paradigm frames the cooperatives' work. Rather than focusing on the limitations of people who are deemed mentally ill or psychologically/socially different, they take as a starting point their human potential.[5] Rather than working on the terrain of psychiatric therapy, they attempt to foster more comprehensive social rehabilitation and empowerment. In Campania, the region has supported the social cooperatives' efforts by allowing them to manage health, social, and educational services and other activities (agricultural, industrial, commercial, and service) aimed at helping vulnerable persons, thanks to special agreement with the local departments of mental health that defines personalized care programs with specific budgets.

This "care for the community" does not simply help individual problems but has intrinsic effects on the entire local community, since it aims to address the social causes of disorders. The natural consequences of seeking to advance community well-being include fighting not only social and environmental injustice but also Mafia culture itself.

For example, the first project of the NCO cooperatives was to collaborate on the Christmas initiative "Let's Give Camorra a Gift," in which they jointly offered for sale the products of 16 cooperatives, associations, and private companies that denounced racketeering or were involved in fighting criminal organizations. The initiative's name ironically quotes the expression *fare un pacco* (literally, "give a gift"), which in popular Neapolitan also means "cheat." The initiative was successful, after which some cooperatives decided to leave their former labels and commercialize their products together under the umbrella brand NCO to increase consumer awareness and improve visibility. Progressively, the cooperatives' strategic alliances yielded organizational and productive assets that facilitated the exchange of knowledge and improved the partnering organizations' performances.

In 1996, Italian law 109/96 came into effect, on the social reuse of property confiscated from criminal organizations. The law allowed for the allocation of confiscated assets and illicit profits to those—associations, cooperatives, municipalities, provinces, and regions—that are able to return them to the citizens. Under this law, the NCO cooperatives obtained access to confiscated lands through a free loan and began to link agricultural practices with care services. They chose farming both because of the land's availability and for the affirmation of the "one-straw revolution," as the Japanese visionary and environmentalist Masanobu Fukuoka framed it: "the ultimate goal of farming is not the growing of crops, but the cultivation and perfection of human beings."[6]

Agricultural activities, they affirm, have a strong potential to involve and integrate "problematic people." All but one of the NCO cooperatives now cultivate lands confiscated from Mafia; the cooperative Millepiedi even created a social farm "Fuori di zucca" on the land of the old mental hospital of Aversa. The one cooperative, Agropoli, that does not practice agriculture runs a restaurant in a villa confiscated from the Mafia. The cooperatives have also begun to implement "green care activities,"[7] which includes elements of health care, social rehabilitation, education, and employment opportunities, for vulnerable groups.

As a result, the social cooperatives have gained importance in the fight against Mafia culture. That importance is both symbolic—assets are a symbol of the Mafia power—as well as material, since they have innovatively opened access to land (and other productive assets) to young people.

The cooperatives focus on agriculture also as an approach to build fairer and healthier relationships with the environment: physically, mentally, spiritually, and also politically, engaged as they are in the practices of Food Activism. They aim not only to break the mechanisms of the criminal economy but also to "challenge the agro-industrial food system and its exploitation of people and resources."[8] Whereas the conventional agriculture sector is marked by unemployment and by irregular and exploited work, the cooperatives promote fair and horizontal work relations, even with marginalized people. They practice mostly organic agriculture, and they try to regenerate and use local seeds and plants, becoming both users and custodians of biodiversity, connecting local knowledge and farming communities. This land use can generate a cognitive and cultural reorientation toward environmental and territorial resources that is not purely instrumental. Agricultural value is thus measured not only in economic terms but also in social value provided for and with the community.

Over the time, the NCO cooperatives have established closer relations with local communities, especially in regard to living with mentally ill people. In some cases, these relationships have been formalized by the official participation of local committees and associations that fight

Mafia culture, such as the Don Peppe Diana committee (an association that nurtures the legacy of a famous anti-Mafia priest killed by Camorra in 1994). These formal and informal links, at both the local and the national levels, also have helped the cooperatives gain support in times of intimidation and damage by the Camorra.

Despite several difficulties, NCO cooperatives have achieved many results, in rehabilitating disadvantaged people, creating jobs, requalifying derelict properties, and preventing illegal waste disposal. The initial four cooperatives have developed in 2014 a total turnover of approximately € 2,500,000 and employ about sixty people, including part-time workers. Furthermore, they have seasonal contracts: one cooperative employs about thirty seasonal workers for three months a year to manage the educational farm. The cooperatives also carry out educational work to spread anti-Mafia culture and to raise citizen awareness, organizing festivals and other public events.

Still, the NCO cooperatives fulfill the more relevant *educational* goals through their daily work and by being immersed in the local community, building relations with their neighbors, with local farmers, and with schools and associations. Their successes derive from their members' whole-hearted commitment and hard work, and from their ability to cooperate jointly and effectively with the public institutions (such as municipalities and health services), private entities (farmers, local entrepreneurs), and civic associations.

More recently they have attempted to institutionalize this network through the Social Economy Network (RES). This ambitious project is a network of thirty-one public and private organizations that seek to use Mafia-confiscated assets to promote and implement the social economy (in food, tourism, and social communication). The project is still in the startup phase, and progress is extremely slow and complex due to the numerous actors involved.

The interests of the NCO cooperatives have converged with the interests of the grassroots movements' coalitions at the crossroads of land reclamation for social and economic purposes. Formal and informal ties among the various actors facilitate the connection between cooperatives and movements. Their action is rooted on a common vision: they share a paradigm shift that accepts the English anthropologist Gregory Bateson's 1972 invocation of the "patterns that connect."[9]

They reject the *logic of exploitation,* the view that nature is a resource to be dominated and exploited, whether by organized crime or by the current economic structure, according to a profit-driven logic. Instead, they propose the *logic of care,* a new ethic of economic, ecological, and social relations based on respect for human rights and recognition of the interdependence of society and nature. Their engagements with transformative politics primarily originate neither from utopias nor from critical theories of social change or environmentalism, but rather from lived experiences of struggle, environmental contamination, social exclusion, and Mafia rule, all perceived as unbearable. By searching for solutions, they realized that these ills were not particular accidents but the result of structural problems.

They joined forces through what the Brazilian educator Paulo Freire called praxis, "reflection and action upon the world in order to transform it."[10] This paved the way for greater politicization of their common struggles, questioning the existing power relationships and promoting community empowerment. They reclaim and assume a more proactive role in the management of common property and resources through collective actions. These collective actions take place through networks involving cooperatives, associations, individuals, and public actors, at the local, regional, and national levels. Through their networking processes they oppose the negative social capital that nourishes the power of organized crime and instead enhance the reproduction of "ethical social capital" and anti-Mafia culture.[11]

NCO cooperatives and environmental movements both promote mutually reinforcing activities for a cultural and physical reappropriation of territory by connecting symbolic, material, and structural dimensions. They are engaged in a real process of revitalization and co-production of *place,* a vision of territory as a set of relationships instead of a mere physical or geographical area. Their alliance aspires to define local communities' new self-narrations, to implement new practices, and to settle an ethical, cultural, and institutional framework. Such processes create a robust basis for place awareness, able to promote an innovative local territorial development in the transition from a criminal economy to a social-ecological economy grounded on the care of commons and on the autonomous self-organization of communities. [12]

The revolutionary challenges outlined are still in progress and leave room for debate. Some critical limits and risks are inherent in these processes. The NCO cooperatives are small-scale economic entities and are not very competitive; their current challenge is to gain economic self-sufficiency on the market, while actually their main source of income is the public contributions received from health care for their rehabilitation activities. These public revenues are problematic because they are not continuous, and too often the payments are delayed. A critical key point is to become economically sustainable without distorting the project in the face of capitalist economy, considering that they provide *community value* and services, some of which are neither accounted nor accountable through market indicators. A related problem is to get out of a niche maintaining full adherence to ethical principles and the vision of community wellbeing. Cooperatives are very often confronted with a trade-off between ethics and market; in addition they risk of being turned into a subsidiary designed by the State to deflect its responsibilities.

Another risk is that capitalist production systems will absorb these experiences and exploit their symbolic power, reducing their subversive potential, or using them as an escape valve for a general system that remains unchanged. Michael Porter and Mark Kramer have suggested that creating "sharing value" is the way to reinvent and revitalize capitalism, but without questioning capitalism's dynamics and injustices, "addressing social concerns in a company's business practices ... can contribute to profit maximization."[13]

Cooperation with the grassroots movements' coalition is thus a potential strategy by which the NCO cooperatives can exercise continuous political pressure in order to change the broader economic and institutional arrangements *maintaining ethical* rigorousness. Resistance to inequalities, informed by a wide critique of the status quo, and coupled with material organization of social reproduction is a risky yet promising path for improving self-determination of communities.

NOTES:

1. David Harvey, *Spaces of Hope* (Berkeley: University of California Press, 2000).

2. Kathryn Senior and Alfredo Mazza, "Italian 'Triangle of Death' Linked to Waste Crisis," *Lancet Oncology*, 5 (2004), 525–27.

3. Marco Armiero, "Seeing like a Protester: Nature, Power and Environmental Struggles," *Left History* 13 (2008), 59–76.

4. Antonello Petrillo, "Le urla e il silenzio: Depoliticizzazione dei conflitti e parresia nella Campania tardo liberale," in Antonello Petrillo, ed., *Biopolitica di un rifiuto: Le rivolte anti-discarica a Napoli e in Campania* (Verona: Ombre Corte, 2009), pp. 13-71.

5. Piet F. Driest, *Care Farms: an Introduction* (Utrecht: Nederlands Instituut voor Zorg en Welzijn, 1997).

6. Masanobu Fukuoka, *The One Straw Revolution* (Pennsylvania: Rodale Press, 1978).

7. Joe Sempik, Rachel Hine, and Deborah Wilcox, eds., *Green Care: A Conceptual Framework: A Report of the Working Group on the Health Benefits of Green Care, COST Action 866, Green Care in Agriculture* (Loughborough: Centre for Child and Family Research, 2010).

8. Carole Counihan and Valeria Siniscalchi, *Food Activism: Agency, Democracy and Economy* (London: Berg Publishers, 2013).

9. Gregory Bateson, *Steps to an Ecology of Mind: Collected Essays in Anthropology, Psychiatry, Evolution, and Epistemology* (Chicago: University of Chicago Press, 1972).

10. Paulo Freire, *Pedagogy of the Oppressed* (New York: Herder and Herder, 1970).

11. Baris Cayli, "Social Networks of the Italian Mafia: The Strong and Weak Parts," *CEU Political Science Journal* 5 (2010), 382–413.

12. Arturo Escobar, "Whose Knowledge, Whose Nature? Biodiversity Conservation and the Political Ecology of Social Movements," *Journal of Political Ecology* 5 (1998), 53–82; Angelo Turco, *Verso una teoria geografica della complessità* (Milan: Unicopli, 1998); Giuseppe Dematteis, *Le metafore della Terra. La geografia umana tra mito e scienza* (Milan: Feltrinelli, 1985); and Alberto Magnaghi, *Progetto locale. Verso la coscienza di luogo* (Turin: Bollati Boringhieri, 2010).

13. Michael E. Porter, and Mark R. Kramer, "Creating Shared Value: How to Reinvent Capitalism—and Unleash a Wave of Innovation and Growth," *Harvard Business Review* 89, nos. 1/2 (2011), 1–17; and Stephen J. Scanlan, "Feeding the Planet or Feeding Us a Line? Agribusiness, 'Grainwashing' and Hunger in the World Food System," *International Journal of Sociology of Agriculture and Food* 20 (2013), 357–82.

ECOLOGICAL CRISIS AND THIRD REVOLUTION

METIN GÜVEN

The current ecological crisis is becoming more visible every day. Even though it appears in many forms such as deforestation, salinization of soil, destruction of ecocommunities due to mining, industrialization, and new energy projects; the most critical one seems to be global warming.

World elites suggest that technological innovations and environmental reforms will restrict global greenhouse gas emissions and stop adverse effects of global warming. In fact these measures only marginally slow down emissions in developed countries; the actual outcome of these measures is mostly moving the sources of greenhouse gas emissions from developed countries to developing countries.[1] They are not effective because global elites try to implement measures compatible with economic growth through investments by multinational corporations. However the main goal of these corporations is more profit and they move industrial production to countries with the lowest cost regardless of environmental impact and greenhouse gas emissions.

Greenhouse gas emissions need to be radically reduced to stop the adverse effects of global warming. This requires not only implementing technological innovations, but also a radical decrease in current economic activity and a thorough decentralization. These requirements are incompatible with capitalism and its demand for endless material growth. Social ecologists argue that the only way to stop global warming is through a radical transcendence of capitalism.

Most of the increase in global greenhouse gas emissions in recent decades came from rapid urbanization with shopping malls and commercial high-rise buildings, and increased transportation due to this urbanization. Political participation is critically important to reversing this trend as people need to decide how to create decentralized cities and rebuild their communities.

Even though these ideas seem utopian, other options do not promise a solution or are authoritarian top down approaches such as population reduction. However, popular participation of such a radical transformation can only be achieved through a social revolution, which will create libertarian power structures and remove the privileges of ruling classes and corporations.

Examining the concrete historical examples of social revolutions that allowed for direct participation in political decision making will give us a perspective on how a revolution that has the potential to create a free society is possible today. Such a revolution would allow us to take real measures to stop global warming and find solutions to other ecological problems.

Many thinkers who consider the concept of revolution often only address revolutions from the modern period. However, the objectives of modern revolutions, such as freedom and equality, were formulated in antiquity. The pursuit of these objectives was first given concrete form in ancient Athens. In his book *From Urbanization to Cities*, Murray Bookchin speaks of the changes that took place in ancient Athens: "Power ceased to be the prerogative of a small, well-born stratum of the population. It became a citizen activity. Athen's historic calendar is marked by seething upsurges of the people, startling fluctuations between aristocratic rule, tyranny, limited popular government, until, by the latter half of the fifth century B.C., Athenian political life stabilized around a face-to-face democracy of the most radical kind."[2]

Writing about this unprecedented development in recorded history, Bookchin noted that "Later ideals of citizenship, even insofar as they were modeled on the Athenian, seem more unfinished and immature than the original," and that "there were impressive attempts to create patterns of civic freedom that approximated the democratic *polis* in medieval city-states and in the American and French revolutions. These attempts were usually intuitive."[3]

Thinkers engaged with the issues of modernization have failed to develop their ideas about the concept of citizenship to the extent of the Athenians. As a result, the criterion of revolution can be substantially attributed to the understanding of direct democracy in Ancient Athens. Accordingly, Bookchin considers the revolutions of recent times as incomplete without what he calls a "Third Revolution."

The concept of the Third Revolution and these approaches will be expanded upon in the following sections. At this point, it should be emphasized that a revolution can only be comprehended as a process rather than an event occurring in an instant. A social revolution, not merely a political revolution, must contain different revolutions within itself and change social life in a fundamental way, creating new values and attitudes in the period following itself.

Athenian democracy can be distinguished from the earlier tribal democracies, not only by their detailed recordings on the concept of citizenship but also the development of a democracy that transcends blood ties. Initially, the former tribal councils were revitalized as institutions with only legislative power, but not the power to enact and execute laws. The enslavement of Athenians was prohibited and all Athenians were given the right of citizenship. This democratization process ultimately resulted in new socially constructed tribes to include all citizens for the functioning of democracy, and in this way the different sections of society were able to express themselves by participating in political decision-making process.

The system that had been functioning for decades consisted of a public assembly that was open to the participation of all citizens, and from this assembly an executive council was elected by lot. The council (*boule*) had five hundred members elected annually by lot who were responsible for carrying out the laws and decisions made by the public assembly. In order to execute the decisions made, administrative boards with various duties were formed under the council. The idea of Athenian citizenship meant that every citizen would be able to take a role in policy making and administration. Direct democracy relied on citizens that acquired administrative skills such as reasoning and problem solving through discussions and debates in popular assembly.

Athenians assembled as an *ekklesia* not only to formulate policies and make judgments; they came together to mutually educate each other in the ability to act justly and expand their civic ideals of right and wrong. The 'political process,' ... was not strictly institutional and inexhaustible, everyday 'curriculum' for intellectual, ethical, and personal growth ... that fostered the ability of citizens to creatively participate in public affairs, to bring their best abilities to the service of the *polis* and its needs, to intelligently manage their private affairs in accordance with the highest ethical standards of the community.[4]

Ten percent of the population of ancient Athens were men with full citizenship rights and eligible to participate in their direct democracy. Wider participation was not permitted due the lack of citizenship rights for women, slaves, and immigrants. It is clear that this narrow and exclusionary form of democracy could not be considered as a model for today. However, it would not be fair to dismiss the democracy of ancient Athens purely on this note. It should not be forgotten that the slave trade in the Middle East had been established over a thousand years at that time, and it wasn't outlawed in Europe until the beginning of the 19th century and until 1865 in the United States. Women's equal participation in political life was achieved only in the 20th century. Therefore, modern revolutions have held the same limited concepts of "equality" and participation.

If we were to look into the daily life of the time, the participation of males in politics was largely due to the responsibility of housekeeping and raising children being given to women, and the use of slavery especially in services and also production, even though slavery was mostly not concentrated in large production units. Women were also responsible for the management of domestic slaves, which were the majority of the slave population. Ancient Greece, unlike ancient Rome, did not have large farms based on slave labor or *latifundias*. Most people were self-sufficient, relying on the production of their farms and homes. People in antiquity had much simpler lives as garments were produced domestically alongside many consumer goods we normally purchase from markets today. Agricultural production was mostly made possible through the labor of the farmer-citizens. However, the lack of mechanical devices either for domestic or agricultural use resulted in lower production and poverty for those who didn't own slaves. The most important reason for this was due to the burden caused by the necessity to defend Athens against aggressive empires and neighboring enemies. The Persian Empire was a constant threat to Greek cities. Athens was often at war with its southern neighbor Sparta. Sparta's production relied on the enslavement of their indigenous population and their citizens dedicated almost all of their time to war preparation. Wealthy Athenians supported war efforts by providing horses, while those moderately well-to-do brought armor, and the poor worked as foot soldiers or rowers.[5]

Immigrants generally worked in the crafts and trades. Within the understanding of the time, a person relying on the market could not make political decisions independently because they sold their products and labor. The vested interests of the marketplace were independent of and contradicted the interests of the entire community. Those engaged in trading were susceptible to prioritize the interests of the market over the community. Our notion of "democracy" today is contradictory to this approach, but we should recognize that a true democracy can only be achieved by a similar understanding. The tension between the common interests of community and the economic self-interests of the individual causes people to ignore the short and long term interests of the community. The Athenian ideal of a citizen was considered to be economically self-sufficient so that they would be autonomous participants in political decision-making.[6] Hence the craft and trade occupations in ancient Athens were largely left to immigrants and slaves.

Athenian democracy collapsed due to the invasions by Macedon and later Rome. Direct democracy in subsequent periods first appeared in rising Italian cities prior to the Renaissance, and then spread to Central Europe, the Netherlands, and the surrounding areas. However, in the intervening centuries, town and country in Europe became thoroughly dissociated from one another as the countryside became heavily dominated by feudalism. A very large section of the city consisted of poor citizens who were not engaged in democracy. These democracies weren't as inclusive as Athenian democracy; moreover, the conflict between the enriched and empowered bourgeoisie and the other sections of society sharpened, leading to the political transformation of democracies into republics. Those cities that were ruled by representative councils lost their significance with the emergence of nation-states.

Nation-states were initially under the arbitrary rule of the king. Kings introduced bureaucracies that grew to become a heavy burden on the people who were taxed to finance the government. Poverty effected a large portion of the population, both in cities and the countryside. Even though feudal serfdom was no longer in effect, feudal obligations to the nobility posed a great burden on the peasants who did not possess enough land. European revolutions of the modern era, while reintroducing forgotten forms of freedom from the past, were a reaction against the parasitic upper classes and the poverty that resulted from them.

The Great French Revolution was one of those revolutions. It restricted the power of the King and started the process to create a new Constitution by the National Convention in July 1789. This was the First Revolution.

The French Revolution largely depended on organizations that initially gathered to elect representatives to the Third Estate. These organizations were formed from councils that were originally created to gather complaints and demands, dispersing when these functions were fulfilled. But they were transformed into organized structures in order to fulfill the demands of the people in 1789.⁷ The most radical of those organizations were the sections of Paris representing the districts of neighborhoods.

When the Monarchy was abolished in 1792, power became seated in the National Convention. This was considered as the Second Revolution. Until that time, the sections of Paris were trying to legitimize themselves while organizing massive marches (*journées*) to bring the revolution forward. Neither the National Assembly nor the moderate Paris Commune of that time wanted to strengthen the sections. By reducing the number of section from 60 to 48 it was thought that they would be weakened. Yet the strength of their political discussions, the decisions they concluded and the actions that they took left them unhindered by the reduction. Each section was developing a distinctive local culture. Some radicalized further and some sections, which included affluent neighborhoods, remained moderate.

The abolition of the monarchy led the Paris Commune to restructure itself. The Commune no longer attempted to be a force on the sections, but instead became an administrative structure that coordinated the implementation of decisions made by the sections. Parallel to this, the popular assemblies of the sections became open to the participation of all citizens by the removal of previous restrictions. Since the First Revolution, committees were formed to organize aspects of daily life such as food and safety. Until the Second Revolution the members of these committees had been appointed by the Commune but now became elected committee members. Thus, a direct democracy similar to the one in ancient Athens was implemented across all of Paris. If we consider the population of Paris at this time to be around six hundred thousand, a much larger community of citizens became able to experience direct democracy.

However, while the sections of Paris were becoming more effective, the monarchist reactionaries organized to crush the Republic. With the eruption of rural uprisings led by monarchists, the dual power could not continue in Paris for long. The liquidation of the Girondins on the 2nd of June, 1793, took place during those circumstances. With the support of the sections, the Jacobins liquidated the Girondins from the Convention. In the following period Jacobins guillotined not only the reactionaries but also all other forms of opposition. The radical leaders of the sections were jailed or suppressed if they hadn't been sent to guillotine. The radicals foresaw this scenario before the 2nd of June, and strove for a Third Revolution by working to eliminate the Convention and to make the direct democracy of the sections the only ruling power. However, they were not able to succeed in this endeavor. Later attempts for the Third Revolution failed, leading to the deterioration of efforts to undo the power of the central government.

Workers, peasants, and soldier soviets appeared as a potentially directly democratic organization after the February revolution of 1917. But they became tools used by the Bolsheviks to manipulate the masses. However, the most radical segments of society created directly democratic institutions in different areas. Factory committees were among them and were especially active in the Vyborg region of St. Petersburg. These committees were elected by all of the workers working in a factory. The factory committees decided the organization of production and all other matters involving the workers.

Another example of direct democracy in the revolutionary tradition was the organization of the Kronstadt sailors. Kronstadt was the military base at which the most radical soldiers in the Russian Revolution were stationed. Their role during critical moments of revolution was unprecedented. They made important political decisions together by discussing and voting. The Kronstadt base had turned itself into a self-managing commune. In February 1921, amidst growing strikes and pressure by the Bolsheviks, Kronstadt sent a group of delegates to closely examine the situation in St. Petersburg with the intention to create a Third Revolution. The observations of the delegates were discussed and resulted in the formulation of 15 demands that were approved by an overwhelming majority. Their demands included the freedom of press, expression, and assembly for workers, peasants, anarchists, socialists, and the Left Socialist Revolutionaries, with freely displayed electoral propaganda to be allowed before new soviet elections.

The Kronstadt base was attacked by approximately 60,000 soldiers before they had the opportunity to organize with the workers of St. Petersburg in solidarity. The Kronstadt resistance lasted 12 days with thousands of people from both sides killed or injured, and thousands of insurgent taking refuges in Finland. Thus, a Third Revolution which could transform the soviets into a direct democracy was completely suppressed, making way for the Stalinist dictatorship that eventually claimed the lives of the majority of Bolshevik leaders.

The revolutionary process that lead to ancient Athenian democracy began as an uprising in response to aristocratic practices of indebting poor small farmers with mortgages, as those who failed to pay back their dues had their land seized and were even enslaved and sold abroad. However, at that time, poverty and misery were not as widespread as it was during the French Revolution. Perhaps the fact that immiseration due to class differences wasn't as widespread or was only nascent, allowed greater possibilities for the formation of democratic institutions. More importantly, finding a solution to the problem of debt and the prohibition of slavery due to debt made it possible to raise the prospect of establishing a democracy. The revolutions of the modern era, involving deeper class conflicts, have been unable to resolve the poverty and misery of their time, and this reveals an important distinction from the revolutionary transformation of ancient Athens.

The exception to this is the American Revolution which aimed to gain independence from Britain. Unlike other revolutions, it was not a product of class conflict or poverty. The rising bourgeoisie at that time was decisive in shaping the newly formed state. The United States was born not as a democracy, but as a republic in which property owners elected their representatives. Only after granting universal suffrage did the United States claim itself as a "democracy." On the other hand, although the soviet revolution ultimately eliminated poverty, it came with the political suppression of freedoms, as the entire country transformed into an environment resembling a labor camp. All decisions were made by a narrow section of elites that composed the leadership of the Communist Party, ultimately leading to the collapse of the Soviet statist system.

However, as it is stressed in all of Bookchin's analyses, the culture one identifies with and how those people view themselves is more important than the economic conditions in determining their political orientations. In ancient Greece the culture of the self-sufficient small farmer and the virtues they developed made way for democracy. The patriarchal values of culture and the view of slaves as objects like washing machines, ovens, or calculators, are not acceptable today. Nevertheless, the idea that citizens dependent on the relations of the marketplace could not make autonomous decisions and are thus unable to properly contribute to democracy is very important.

In the other democracies since antiquity, the importance that citizens have placed on their own independence has played a significant role. During the Great French Revolution, those who were the most radical agents were not industrial workers but artisans. They were recently removed from their village life and had not yet been dramatically affected by the anonymity found in cities. They created the same sense of community in the neighborhoods as it was found previously in their villages. In contrast to ordinary assembly line workerism their outlook carried self-confidence from both their communal solidarity and their artisanship. The workers who led the revolution in St. Petersburg possessed similar characteristics. Although they worked in large factories, they had not yet been transformed into assembly line workers, continuing as they did to practice their crafts at the workbench.

Germany and the United Kingdom experienced rapid industrialization, while the rest of the Western world followed in the second half of the 20th century. By then, the factory worker had fully become a cog in a machine. Their work environment didn't permit them to view themselves with the same confidence as the artisan worker. In these circumstances, rather than finding solutions to their inequality and disempowerment, they were content to merely improve their work and economic conditions.

So why did the revolutionaries who had self-confidence fail to achieve the Third Revolution? Although it isn't possible to fully answer this, we must recognize that well-developed organizations which could accomplish the Third Revolution hadn't emerged at that time. Perhaps those who came closest to achieving the Third Revolution were the syndicalist CNT-FAI organization who suppressed the fascist assault in Barcelona in 1936. However, their anarchist views, which desired the dissolution of power completely, caused confusion between the distinction of a state and government, fearing as they did that they would lose their identity and become an authoritative party or state. Despite the fact that the power was in their hands, this prevented them from institutionalizing it and led them to return it to the government. On the other hand, the central government took up the first opportunity to rule out the possibility of the Third Revolution by crushing them.8

As we can see in this last example, the people who will succeed in actualizing the Third Revolution and their organizations must first and foremost clarify the concepts such as government and power. The success of democracy in ancient Athens was largely a result of the people's opposition to bureaucratic governments and statehood. Instead, they adopted administrative duties by a system of rotation. In this way, the emergence of a government that was composed of professional officers and the hegemony of such a government was prevented. However, due to the events in Russia, the concrete product of thinking that a central power would be the most successful in fighting against reactionary forces and solving economic problems is well known.

Considering these examples, we must not forget that when opposing a bureaucratically centralized power, a society without power and institutions to make political decisions cannot be conceived. As in the example of Barcelona, power cannot be eliminated. If the people who hope to achieve a direct democracy do not form institutions and take power, a force that aims to form a class or state domination will fill this vacuum and take power. The opposition of this force against the dominating class is not an indication that it does not aim for state domination. In other words, if the people are unable to exercise this power and fail to build long lasting decentralized democratic institutions the people's power will evaporate.

If we are to evaluate the past revolutions in terms of the present, we must understand that these revolutions acted on a narrow set of problems in comparison to the issues of today. The spread of capitalism within the last century to every corner of the world and the commodification of all natural resources as assets to be bought and sold renders the ecological and social crises today, and the need for a fundamental transformation that will overcome these issues, as urgent. If the destruction of nature, fossil fuel consumption, and air, water, soil pollution all continue at the current rates the Earth will cease to be a habitable environment for human life. Capitalism, which puts profit and the accumulation of capital ahead of all other concerns, is not only destroying biological nature, but is also debasing human nature by transforming people into robots only concerned with economic interests.

The large scale, multi-dimensional crisis that is being experienced can be solved through a Third Revolution that comprises an approach that aims for the elimination of the intertwined domination of class, gender, state, nation, and the idea of the domination of nature. The advancement of technology has made it possible "to replace the one dimensional worker with the multidimensional citizen as the agent for social administration and change."[9] In contrast to past revolutions, this holistic perspective allows women and marginalized minorities to play a significant and important role in creating a new society. To achieve full citizenship for all, today's revolutionary utopia will need to go beyond the utopias of the past.

NOTES:

1. Suzanne Goldenberg, "CO2 Emissions Are Being 'outsourced' by Rich Countries to Rising Economies," *The Guardian*, January 20, 2014.

2. Murray Bookchin, *From Urbanization to Cities: Toward a New Politics of Citizenship* (London: Cassell, 1996), 48.

3. ibid., 83.

4. ibid., 64.

5. For more information, see H.D.F. Kitto, *The Greeks* (London: Penguin Books, 1951).

6. Bookchin, *From Urbanization to Cities*, 67.

7. Murray Bookchin, *The Third Revolution: Popular Movements in the Revolutionary Era*, Vol. 1 (London: Cassell, 1996), 274.

8. Murray, Bookchin, *The Third Revolution: Popular Movements in the Revolutionary Era*, Vol. 4 (London: Cassell, 2005), particularly 236-260.

9. ibid., 267.

TOWARD AN
ECOLOGY MOVEMENT
IN THE MIDDLE EAST

JOHANNA L. RIVERA
& TOON BIJNENS

I s it meaningful to talk about an ecology movement in the Middle East? For the most part, ecological movements have been limited to the developed world. Although natural resources in the Middle East have been stretched to their limits, and the whole region has felt the impact of climate change in recent years, yet a distinct ecology movement did not emerge until the turn of the century.[1] Globalization processes and environmental dislocations have indeed affected the area, but most governments have turned a blind eye to the perilous environmental situation in front of them. To them, ecology has never been a pressing issue.[2]

Today, ecological issues are becoming increasingly relevant, particularly related to the current political instability and the water crisis in the Middle East. Access to clean water is being used as a weapon of war in Iraq and Syria. Yet, some scholars claim that the region lacks what it needs to be at the forefront of ecological movements.[3] But emerging movements challenge this notion. In this essay, we would like to highlight the Save the Tigris and Iraqi Marshes Campaign, a campaign to protect the Iraqi Marshes and to expose dam development projects and its impact in the region. Such campaigns are needed to increase ecological awareness, to transform public opinion, and to influence government officials.

I n his book, *The Middle East Water Question*, geographer John A. Allan discusses the fact that in the North, civil society is aware of environmental issues; the media regularly addresses public concerns and anxiety about the environment, and ecological activists have transformed popular perceptions of water resources. Political elites and institutions in the North seem to be acutely aware of environmental risks. This, Allan argues, is in sharp contrast to the Middle East, where societies have been less aware of environmental issues. He explains how the question of water use and allocation in the region is determined by a "complex interplay of unrecognized economic solutions, belief systems and political processes."[4] The region risks major water shortages, but has little political will to tackle the problem.

From our experience, in order to be effective, ecological movements in the Middle East need to focus their efforts on two areas: awareness and advocacy. First, it is important to raise awareness among people and societies about the very real dangers involved in ignoring environmental issues. Second, it is necessary to press policy-makers to advocate an ecological transition. This, Allan explains, will require both the capacity to create awareness and mobilize civil society, and to lobby and influence national and regional environmental policies. To achieve this, ecological issues will have to become visible in the public sphere, and civil society will have to create an open and democratic space where environmental policies can be discussed.

The more a movement is able to assert itself into the political process, Allan claims, the more likely it is that its demands will be taken into account in the policy formation process. In order to achieve this, the civil society in the region must be involved in the international exchange of ecological knowledge, and they need to be acutely aware that ecological issues stretch beyond nation-states and regions, and across north-south borders. Thus, ecological activism in the Middle East will have to be embedded in a global, democratic ecological movement, where a sustained and active exchange of ideas and practices on ecological sustainability is possible.

Building on Allan's claim, Sanjeev Khagram argues in *Dams and Development* that transnational alliances alter the dynamics of a movement not only in terms of scale but also in terms of policy impact.[5] A movement that extends beyond its borders will have a greater chance of influencing environmental policies and make them comply with international standards. We will build on Allan's and Khagram's work to explain how civil society in the Middle East, and particularly in Iraq, is growing more aware of ecological issues and is consolidating its activism by building alliances, exchanging knowledge, and reaching political spaces where it is possible to discuss water policy.

Iraq is an interesting place to study new ecological movements in the Middle East. Several factors have influenced the emergence of ecological movements in Iraq during the last decade. First, after 2003, a new political system was built with more space for social movements and non-profit organizations to operate, and new civil society groups appeared. The Iraqi Social Forum is an example of an open political and social space advocating social justice and opposing neoliberal policies. Second, during the Arab Spring protests that took place in Iraq in 2011 and 2012, for example, there was an increase in political mobilization. Third, we have seen several natural disasters and effects of climate change: few other countries in the Arab World have suffered more environmental damage than Iraq, which has made the rise of ecological movements all the more relevant and urgent. At the same time, a clear link between human security and ecology has recently become more evident there.[6] Large groups of people in Iraq are increasingly vulnerable to natural disasters, like floods and droughts. Fourth, as a consequence of years of war and heavy neglect, the environment is in a critical condition. The Mesopotamian Marshes probably best demonstrate how rapidly the Iraqi environment deteriorated toward the end of the previous century. The Marshes are one of the country's most important ecosystems, and used to be one of the largest wetlands in Asia. At the beginning of the 2003 Iraq War, the Marshes were only 10% of their original size. This was a direct result of Saddam Hussein's deliberate drainage of the marshes to crush Shi'a resistance during the Iran-Iraq war. After the war a new grave threat emerged: upstream dams in Syria and Turkey. The construction of big dams poses a threat not only to the Marshes, but also to Iraq's water resources. The first water shortages started in the 1990s when Turkey built several dams on the Euphrates River.[7] This caused a decline in freshwater availability and an increase in water salinity, making water unsuitable for agriculture and human consumption. Turkey is currently constructing more dams on the Tigris River, such as Ilisu. The effects of this dam project will have grave ecological consequences in the years to come.[8]

After the war in 2003 ended, new organizations and initiatives have been established. A landmark for Iraq was the New Eden project, which, in collaboration with the Ministry of Environment and local communities, partially restored the Marshes in the years following the American invasion.[9] In 2004, Nature Iraq was founded. This is the country's only conservationist organization, which focuses primarily on environmental research. Furthermore, there are numerous local environmental organizations operating in the country. However, few organizations have been involved with advocacy campaigns and raising environmental awareness. This is changing in recent years as the landscape of ecological organizations in Iraq continues to expand. Waterkeepers Iraq, active since 2011, has been implementing activities with the aim of raising awareness about the need to protect Iraq's rivers. The transnational Ekopotamya Network was founded in 2012, and serves as an international platform for Kurdish ecological organizations in the region, including Iraq. It meets twice a year to scrutinize environmental policies in the region. The Arab Youth Climate Movement has been mobilizing since 2012. It features Iraqi campaigners who participate in the Conference of the Parties (COP) and climate change negotiation talks, and it tracks what role the Iraqi government plays in negotiations.

The Save the Tigris and Iraqi Marshes Campaign is a transnational advocacy campaign that demands accountability and transparency from the Iraqi government on water policies, and on monitors how the Ilisu Dam in Turkey poses a threat to the environment in Iraq.

We believe the Save the Tigris campaign is a prime example of how new environmental networks are becoming increasingly relevant and paves the way for a real ecology movement in the Middle East. This campaign has galvanized environmental struggles within Iraq. Importantly, it has also gathered strength from the international environmental movement and from transnational networks working against dams, and it has benefited from expert legal and environmental advice that has, in turn, shaped its advocacy work.

Founded in 2012, the campaign focuses on protecting the Tigris River and the Iraqi Marshes from the negative impacts of the Ilisu Dam, which is currently under construction in Turkey. Recognizing that there are multiple challenges to water resources in Iraq, like water management and lack of modern technology, the Save the Tigris Campaign focuses on transboundary water issues: it advocates policies that secure the sustainable and equitable use of water, and opposes the privatization and commodification of water supplies and natural resources.

We cannot, here, discuss all political aspects of the Ilisu dam project. Suffice to say that the Ilisu dam construction creates the potential for the escalation of international conflict in a region that is vulnerable to both drought and political instability. Turkey shares the Tigris River basin with Syria and Iraq, and when the Ilisu dam is fully operative, Turkey will have complete control over Iraq's water resources. Through projects like the Ilisu dam, Turkey will strengthen its economic and political power, and secure its hegemony in the region. There exists no transboundary water agreement between Turkey and Iraq over the Tigris River, and the dangers of Ilisu dam to Iraq's water resources remains unaddressed by the Iraqi government.[10]

The Save the Tigris campaign is led by the Iraqi Civil Society Solidarity Initiative (ICSSI) and the work on the ground in Iraq is carried out by both internationals and Iraqi activists. International activists involved in the campaign provide expertise and skills, such as in international law or advocacy, to consolidate the campaign. Most Iraqi NGO's do not have ecology as one of their core issues, but this campaign has been able to partner several local NGO's, hereby expanding their radius of action to include environmental issues as well. In addition, an important component is "The People of Iraq Campaign to Save the Tigris," a collective that includes Iraqi activists and intellectuals. The Save the Tigris Campaign contradicts Allan's argument that Middle East activists are unaware of the growing water problem in the region.

The campaign aims to strengthen the capacity of the Iraqi people to participate in the political decision-making process. To this end, the Save the Tigris has worked to expand environmental awareness among Iraqi civil society and to empower them to make meaningful contributions to the policy-making process. To get Iraqi civil society engaged in the issue of Ilisu Dam, much work is put into raising awareness among local civil society groups, NGO's, academics, and students. Activists from the campaign held workshops and seminars in the provinces of Basra, Amara, Nasiriya, and Sulaymaniyah, at the University of Basra and the Universities of Duhok and Sulaymaniyah. Moreover, the campaign has engaged with the Iraq Social Forum, one of the country's largest civil society platforms. These efforts support Allan's argument that awareness is key to changing perceptions on the water problem.

According to Portuguese sociologist Boaventura De Sousa Santos, each environmental struggle is organized according to a particular scale, be it local, national, or global.[11] De Sousa argues that any movement will have the option of instigating change via direct or political action—or both. Due to the existing political conditions in Iraq, the Save the Tigris Campaign work choose political and legal action, in order to influence the national government. Iraq has a Ministry of Environment, but ecological issues are put aside with the excuse that the current situation makes them less pressing than other aspects of the political crisis. Water policy is not a priority for the government. Furthermore, in Iraq it is difficult for individual NGO's to criticize the government without getting censored, and it might be difficult for others with close ties to the government to be critical of it as well. Nonetheless, the Save the Tigris Campaign has shown that it is possible for ecological movements to influence public policy.

To be sure, the national advocacy work of the Save the Tigris Campaign has faced many challenges. These include restrictions on the freedom of expression, Iraq's poor governance (including high levels of corruption), inherent weak position vis-à-vis Turkey as a downstream state, its inexperience in international legal matters, and the lack of political will in the government to bring the water issue to the top of the agenda. Although it has been difficult, the campaign has succeeded in strengthening Iraqi voices in public institutions, advancing concrete water policy proposals, and has gradually gained access to ministries and local government officials. Khagram argues that popular movements only succeed when they are in strong democracies, but emergent movements in Iraq demonstrates that this is not necessarily the case.

The struggle to protect and preserve the environment involves a global movement against mega-dams. We believe that the fight against such dams constitutes an important part of community struggles to control over their own water and other natural resources. This movement has challenged powerful interests and institutions, and contested hegemonic ideas about development.[12]

The Save the Tigris and Iraqi Marshes Campaign has learned from other struggles in southern nations, such as India and Brazil, that the potential success of any ecological movement depends in its capacity to associate and collaborate with other transnational movements and activists, to learn from their forms of organization, and to unite in common objectives.[13] This campaign therefore includes activists from both the North and the South, and aims to bring together ecological movements across borders. Partners from the North are organizations such as The Corner House (UK), GegenStrömung (Germany), and the

Environmental Defender Law Center (USA). From the global South, organizations include the Center for Sustainable Development (Iran) and the Initiative to Keep Hasankeyf Alive (Turkey).

Since the issue of Ilisu Dam affects both Iraq and Turkey, the campaign has established firm links with dam-affected communities in Turkey. Delegations have visited the site of Ilisu Dam, and the town of Hasankeyf (Turkey), which will be flooded when Ilisu Dam becomes operative, and there are exchanges with Turkish organizations such as Hasankeyf Matters and the Initiative to Keep Hasankeyf Alive. To link Turkey and Iraq to the global struggle for water justice, the campaign has organized events to raise awareness both in the North and in the South, in countries such as Italy, Jordan, and Tunisia.

Anti-dam organizations meet at international gatherings such as the World Social Forum (WSF), which has released several documents on the global anti-dam struggle.[14] Numerous activists, campaigns and non-profit organizations from the Middle East have found their way into the World Social Forum. In 2013, the World Social Forum was held in the Middle East for the first time, in Tunis, underscoring the importance of resistance and mobilization in the region. From the World Social Forum other thematic and national forums emerged. The Iraqi Social Forum was founded in early 2013, and other social forums followed suit, such as the Egyptian Social Forum for Youth in December 2013. Growing ecological awareness is increasingly expressed through such forums, protests, and campaigns.[15]

The Save the Tigris Campaign is one of the very first ecological initiatives in Iraq to focus on broad, nationwide advocacy. The campaign is part of a new, bourgeoning ecological movement, not only in Iraq but also in the whole Middle East. It has established an important link between global and local civil society, thereby paving the way for other initiatives to follow suit in Iraq. A genuine ecological movement must be able to influence political processes, and the Save the Tigris Campaign has succeeded in putting an urgent ecological issue on the national agenda. Local and international media are increasingly reporting about Iraq's water issues, and the Iraqi Marshes are likely to be included in

UNESCO's World Heritage list. At the same time, Iraqi civil society has expanded their scope. By being closely involved in the campaign, local activists have been empowered to act not only upon the issue of Ilisu Dam, but on ecological issues in general.

The Save the Tigris Campaign demonstrates the importance of international solidarity. It has inspired Iraqi activists and given them a sense of being part of a bigger and enduring international movement that successfully struggles to promote human and environmental rights. Iraqi environmental activists are now part of the global ecology movement. We believe their experience will be much valued in the global exchange of ideas.

NOTES:

1. John A. Allan, *The Middle East Water Question: Hydropolitics and the Global Economy* (New York, I.B. Tauris, 2002), 199.

2. Joseph G. Jabbra and Nancy W. Jabbra, "Challenging Environmental Issues: Middle Eastern Perspectives," in Joseph G. Jabbra and Nancy W. Jabbra, eds., *Challenging Environmental Issues: Middle Eastern Perspectives* (Leiden, Brill, 1997), 13.

3. See, for example, Allan, *Middle East Water Question*.

4. Ibid., 37.

5. Sanjeev Khagram, *Dams and Development: Transnational Struggles for Water and Power* (Ithaca, Cornell University Press, 2004), 3.

6. Odeh Al Jayyousi, "Water as a Human Right: Towards Civil Society Globalization," in Asit K. Biswas, ed., *Water as a Human Right for the Middle East and North Africa* (New York, Routledge, 2008), 129.

7. Toon Bijnens, "The Basra water crisis and increasing salinity of the Shatt al-Arab," February 26, 2014 (available at iraqicivilsociety.org).

8. Susanne Gusten, "Construction of Disputed Turkish Dam Continues," *New York Times*, February 27, 2013.

9. Erica Gies, "Restoring Iraq's Garden of Eden," *New York Times*, April 17, 2013.

10. Save the Tigris and Marshes, "Ilisu Dam and Legal Considerations in Iraq," Policy paper, March 22, 2014, 2.

11. Boaventura De Sousa Santos, *The Rise of the Global Left: The World Social Forum and Beyond* (New York, Zed 2006), 116.

12. Khagram, *Dams and Development*, 3.

13. Franklin D. Rothman and Pamela E. Olivier, "From Local to Global: The Anti-Dam Movement in Southern Brazil," in Jackie Smith and Hank Johnston, eds., *Globalization and Resistance: Transnational Dimensions of Social Movements* (Lanham, Rowman and Littlefield, 2002), 128. See also De Sousa Santos, *Rise of the Global Left*, 139.

14. Glenn Switkes and Elias Diaz Pena, "Water—A Common Good," in William F. Fischer and Thomas Ponniah (eds.), *Another World is Possible: Popular Alternatives to Globalization at the World Social Forum* (London, Cox and Wyman, 2003), 132.

15. Moshe Terdiman, "Environmental Protests of the Middle East show Eco Awareness in the Arab World," *Green Prophet*, June 18, 2013.

THE GEZI FORUMS: TOWARD DIRECT DEMOCRACY?

CAĞRI ERYILMAZ

I n 2013 Istanbul's Gezi Park was slated to become just another site for a neoliberal project of urban renewal (or urban removal, as Henri Lefebvre calls it), transferring capital to sustain the growth of capitalism. The project would have destroyed one of the city's last remaining green spaces. In many cities around the world, such transformations have given rise to urban struggles, and so this one did in Gezi Park: on May 28, 2013, a protest erupted there that emerged from the grassroots and, without leadership from any party, union, or other organization, spread from Gezi Park to Istanbul's squares and other parks and then to other cities in Turkey, until it became a full-fledged resistance movement. For an entire month, the movement occupied Taksim Square (adjacent to Gezi Park) and also parks of İstanbul and other cities. In some cases violence erupted between protesters and police.

The movement comprised the whole range of opposition groups. Indeed, the composition of protesters was unique in Turkish history in that many different groups acted together for the first time. Öğütle has defined six types of participants: nongovernmental organizations

(NGOs); the revolutionary left; the Kurdish movement; Kemalist groups (the name refers to the founding ideology of Turkey, developed by Mustafa Kemal Atatürk); people on Istiklal Street (Istanbul's most famous avenue, which ends in Gezi Park); anticapitalist Muslims; and "flagless" people (lacking ideology, identity, or aims).[1] They were protesting, among other things, the government's authoritarian policies, which they saw as making protest necessary. In the 2014 local and presidential elections, the opposition parties failed to respond to or represent the demands of the protesters, and half the population strongly supported the government. The diversity of the protests against the government and the polarization of the country show that the current representative democracy fails to address popular demands.

The protests, and the deficiency of the opposition parties, led a few protesters in Istanbul to develop forums. Soon hundreds of forums sprang up, throughout the country. Nightly and later weekly, in the occupied parks and squares, issues of common concern were discussed at these forums. Any group or individual could take part.

> Following the Gezi Resistance, people come together at forums where they freely discuss issues ranging from the streets where they live to the whole country. To people in these forums, the tiresome old policy-making—which depends on tricks and personal interests behind cold parliament walls— seems inadequate. From now on, a new policy making based on local democracy appears in parks and streets where everyone listens and tries to understand one another and nobody is held to be superior or inferior. We, living in Şisli central neighborhoods, and others through our forums met with the people of our neighborhood to rebuild a lost neighborhood culture and to discuss the serious agenda of neighborhood and nationwide issues as well as to have fun together.[2]

For the first time in Turkish history, an opposition moved beyond protest to generate a platform that was intended not to dominate but to share ideas and listen to others. The 2011 events in Tahrir Square in Cairo were similar, but the majority there in the end preferred a liberal and representative democracy. The Gezi protests, however, and the forums that resulted, may be a starting point to extend and expand participatory and even direct democracy. Forums provide a base for transformation of temporary protests into permanent structures. Hence, they have a potential to develop local policies that affect local governance.

Benlisoy implies that there is a need for establishing forums of direct democracy that can provide a dynamic and a representative structure.[3] However, the forums were late to enable people to join the decision-making processes. Hence, many lost their motivation before they could fully participate.

In this essay, I have used forum notes on the Internet and social media accounts as data sources. Although the discussions and atmosphere cannot be transcribed entirely, such notes present details of discussions of many meetings of hundreds of forums. This study is a first phase in an analysis that should be improved with in-depth interviews and observations.

Social ecology, developed by Murray Bookchin, provides a coherent and radical critique of environmentalism as a capitalist discourse. Environmental actions, projects, and campaigns, Bookchin argues, cannot solve the ecological crisis; nor can green production and consumption, because the domination of nature stems from domination of human by human. Environmentalist activities not only veil the roots of ecological crisis but also obscure the need to construct a rational ecological society through a much farther-reaching political program.

An ecological and rational society, according to social ecology, can be organized from bottom up at the neighborhood level through citizen assemblies in a face-to-face democracy where "people act directly on society and directly shape their own destinies."[4] This bod of ideas is based on citizenship, the ecocommunity, direct democracy, and the municipality. Social movement approaches that address political opportunity, resource mobilization, and ideology formation are insufficient to assess it. Because social ecology's aim is to change society in radical ways, protest is not sufficient to implement it.[5] Moreover, social ecology's direct democracy approach, based on citizen assemblies, is more radical than a liberal democratic framework, even one that is deepened and enlarged into a radical and pluralist democracy.[6] Social ecology, instead, offers a slow but a revolutionary change toward a libertarian society.

Bookchin's model for direct democracy, libertarian municipalism, rests on the formation of citizen assemblies within neighborhoods to discuss community issues within the public realm.[7] David Harvey's call for cooperation between worker and citizen for "the right to city" resembles libertarian municipalism in its invocation of the city as the arena for struggle.[8] However, his program also differs significantly. First, where Bookchin defines the spatial unit as the neighborhood, Harvey refers to the whole city comprising millions of people. Second, Bookchin uses the concept of citizens of a community within a neighborhood, whereas Harvey refers to citizens of a city and workers within a class. Finally, Bookchin offers a confederal approach from bottom to top, in contrast to Harvey's centralist approach.

Andrew Dobson implies that the space for ecological citizenship is not the boundaries of nation-states or EU but is "produced by the metabolic and material relationship of individual people with environment."[9] Social ecology claims that this space is the neighborhood: a political realm governed by a citizen assembly. The administrative structures should be embedded in the municipality. Dobson's metabolic relation between ecological citizens and their environment is possible only with a direct democracy that generates genuine self-governance. The municipality can represent the city in a way that trade unions cannot. The municipality is the basic unit of political life where "citizenship, interdependence, confederation and freedom emerge."[10]

The municipality executes the decisions made by the citizen assembly. However, the municipality as currently structured requires radical change in order to underpin an ecological society. Current municipalities differ in quality and quantity. Although they have a "residual" democratic tradition, they are management bodies of current capitalist system. In most developed countries in the age of global capitalism, they have been transformed into town/city companies governed by patriarchal entrepreneurship, production and consumption spaces where citizens live as consumer monads.[11]

There are two ways reforming current municipalities to make them as the political realm of community: decentralization and democratization. As Biehl and Bookchin have detailed, decentralization is to be both institutional and physical. Institutional decentralization aims to reorganize municipalities into a smaller, more manageable unit like the neighborhood. The metropolis should be divided into neighborhood municipalities so that communities can govern themselves. Bookchin's understanding of community resembles *Gesellschaft* more than *Gemeinschaft*.[12] Rural towns are too small for physical reorganization. City halls are changed into neighborhood centers.

According to Biehl and Bookchin, the democratization of the present gigantic municipalities is paralleled by the decentralization of city government bodies.[13] Smaller municipalities provide space for direct democratic approach, through citizen assemblies that meet regularly, even weekly, for widest possible participation of concerned citizens. Institutional decentralization can be achieved only through direct democracy. In his study of neighborhood councils, Hillel Schmid defines a council as a mediator between "residents and neighborhood authorities."[14] He positions the self-management councils as a participative tool for reforming centralized authority. These councils can play a reforming and mediating role within the state structure.

As to the different approaches to decision making, Biehl and Bookchin say that consensus process may be good for small groups but may also oppress minorities by coercing their acquiescence to reach a majority decision.[15] Even when the majority-voting limit is 80 percent, it still dominates the minority. Biehl and Bookchiun prefer instead a majority rule system where dissenters can object openly, inscribing their objections into the community record, and keeping the issue alive in order to ensure that citizens in the assembly do not have to think the same way.

The creation of a movement for libertarian municipalism can be broken down into several phases. In the first, several interested people who recognize their commonality of views meet regularly and form a study group to discuss social ecology, democratic traditions, and social criticism. The group's more experienced and mature leaders motivate the others. In the process, they educate one another, becoming an intelligentsia.[16]

During a second phase, the core group seeks out new members among friends and interested people. The group establishes bylaws defining its decision-making processes and other institutional procedures. It chooses a recognizable name for itself, so that it will have a distinct identity within the community. The group members focus on a popular community issue. They produce position papers, reports, posters, and leaflets, linking it to libertarian municipalist ideas; they organize demonstrations and protests both to call attention to the issue and educate the public in their ideas.

According to social ecology, continuous education, face-to-face inter-action, and local elections are necessary to construct a public realm grounded in citizen assemblies at the neighborhood level. The third phase is to initiate the call for a citizen assembly, by linking the chosen community issue to the need for direct democracy or by using a local election campaign as a tool. The citizen assembly is the traditional form of town management. If their town has no such assembly, they should call for the formation of one.

The citizens' assembly is not limited to addressing specific issues but is a permanent structure, where citizens discuss community issues face to face and exercise direct democracy. It is a decision-making body, with a name, a moderator, a coordination committee, as well as a system of communications, all of which contribute to the institutionalization of the assembly.[17]

The creation of a municipal citizen assembly ignites the process of institutional decentralization. More neighborhoods form assemblies that go on to confederate, as did the Parisian sectional assemblies of the early 1790s. Each assembly choses delegates, so that decision making remains bottom-up.

Libertarian municipalism aims for a rational, ecological, and democratic society. This aim seems attractive and unique, but it has also offers significant problems. For one, the process of creating libertarian municipalism requires the presence of a core enlightened group of citizens who passionately work to construct the citizen assembly. For another, the risk of parochialism threatens humanitarian principles. Finally, the assumption that direct democracy will make decisions that favor ecology is a problem, since the assembly may also make decisions that cause the destruction of nature.

In 2013 hundreds of forums emerged throughout Turkey, starting with the Gezi Park protests. Forums, as defined by Farro and Demirhisar, are "alternative living constructs" to neoliberal authoritarianism where people can stay, share, speak, and listen without oppression.[18] Although forums do not consciously prioritize the municipality as the main unit, they focus on existing municipalities. Some forums are organized at the district level, but the formation of most forums at the neighborhood level rather than the district fits the principles of decentralization and democratization.

In terms of the phases of movement building, a group of people interested in direct democracy is needed in neighborhood. The first participants in the forums came mostly from the neighborhood, or at least from the district, because their first aim is to continue the forums and to extend the protests to their neighborhoods. However, the participants held different political perspectives. Moreover, no education about democracy, ecology etc., took place; hence they did not constitute a study group. There were no specific leaders, but there were always prominent people in the forums who they lead activities. The forum participants and also the core groups might have included intellectuals, but leadership by intellectuals was hardly seen in the forums.

Forums are not closed to participants coming from outside the neighborhood or district, but most of the participants were local. All forums had a name implying the neighborhood scale. Some of them included the word *solidarity* (Turkish: *dayanışma*). Forums had Facebook, Twitter, and Tumblr pages where they identified themselves, announced activities, and shared their views. The forums prepared stickers, badges, fanzines, and leaflets to introduce themselves to increase participation. They were willing to use both social media and printed matter. The desire to increase participation was a top issue at forum meetings. Ways to increase participation were discussed, such as inviting residents personally.

> The local forums propose extending direct democratic participation. Some offer ideas about expanding the movement and using democratic forums in the upcoming election period. A few speakers talk about the need of the establishment of the Gezi Party. Other speakers talk about supporting current organizations and parties. No concrete decision is taken. The result of the forums' first day seems ambiguous.[19]

The forums had three principles: popular assembly, solidarity, and praxis. Everyone had a right in to participate in decision making about the places where they live. From the neighborhood to the city, solidarity means resisting repression. Praxis makes participants active in their lives.[20] A general website of the forums expressed these common principles, and the meetings showed their implementation in real life.

Forums were to be open to everyone in the neighborhood. For example, the Şişli Forum called for everyone to join—neighbors, teachers, workers, doctors, musicians, and photographers—and said, "We are women, men, gay, children, young, old, ageless ... in summary we are you, like you, very similar to you."[21] Community issues were key to attracting people to the local assembly. Many issues were discussed at forum meetings, especially the urban renewal projects that ignited the Gezi protests. Other community issues were garbage, animal shelter, biodiversity, new alcohol regulations, tourism, joining Peace Day, an antinuclear platform, and a campaign against drug, theft, and prostitution gangs. Many forums built orchards in their neighborhoods: by meeting and working together on a communal issue, residents increased their ownership of their neighborhoods.

At each forum, moderators facilitated meetings, and a kind of core group facilitated the whole process. The forums and their meetings made significant improvements in the public realm, but that was far from the desired status. A year after the Gezi protests, the forums continue, although participation has decreased. But their survival is significant, revealing a popular civic demand for something beyond protests. The enthusiasm for the forums has waned over time, however, and the traditional political groups have come in to dominate the forums.

Forums are extralegal assemblies, necessary because participation in legal ones is restricted, hence training seminars on ways of joining the city council were organized. Speakers discussed joining elections but had no clear idea how to take part. There were complaints about current political system, and some were willing to support a current candidate on condition to accept their demands. Forums chose representatives to a group to meet the leader of opposition party to say that they want only direct democracy. They also demanded that mayors should be chosen directly by the people; they should not be nominated by the party leaders, which is the case today.

Speakers at some forums were willing to interact with others on issues like solidarity with the Kurdish and Alevi population, who has been subjected to a series of violent attacks. Forums organized joint meetings that can be seen a preparation for a confederative framework. Although there were attempts to organize and strengthen joint meetings, the confederative organization of forums needed much further work.

The evolution of the forums out of the protests was as unique as the eruption of the Gezi protests in the first place. For the first time in Turkish history, direct democracy at the neighborhood scale was discussed and attempted. Protests are limited to opposition, but forums have a potential to shift society toward direct democracy. Forums may become a significant tool to increase participation in representative democracy, as Schmid argued, or else they may become a step toward radically changing society. In a dialectical understanding, both ways are possible, and so is the disappearance of the forums.[22]

The core actor in social ecology's direct democracy is the citizen of the ecocommunity. The more people join neighborhood forums and the more they participate in decision-making processes, the more they become citizens of the ecocommunity. But the forum meetings should be shielded from all professional parties, leaders, and other organizations in order to preserve the base of the neighborhood ecocommunity.

NOTES:

1. Vefa Saygın Öğütle, "Adına Layık Bir Sosyal Bilimin Gezi Gündemleri," in Vefa Saygın Öğütle and Emrah Göker, eds., *Gezi ve Sosyoloji: Nesneyle Yüzleşmek, Nesneyi Kurmak* (Istanbul: Ayrıntı, 2014), 142-43.

2. Şişli Forum, public announcement, August 24, 2013.

3. Foti Benlisoy, *Gezi Direnişi: Türkiye'nin Enteresan Başlangıcı* (Istanbul: Agora, 2013), p. 71.

4. "Interview with Murray Bookchin," in Janet Biehl, *The Politics of Social Ecology: Libertarian Municipalism* (Montréal: Black Rose Books, 1998), p. 163.

5. Ibid., p. 176.

6. Ernesto Laclau, and Chantal Mouffe, *Hegemonya ve Sosyalist Strateji: Radikal Demokratik Bir Politikaya Doğru* (Istanbul: İletişim, 2012), p. 270.

7. Bookchin's model is outlined in Biehl, *Politics of Social Ecology*.

8. David Harvey, *Rebel Cities: From the Right to the City to the Urban Revolution* (London: Verso, 2013).

9. Andrew Dobson, *Citizenship and Environment* (Oxford: Oxford University Press, 2003), p. 106.

10. Biehl, *Politics of Social Ecology*, p. 175.

11. Murray Bookchin, *Kentsiz Kentleşme: Yurttaşlığın Yükselişi ve Çöküşü* (*Urbanization Without Cities: The Rise and Decline of Citizenship*), trans. Burak Özyalçın (Istanbul: Ayrıntı Yayınları, 1999).

12. Stewart Davidson, "Ecoanarchism: A Critical Defense," *Journal of Political*

Ideologies 14, no. 1 (2009): 57.

13. Biehl, *Politics of Social Ecology*, p. 58.

14. Hillel Schmid, *Neighborhood Self-Management: Experiments in Civil Society* (New York: Kluwer Academic/Plenum Publishers, 2001), p. 145.

15. Biehl, *Politics of Social Ecology*, p. 59.

16. Ibid., pp. 164-66.

17. Ibid., p. 175.

18. Antimo L. Farro and Deniz Günce Demirhisar, "The Gezi Park Movement: A Turkish Experience of the Twenty-First-Century Collective Movements," *International Review of Sociology* 24, no. 1 (2014), p. 184.

19. "Parklar Bizim," available at www.parklarbizim.blogspot.com.tr/2013/07/ankara-batkent-forum-notlar-21-haziran.html.

20. Gezi Forumlari Dayanismasi, at www.geziforumlari.org.

21. *Refüj*, June 2014.

22. Schmid, *Neighborhood Self-Management*.

SOCIAL ECOLOGY AND CONTEMPORARY URBAN STRUGGLES

FEDERICO VENTURINI

All around the world today cities face a series of uprisings where urban social movements play a key role. Social ecology can help us understand contemporary urban struggles and articulate their opposition to capitalism and domination. Social ecology provides a powerful set of ideas that can strengthen these movements. However, a more extensive dialogue between the theory of social ecology and the practice of social movements still needs to be developed.

This is important because cities, where the majority of the world population lives, are today at the forefront of the environmental and social crisis. They are not only an arena for intense social and ecological conflicts, but are also, as observed by David Harvey, the frontier of capital reproduction. At the same time, cities are major sites for re-imagining more ecologically and socially sustainable futures: "Cities are the world's greatest assets for pursuing sustainable development. How we plan, build and manage our cities today will determine our future."[1] Living in cities is, indeed, the only way in which our densely populated world can dramatically reduce waste and consumption, share resources, stop sprawl and save energy, due to the greatly reduced ecological footprint cities may offer. Social ecologists are keenly aware of this, and Murray Bookchin certainly appreciates the importance of the city for human development. Indeed, human civilization primarily developed in cities; they constitute a basic arena for cultural development and a precondition for politics. Bookchin defines the city as "a space in which we work and engage in everyday consociation [and] as a public arena."[2] To the general idea of urbanization, a phenomenon in which the urban environment absorbs all space, he prefers the idea of "citification," recognizing how real urban lives presume an idea of a political community, a civic sphere. However, cities today have lost their ability to guarantee political community and a genuine social life: people are highly individualized, reduced to fragmented individuals. Citizenship has vanished and the city becomes a space where the state affirms its power and control: indeed, we now reach a point where city negates itself as a political embodiment of society. The solution to these problems depends not on a new urban design or technological fix, social ecologists argue, but on fundamentally changing the institutions and culture of urban society. Social movements are crucial to initiate and build this change.

Since the battle of Seattle in 1999, there have been a continuous series of urban uprisings around the world, led by social movements: most recently the 2008 Greek uprising, the Occupy movement, the Spanish 15-M, the Arab Spring, urban struggles in Latin America, and the international student movements. All of these can be included in a series of worldwide mobilizations or urban insurrections that take inspiration from the principles of autonomy, direct democracy, solidarity and direct action, key points that resonate also in social ecology.[3] These movements are united, above all, by their discontent with the current model of capitalist development. This discontent assumes the same global scale of the system they contest. At the same time, these movements are built on a very local scale. Behind all these expressions of dissent, which share a set of similar characteristics on a global scale, stand the overlapping effects of local grassroots work that piece by piece, like the work of termites, make big things possible: at certain moments and places, they escalate into massive popular mobilizations. Two aspects distinguish these movements: they are urban and they aim at emancipation through collective action. They aim at addressing the urban questions, and establish the right to the city for all.

These urban social movements are acting on a local scale, within their own urban context. At the same time their struggles resonate with a global perspective, through which they are able to build transnational links and solidarity networks. Social ecology can provide a solid theoretical ground for all these struggles, thanks to its generalized analysis of hierarchy and domination. A social ecological elaboration of how domination plays out on a global scale can accompany these movements and help unite them in a common, global struggle. Until now, indeed, Bookchin and other social ecologists have remained concentrated on European or North American experiences and viewpoints, loci in which their thoughts were born.[4] Thanks to their elaboration we now have a body of theory that is ready to embrace a global scale, to be used also to analyze other contexts and, at the same time, become informed by them. If we want to develop a meaningful explanation of current struggles, I believe a worldwide vista is necessary: we must use it to surpass a Western-centered mindset.

This process, I think, could start with conceptually classifying the world into core, semi-periphery and periphery countries, as suggested by Immanuel Wallerstein's World-System Theory. These concepts are useful and can help explain the complicated power-economic relations between countries of the world today. Moreover, it would be important to also consider the concept of neocolonialism. This is a form of domination based on the indirect control of the economy and culture of periphery and semi-periphery by the core countries. A distinct social ecology perspective on global patterns of dependency and exploitation would not only provide more powerful explanations, but could also reinforce local communalist politics, which indeed feeds on cosmopolitanism. At the same time, a genuinely ecological perspective must always consider the global scale of ecological crises, and put forward a social analysis of how these crises unfold unevenly in the core, the semi-periphery, and the periphery.

Brazil is a perfect example of a system slowly exhibiting all its contradictions. It is a society marked by an uneven development, where the polarization between rich and poor classes is one of the highest in the world. Violence by the military police—a legacy of the military dictatorship—or by drug dealers is a part of everyday life. Political and financial scandals are continuous. The Amazonian forest faces increasing destruction. The transport system is poor and expensive, and so too are the health care and school systems. This uneven development is reflected in the socio-political fragmentation of urban space; a dramatic segregation where some neighborhoods are specifically designated for rich people and others for the poor, and the poorest are banished to the precarious situation of the favelas.[5] In Rio de Janeiro, a metropolis of six million people, these problems have reached a magnitude of dramatic proportions.

In June 2013, the protests against a general increase in public transport fares exploded in Brazil. In a few weeks, small initial demonstrations became oceanic, with millions of people taking to the streets across the entire country. Explaining the multiple reasons for the protests is complicated and certainly there are a series of concomitant factors, but this public transport fare became the "straw that broke the camel's back." The protests built on a growing political discontent with the neoliberal drift of the government, and with the devastating impacts of mega-events and persisting social inequalities. At the same time, since the very beginning, these protests were violently repressed by the police. This generated an emotional public reaction that increasingly came to support the protesters. These mobilizations were unusually large for Brazil, and continued to grow. Alternative technologies also played an important role in broadening the protests: social media helped to quickly spread the campaigns to millions of people, denouncing police violence and deconstructing the corporate media discourses.

This was unprecedented, as Brazil boasts a strong corporate media that systematically distorts information about social movements. However, in line with the patterns that I have explored, it is clear that behind this street explosion there is the persistent, ongoing grassroots work of urban social movements. They have been present from the beginning, and have been able to give structure to the protests, radicalize their demands, and build a broader movement to sustain the struggle over time. From a general critique of the current public transport system, this movement started opposing the development of modern Brazilian cities and the entire capitalist system.

In the specific context of Rio de Janeiro, social movements pushed for the first protests in June 2013. In this city, these mobilizations have maintained momentum, reinforced by a critique against mega-events—like the FIFA World Cup 2014 and the forthcoming 2016 Olympic Games—as well as various important strikes. Driven by necessity, the Rio de Janeiro movements have adopted numerous forms of resistance, such as direct action, encampments in the Occupy style, alternative media, and popular assemblies. They reject traditional political parties and connect their horizontal approach to a broad range of social issues, such as, for instance, the struggles of indigenous peoples.

The assembly has been at the core of these social movements, a forum where all issues are debated, discussed and decided. Well-structured and hosting often hundreds of people, the assembly has provided a space of political elaboration and organization of events and actions. Moreover, from the assemblies of these social movements, spread during the peak of the protests, there have also been developed geographically localized assemblies. Rio de Janeiro has been a political laboratory with decentralized and confederated assemblies of both neighborhoods and work-places.

This attempt to build direct democracy has also been supported by the repeated use of Occupy-style encampments, which clearly show the transnational links among movements. The inspiration from Occupy has been used to add a stronger political meaning to a common Brazilian practice of squatting and land occupation. The Occupy camps have been public, in visible urban spaces, and they have been key in providing a base for demonstrators to publicly meet, assemble, debate and organize their actions. They have acted as liberated spaces, semi-temporary autonomous zones, where movements have put into practice the principles they proclaim, interacting with the urban poor, exploring the challenges and difficulties they face, and celebrating common victories.

These movements had also to develop a tactic to resist the brutal police violence. In order to do so some protestors employed the black bloc, whose main aim has been the protection of demonstrators through the use of direct actions against the police and their weapons. First, despite a massive denigrating campaign by the state and corporate media, this tactic has retained much greater popular support in comparison with core countries. Common people in Brazil have seen and suffered daily police brutality; they recognize a response to violence or use of direct action as a necessary condition for the protesters to self-guarantee their right to demonstrate. Second, the direct actions of these black blocs are normally not mere lifestyle choices or acts of self-glorification, but rather a fully-cognizant political decision—part of the movement strategy. From Tahrir Square to the streets of Rio de Janeiro, protests around the world have proven that barricades have not yet completely left the necessary repertoire of civil resistance.

With its critique of domination and emphasis on the desire for freedom, social ecology offers two important contributions. On the one hand, it challenges the current capitalistic system as a whole, and all other forms of oppression and exploitation. On the other, it offers a liberatory vision for a future society, free of scarcity and hierarchy. Social ecology tells us "where to look," identifying areas of intervention, and understanding the reality of current modes of domination and struggle; such as, for instance, the city, the countryside, the natural world, and the role of science and technology. At the same time it puts forward also "what should be done," how we can construct a new society: suggesting a communalist politics, affinity groups, collective actions, and alternative education. Moreover, it gives us the principles that lay at the foundation of this revolutionary project: such as feminism, anti-statism, horizontalism, egalitarianism, cooperation, mutual aid, self-determination, an ethics of complementarity, and decentralization. This, I believe, is the real power of social ecology: it provides a coherent and comprehensive system of thought that offers analyses of the current crisis, a vision for the future, and the tools to achieve it. But for social ecology to become truly relevant, and live up to its great promise, it must engage in an open a dialogue with contemporary social movements.

The Brazilian experiences shows how a more developed knowledge of social ecology theory could reinforce these movements and help them formulate more comprehensive challenges to the current political and economic system. They already embody many elements that reflect the core principles of social ecology, but do not yet fully embrace it as a new urban politics. At the same time, I would say that further reflections on the novelty of these movement practices also offer ideas for advancing social ecology, stimulating a debate that can bridge urban struggles and worldwide movements with a social ecology perspective.

One of the key aspects that urban social movements in Brazil can learn from social ecology is the need to also focus on the environmental damage caused by the model of development they already oppose. The Brazilian national economy today dictates the unrestricted and uncontrolled growth of Brazilian cities, with grave environmental consequences. Despite the massive environmental problems that affect Rio de Janeiro and Brazil, few activists pay attention to environmental issues. Contemporary social movements focus their attention on the urgent question of survival, which is still not guaranteed for a great part of the urban population. In a society of sharp class divisions, they prioritize the fight against class domination, and they see environmental problems as secondary to the basic needs of human life. It seems, then, that it is only when basic standard of living is ensured and minimal working rights are guaranteed, that movements can start claiming other rights and concentrate on environmental problems.

But this failure to address ecological issues clearly weakens the struggle against capitalist domination, and fails to identify the nature of the current crisis and comprehend its full range. This also makes it difficult for us to find viable and holistic alternatives. As social ecology explains, only by addressing the concept of domination over nature as well as over human beings can we work for a real alternative that reconnects humans to nature. Only by acknowledging that our current social and environmental crises are structurally built into the very system of capitalism can we start building holistic and viable alternatives. Moreover, the class struggle that is still intensely present in countries like Brazil, will, in a social ecology framework, assume a new centrality and meaning. Without falling into an old-fashioned Marxist understanding of the role of the proletariat, social ecology could advance the class component in social movement theory. Again, it is the broader concept of domination that provides the framework for explaining social struggles in their specific movement contexts, as well as their geographical, cultural, and historical peculiarities. According to this analysis, social movements primarily struggle against domination, even though this struggle is framed differently in different contexts. Class struggle is then integrated into a coherent struggle against all forms of domination. However, when we allow the struggle over economic concerns to exclude ecological concerns, which is what Brazilian activists practice, we greatly limit our vision and sphere of action. Here, I would suggest that the holistic perspective of social ecology could broaden our scope, also in very practical ways.

These urban social movements also convey an important lesson for the whole political Left. In many countries, the Left seems to have abandoned its longstanding tradition of forging strong relationships with the political base. Too often, the Left is entrenched in dogmatic discussions or narrow campaigns, while the development of genuine grassroots projects is left in the hands of right-wing or religious organizations. Rio de Janeiro reminds us of the importance of action from below, and this resonates with the basic principles of social ecology. Here, an articulated undergrowth of grassroots initiatives, such as community centers, popular education projects, land and housing occupations, all built on their own networks to mobilize for the protests, giving these protests both a structure and radical content. This is an important lesson for movements in core countries: continuously working in community organizations to build grassroots self-governing structures offers the possibility of mobilizing the population and creating a "political climate" favorable to radical social change. It also opens up spaces where alternative futures and social ecology principles can be put in practice, visible to the whole society. With the support of social ecology, such public arenas could help ground and solidify the moments of street protests and popular insurrection.[6]

Bookchin reminds us that novelties often emerge from the periphery and two of the most extraordinary contemporary examples of realized utopias are the Zapatistas' autonomous municipalities in Chiapas and the experience of Democratic Confederalism in Kurdistan.[7] These experiences underscore the importance of a vision for the future such as the ones provided by social ecology. At the same time they show that this vision should not be a strict blueprint, but act as a guide, modified and adapted to each specific geographical, historical and social condition. Social ecology's political approach provides a powerful tool for social change, something even a Marxist scholar like David Harvey acknowledges. In order to take maximum advantage of its potential, however, it needs to be adapted to specific times and places, also reconsidering, where needed, its electoral strategy. We should take into account the reasons why many contemporary social movements reject traditional political parties and representative democracy, and make sure we do not reproduce them. In Rio de Janeiro, for example, municipal elections would present many similar problems to elections at the statewide level. This city of six million people lacks any institutional framework at the community level. Therefore these urban social movements are now building their political structures entirely outside of the existing institutions. Social ecologists need to elaborate new ways to accompany them in their struggles, adapting a communalist politics to different contexts. Communalism, Bookchin reminds us, "is not a fixed electoral dogma that depends upon the state, in whatever form, to initiate municipal institutional changes. In practice, it will obviously vary from locality to locality and country to country."[8]

The importance of adapting ideas and practice to each historical and geographical context is crucial. "The Left cannot fetishize either the state or the street but must rather engage in a variety of struggles for power where tactics emerge from a broader strategy that moves us toward a clearly articulated vision of a different society."[9] To this end, it is important that it "can experiment with alternative institutions, like worker cooperatives, to practice self-management, while also recognizing limits imposed by present realities. It must address existing social inequalities of race, class, and gender both in the movement and society, without becoming paralyzed by their intransigence or individualizing deep-seated social problems."[10]

Social ecology has the potential to be central in this process, due to its coherent and comprehensive analyses. At the same time we have to bear in mind that "it is difficult to provide a 'handbook' for achieving a successful revolution. No schematic formulas or laws can apply to all revolutionary developments, although parallel events are strikingly present."[11] Social ecology also has much to learn from contemporary urban struggles, and I believe that we should continuously work to link social movements and social ecology, trying to bridge different experiences and tactics in different cultures.

The current social and environmental crises perpetuated by the capitalist system offer everyday challenges that must be fought on a variety of fronts. It requires that we have the ability to learn from the past and continuously analyze the present. Moreover, it demands a fervent imagination to prefigure and actively seek out alternative ways of living and doing politics. This is a struggle that happens everywhere and at all times, and social ecology, entering in dynamic dialogue with our everyday practices, will be able to support us in each moment of this process. Social ecology is a key tool for social change: it helps us to analyze and understand the current crises, and, above all, provides us with a bold vision for a future yet to come.

NOTES:

1. World Urban Campaign, *Manifesto for Cities: The Urban Future We Want* (2012), 3. (Available at worldurbancampaign.org.)

2. Murray Bookchin, *From Urbanization to Cities: Toward a New Politics of Citizenship* (London: Cassell, 1995), 4.

3. The concepts of autonomy, direct democracy, solidarity, and direct action in social movements have been explored by George Katsiaficas in *Asia's Unknown Uprisings, Volume 2: People Power in the Philippines, Burma, Tibet, China, Taiwan, Bangladesh, Nepal, Thailand, and Indonesia, 1947–2009* (Oakland: PM Press, 2013).

4. This exposed them to criticisms such as the one by Brazilian scholar Cavalcanti, who says that "the main criticism to Bookchin could be … the scant attention that he devoted to problems of social ecology in Third World countries," like problems of neocolonialism and megalopolis. See Mauro José Cavalcanti, "Introduction," to Murray Bookchin, *Ecologia Social e Outros Ensaios*, edited by Mauro José Cavalcanti (Rio de Janeiro: Achiamé, 2010), 15. My translation from Portuguese.

5. On the concept of socio-political fragmentation of urban space, see Marcelo Lopez de Souza, "Social Movements in the Face of Criminal Power: The Socio-Political Fragmentation of Space and 'Micro-Level Warlords' as Challenges for Emancipative Urban Struggles," *City* 13:1 (2009), 26–52.

6. As pointed out by Dan Chodorkoff, *The Anthropology of Utopia: Essays on Social Ecology and Community Development* (Porsgrunn: New Compass, 2014), particularly 173-185.

7. Murray Bookchin, *The Modern Crisis* (Philadelphia: New Society, 1986), 148-149.

8. Bookchin, *From Urbanization to Cities*, 12.

9. Blair Taylor, "To Be Realistic, Demand the Impossible: Toward a Visionary Left," *Tikkun*, Spring, 2014 (Available at tikkun.org).

10. Ibid.

11. Murray Bookchin, *The Third Revolution: Popular Movements in the Revolutionary Era*, Vol. 4 (London: Continuum, 2005), 261.

PARTICIPATORY DEMOCRACY ALLOWS US TO THINK WHAT WE ARE DOING

CAMILLA HANSEN

The ecological crisis looms over us and threatens our very survival. Yet, there is no decisive action, no effective response. International climate summits and diplomacy fail repeatedly, and no government has initiated a radical transformation of our current course. Although we recognize the gravity of the situation, we seem unable to assume responsibility for it.

This situation has led some to see ordinary people and democracy as part of the problem. People are typically portrayed as narrow-minded consumers driven by short-term self-interest and unwilling to make the necessary changes to their consumer lifestyles to avert global ecological collapse. As the lack of political action to tackle global warming continues, calls for authoritarian solutions have become more common. It is argued that the crisis is too serious and too urgent to be left to citizens and that "democracy must be put on hold for a while" or suspended altogether and replaced by various forms of authoritarian expert rule.[1]

This essay sets out to contest eco-authoritarianism and argues that radical participatory democracy is a better alternative to address the ecological crisis.[2] While they differ on many issues, I will dispute the two main arguments that are put forward by most eco-authoritarians; namely that of the human propensity towards short-term self-interest and the lack of sufficient knowledge and objectivity, among ordinary citizens, that are required to understand and address environmental problems.

Eco-authoritarians tend to overlook or downplay the political and societal causes of ecological destruction and the fact that ordinary people are denied the capacity to act politically, and collectively change the societal structures, institutions, and practices that are necessary to tackle the crisis. Drawing on the political ideas of Hannah Arendt, I argue that a participatory politics oriented towards the common interest will be able to transcend short-term self-interest and foster collective responsibility and action.

Furthermore, looking at Arendt's view of what constitutes political issues and her thinking on political judgement and its cultivation, it becomes clear that the environmental problems should be subjected to the political processes of public deliberation and collective decision-making. This, I contend, requires a form of participatory democracy in which all citizens have the right and opportunity to participate directly in public affairs.

One of the most common arguments raised against democracy and for the need for authoritarian measures to address the ecological crisis is that ordinary people are driven by short-term self-interest; they are supposedly unable to see beyond their own interests, and they are certainly not willing to make sacrifices for the future.[3] Political leaders trying to implement long-term policies that demand the forgoing of pleasures today for benefits in the future will inevitably lose power. This puts strong limits on what politicians can do in terms of wise environmental policies. The alternative then, eco-authoritarians claim, is "forward-looking authoritarian regimes that have the liberty to consult more rarely with their populations."[4]

This view is misguided for several reasons. It is based on the premise that the root of the ecological predicament lies in the attitude of private and isolated individuals and does not take into account the systemic and societal causes of the environmental problems. Ecological degradation is to a large extent caused by the operations and activities of collective institutions like multinational corporations. Industrial society and the capitalist economic system based on unlimited growth are dependent on increased production and massive levels of consumption. Consumerism, in turn, is fuelled by the omnipresent advertising and marketing applied by these corporations.

Furthermore, the argument about "the short-term nature of the voter" does not recognize that in liberal representative regimes, the biggest threat to ecologically-minded politicians and the strongest limits to environmental action comes not from ordinary people, but from powerful elites and special interests, often the very same industries and corporations that account for most of the environmental destruction. Through powerful lobby groups and privileged access to political decision-makers they have a great bearing on environmental politics. Citizens and popular movements, on the other hand, are often sidelined.

Contrary to the eco-authoritarian assumption, people in liberal representative "democracies," do not have "too much" democracy and freedom. While people are liberated from oppression and coercion and civil liberties protect the right of isolated individuals to pursue their interests in the private sphere, the vast majority of the population are denied the capacity to act in a political capacity and is bereft of political community. As consequences of the structures and practices of modern industrialized society, the environmental problems must be addressed collectively. This requires, however, involving the citizenry in public affairs, giving them the power to act politically. Before turning to this point, let us have a look at Arendt's conception of politics.

Here, I would like to highlight two central aspects of Arendt's conception of politics. First, that politics should be understood as free action and second, that politics is oriented towards the common world and the common interest. To *act*, as Arendt understands it, is to initiate the new and unexpected, "to call something into being which did not exist before."[5] All humans have this capacity to initiate the new because we are plural, that is, we are all distinct persons with unique biographies and perspectives on the world different from everyone else's. Action when it is political, is intersubjective and public, and coordinated by speech. We can only act together with others in a public realm, a politically organized community where our actions gain publicity and can be seen and heard and talked about, and responded to by others. Political action always either comes in the form of words or is followed by them. We start the new and unexpected through our words as plural individuals exchanging and discussing our opinions and our perspectives on the world, trying to persuade each other in the hope of arriving at collective agreement and decision. Political freedom, as distinguished from the negative freedom in the private sphere, is the freedom to act politically; to enter the public realm constituted by our equals and to participate in "those activities of 'expressing, discussing, and deciding' which, in a positive sense, are the activities of freedom."[6]

Politics, as Arendt understands it, is "the judicious exchange of opinion about the sphere of public life and the common world, and the decision what manner of action is to be taken in it, as well as to how it is to look henceforth, what kind of things are to appear in it."[7] The common world is our humanely constructed world of artifacts and institutions that we share with others. Since it existed before we were born and will continue to exist after we die, it is common in the broadest sense; we share it not only with everyone who inhabits it now, but also with those who were here before us and those who will come after us. Our public interests as citizens are different and often at odds with our private interests as individuals. While we as private individuals pursue our own interests and those of our family and partial group, *as citizens* we are oriented towards the common good, the interests of the shared world and all its inhabitants, including future generations. Only through acting collectively in the public realm, debating, deliberating and jointly deciding about common concerns with our equals will we be able to transcend our narrow self-interests and see the world from perspectives other than our own.

While the common world in Arendt's thought is sharply distinguished from nature, the way we organize and shape our common world and its affairs impacts the natural environment. The organization of modern industrialized society has resulted in ecological destruction which in turn impacts on our common world. I contend therefore that the ecological crisis and the environmental problems are matters of common concern, deeply affected by and affecting our common affairs.

Arendtian politics as that which concerns the common world and the common interest is different from the kind of politics practiced in liberal regimes which is based on the aggregation of private preferences and the pursuit of, usually economic, self-interest. The public sphere is no longer truly common, but has been invaded by private interests. Politics , in turn, has been degraded into bureaucratic administration and the maneuvers of lobbyists and pressure groups. Thus, environmental politics is largely dominated by national and global elites, technocratic managers, and centralized institutions, and it accentuates technical fixes, market mechanisms and vast top-down solutions that do not involve citizens and local communities. The population, rather, is constructed as a mass of atomized and passive consumers, whose behaviour is to be analyzed, predicted, steered, and influenced by the authorities. Seen as incapable of acting on their own initiative in the shaping of their common affairs, the role of people in addressing the ecological crisis has been confined to private choices in the market and the household. There are no public arenas for genuine citizen participation, and people's opinions and actions are not welcomed.[8]

But to confront today's ecological challenges, we need to make possible collective action. The solution, I think, lies precisely in giving people the right and opportunity to take part in formulating, shaping and deciding environmental politics, and for us to act together as citizens of a political community. This would transform politics from a battlefield of private interests to an activity concerned with our common affairs and enable us to together take responsibility for addressing the ecological challenges that face us all.

The second major argument put forward by the eco-authoritarians is that environmental problems are too technical and complex for ordinary people to make informed judgement and sound decisions: they lack the necessary knowledge. Experts on the other hand, it is claimed, are better equipped to rule in these matters, because they supposedly possess objective and universal knowledge, and that their technical expertise makes them neutral and disinterested.

This argument is based on the premise that the ecological problems can be reduced to purely scientific or technical questions with answers that are objectively and demonstrably true. However, even though most environmental problems have technical aspects, they are also, I contend, highly political and social. Here I will turn again to Arendt.

According to Arendt, matters that are political cannot be solved through scientific means, but must be subjected to public debate and collective decision-making. She distinguishes between political concerns and matters of scientific truth or technical administration. Political concerns are those about which there is disagreement and different opinions, while scientific and technical problems have answers and solutions that can be demonstrated to be true or false through mathematical formulas or technical evidence.

Scientific statements that are demonstrably true cannot be refuted and disagreed with: We cannot disagree with the statement "2+2=4" or with the theory of gravity. Truth claims therefore have a coercive and despotic character, they preclude debate and demand only recognition and obedience. Political opinions, on the other hand, have many possible answers and alternative choices of action. They are connected to a specific location and time and can be changed and enlarged through debate and persuasion. Unlike the compelling validity of scientific statements, the validity of political opinions is intersubjective and rests on the free agreement and consent between the many.[9]

Arendt wants to protect politics against those who want to reduce political questions to matters that can be resolved through scientific means or technical administration. But she also warns against the tendency to transform scientific and factual truths into political opinion.

The climate deniers' attempts to convert the scientific truths about global warming is an example of this. Arendt underscores that respect for the nature and dignity of rational and factual truth is necessary for an enduring political community.

However, nothing follows from the facts; they cannot tell us what to do and how to act. That global warming is happening and that it is caused by human activity is a fact that can be demonstrated through scientific means. We cannot change this fact; it is a factual truth that has to inform political debate. However, the question about what we are going to do—how to respond to and act on climate change, is a political one. It is a question about which there is disagreement and many different opinions. Should we prioritize big cuts to carbon emissions above economic growth? Should fossil fuels be replaced with renewable energy sources or with nuclear power? Should we opt for large-scale, centralized technologies or more decentralized, intermediate ones? Should we go for market mechanisms or commons to conserve and protect natural resources? How should the responsibility for reducing emissions be shared among and within countries and communities? These are all political and "pre-scientific" questions and they inescapably touch upon principles of justice, solidarity, freedom, and equality— principles about which there are no absolute standards, no answers that can be demonstrated to be true by scientific means.

When scientists and experts discuss principles like these, they leave their roles as scientists and become *citizens* with diverging opinions and perspectives. The answers to the many political and normative questions inherent to the ecological challenges can therefore be valid only if they are agreed on by the political community of citizens—an agreement arrived at through debate and deliberation taking into consideration as many perspectives as possible.

When we participate in public debate, we express how the world appears to us from our perspective. Our opinions, in turn, are challenged by the opinions of others with very different perspectives and experiences from our own. In the process our own opinions are tested, modified and refined. We learn to appreciate the perspectives of others and to take them into consideration when we are forming our own opinions. By taking into consideration the opinions and perspectives of others, we imagine ourselves in their position and see the world from their perspective.

In this way we can develop political judgement, what Arendt terms an "enlarged mentality." Only in this way are we able to transcend our own subjective circumstances and private interests, and see the problem or the issue being discussed from many different perspectives. Political judgment then, starting from our own personal and narrow perspective, extends through public debate— through "the inexhaustible richness of human discourse"[10]—to incorporate evermore perspectives, so that we gain a multi-perspective understanding of the problem and the situation. The point here is that through participating in plural public deliberation, ordinary citizens are able to transcend self-interest and narrow thinking and to make considered and disinterested judgement.

This kind of political speech has an important meaning-giving function according to Arendt. It is by talking together that humans are able to make sense, to comprehend and find meaning in what we experience, know, and do. Arendt fears that if we renounce our capacity for speech, then would end up as thoughtless creatures, merely calculating, not thinking. We would become helpless slaves to our know-how, "thoughtless creatures at the mercy of every gadget which is technically possible, no matter how murderous it is."[11]

Modern science consists of a "language" of mathematical symbols that cannot be expressed in normal thought and speech. Science, Arendt contends, has thus emancipated itself from humanistic concerns.[12] When the scientist enters the laboratory, he begins to communicate in mathematical symbols and he is forced to leave his role as a citizen and his power of human understanding. This is why Arendt warns us against trusting the political judgement of scientists *qua* scientists:

The simple fact that physicists split the atom without any hesitations the very moment they knew how to do it, although they realized full well the enormous destructive potentialities of their operation, demonstrates that the scientist *qua* scientist does not even care about the survival of the human race on earth or, for that matter, about the survival of the planet itself.[13]

This does not, of course, mean that scientists are immoral and lack concern for humanity and the earth. However, it implies that when scientists do care about political and normative concerns like the environmental issues, they act *as citizens*, not as scientists. In political matters, scientists are themselves laypersons.

That scientists act as citizens, not scientists when engaging in political matters is illustrated in the process of "counter-expertise" so common in environmental politics, in which scientists from industry and the environmental movement are pitted against each other. As Frank Fischer adds, in environmental disputes, scientists have, "under the guise of scientific neutrality,"[14] often made social and political choices and taken sides.

The ecological crisis concerns us all, it raises a broad range of complex and contingent political, social, cultural, and ethical questions that cannot be answered through the language of mathematical calculation. Recent attempts to do so, such as in technocratic approaches like risk-benefit decision-making, trade in carbon credits, and "payment for *ecosystem services*" schemes such as REDD, are bound to fail.[15] While science and technology certainly have a role—not only in identifying and measuring environmental problems, but also in searching for solutions and in developing alternative ecological technologies—it is important to remember that questions concerning the very goals of scientific research, how the knowledge might be used, and what kind of technologies that should be developed, are all political questions that must be answered "in terms of common sense and in everyday language," through the political processes of public deliberation and collective decision by citizens.[16]

Political judgment needs a political realm containing a plurality of perspectives. The public realm can only exist in a diversity of perspectives;

it depends on being seen from multiple locations. Cultivation of political judgement therefore requires a political community consisting of concrete public spaces open to all citizens, "spaces of appearance" where opinions and views are made public, and are challenged and enlarged through debate and deliberation.

The public realm as Arendt conceives of it, is a sphere of equals, "constituted by one's peers."[17] Free and spontaneous collective action is only possible among equals. Where there is a distinction between rulers and the ruled, where there is command and obedience, there cannot be free debate and free agreement. Like the ancient Greek *polis*, the public realm is an *isonomy* where no one rules over others and decisions are not decreed from above by an external government, but where policies are proposed, deliberated, and decided upon by "citizen co-rulers" acting together.[18] What this implies is that the Arendtian kind of participatory politics enhancing the cultivation of political judgement requires a form of government that is radically democratic.

Ecological problems are collective problems, they are the results of societal structures and practices, and that they need to be changed through collective political action. Arendt's political thought emphasizes participation by citizens in public affairs, and how the political is fundamentally oriented toward the common interest rather than pursuit of short-term self-interest. Because the ecological challenges we face are political issues about which there are disagreement and different opinions, they must be subject to public debate and deliberation and to collective agreement and consent among citizens.

A participatory form of democracy in which the plurality of citizens participate directly in the public deliberation and decision, is the form of government that will enable us, as a community, to jointly "think what we are doing." This implies a decentralized political system in which citizens have the right and opportunity to act together, to discuss and make decisions in a variety of concrete, tangible, public spaces.

Arendt herself envisioned a new form of government, a confederation of popular councils that make possible the direct participation of every citizen in the public affairs.[19]

Radically democratic proposals like Arendt's are often rejected as naïve and unrealistic. However, in a situation where we need to make profound political and societal changes in order to tackle climate change and avoid ecological catastrophe, it seems that a participatory democratic form of government is more realistic than the perpetuation of the status quo. It is also a more humane and responsible alternative than the one proposed by the eco-authoritarians.

NOTES:

1. Leo Hickman, "James Lovelock: Humans Are Too Stupid to Prevent Climate Change," *The Guardian*, 29 March 2010. See also how Shearman and Smith, for example, advocate an authoritarian technocracy inspired by the Singapore system of governance by "a team of technocratic elites supported by educational structures." David Shearman and Joseph W. Smith, *The Climate Change Challenge and the Failure of Democracy* (Westport: Praeger, 2007), 126.

2. Calls for authoritarian solutions to the environmental problems are not new. They were a vocal strand of the environmental discourse in the 1970s, but were eventually rejected. The recent years however, eco-authoritarianism has re-emerged. Prominent eco-authoritarians today include James Lovelock, David Shearman, and Jørgen Randers.

3. Jørgen Randers, *2052: A Global Forecast for the Next Forty Years* (White River Junction: Chelsea Green, 2012), 347.

4. Ibid., 166.

5. Hannah Arendt and Jerome Kohn, *Between Past and Future: Eight Exercises in Political Thought* (London: Penguin Group, 2006), 150.

6. Hannah Arendt, *On Revolution* (London: Penguin Books, 1990), 235.

7. Hannah Arendt and Jerome Kohn, *Between Past and Future*, 220.

8. Ingerid S. Straume, "Depoliticizing Environmental Politics: Sustainable Development in Norway," in Douglas Torgerson and Robert Paehlke, eds., *Managing Leviathan: Environmental Politics and the Administrative State* (Peterborough, Ontario: Broadview, 2005), 5.

9. Arendt and Kohn, *Between Past and Future*, 243.

10. Ibid., 229.

11. Hannah Arendt, *The Human Condition* (Chicago: University of Chicago Press, 1998), p. 3.

12. Hannah Arendt, "The Conquest of Space and the Stature of Man," *The New Atlantis,* 18 (Fall 2007), 43.

13. Ibid., 51.

14. Frank Fischer, *Citizens, Experts, and the Environment: The Politics of Local Knowledge* (Durham: Duke University Press, 2000), 104.

15. See, for example, Chris Lang, "Nine reasons why REDD is a false solution: Friends of the Earth International," *REDD Monitor,* 15 October 2014 (available at redd-monitor.org); emphasis in original.

16. Arendt, "The Conquest of Space and the Stature of Man," 43.

17. Hannah Arendt, *The Human Condition* (Chicago: The University of Chicago Press, 1998), 49.

18. Arendt borrows the term from the Czech author Pavel Kohout who defined a "free citizen" as a "Citizen-Co-ruler." See Hannah Arendt, *Crises of the Republic* (New York: Houghton Mifflin Harcourt, 1972), 180.

19. Arendt, *On Revolution*, 263.

THE POLITICS OF ECOLOGY AND THE ECOLOGY OF POLITICS

DIMITRIOS I. ROUSSOPOULOS

Consider the historical record of States to protect the natural environment from being damaged. The first State pollution agency was established over 150 years ago. It is more than a century since the first international environment agreement between nation-states was signed. In the twenty year period before the publication of the Brundtland Report in 1987, more than 130 States created environmental agencies; more than 180 international agreements were signed; and the United Nations has long since created a global environmental agency and program.

By the end of the last century, few speeches made by the heads of States of the "developed" nations would fail to evoke the environmental crisis. It is one thing, however, to establish and sign international treaties, national laws, and promote environmental ministries and agencies; it is quite another to effect the concrete changes in attitudes, practices and institutions necessary to resolve the ecological crisis. It is true, to date; there have been environmental improvements, at least temporarily, in a few critical areas. But overall, the scientific indications paint a very grim picture, in particular as regards the basic changes in the world's climate and its increasingly visible consequences.

The best indicator is nature itself. It is clear with each passing month exactly how much trouble we are in. There is an endless series of ever more dramatic symbolic moments. The north has heated up more dramatically than any place on Earth. The physics of climate change make the poles heat faster, an entirely different condition is the result than even ten years ago. The Northwest and Northeast passages open up almost every summer. The summer of 2014, the Northwest Territories of Canada had fires that were biblical in dimension.[1]

A new study recently in the Proceeding of the U.S. National Academy of Sciences suggests that the oceans have been surprisingly static since 4,000 BCE. But that changed 150 years ago. There are two main forces that can drive sea levels higher. One is something called the thermal expansion of ocean water as it warms. The other is an influx of additional water, ushered into the sea by melting ice sheets and glaciers. And the ice sheets are melting at a faster rate than previously understood.[2]

Despite the substantial growth of environmental awareness among people throughout the world, the health of the Earth continues to deteriorate at an unprecedented rate. The attempts at State management of the environmental crisis have, at best, yielded questionable results. Recent international conference like the Copenhagen conference on climate change in 2009 as well as the more recent Rio+20 conference on sustainable development in 2012, demonstrates over and over again the incapacity of the current economic and political system to be reworked. Yet the results of this flurry of activity are far from satisfactory. The dominant proposals have been for political action without radically transforming the developmental trajectories of contemporary societies. Globalized capitalism persists in spite of accumulated evidence of the destructiveness of its perpetual economic growth.

We must conclude that for genuine reversal of global patterns to occur, more far reaching political and economic changes in the dominant institutions of our society must be made. These fundamental changes must, moreover, be undertaken by the current generation, as it may be too late for the next. Whether this generation will indeed be willing and able to take the necessary actions "from below" that our ruling elites have demonstrated themselves reluctant to take remains an open and urgent question. More than ever, thoughts and engagements at the edge of conventional politics and environmentalism are being called on to answer present and future challenges.

In the last forty years or so, many citizens have become acutely aware of the immediate and long-term consequences of environmental deterioration, and have begun to organize in response to the plight of the Earth. Already in 1983, it was estimated that the British environmental movement comprised some three million members (almost six per cent of the total population), making it the largest movement in that country's history. It is important to realize, that environmental activism is not a phenomena exclusive to the advanced industrial nations. According to recent U.N. estimates there were more than 25,000 environmental organizations worldwide. [3] Estimates by other organs claim that there are over 100,000 such organizations, with 100 million members, in the "developing" nations alone.[4]

The emergence of the new environmental activism of the 1960s and 1970s was a response to powerful historical forces that preceded it. Substantial changes took place in industrial societies after the Second World War, ushering in a period of intense economic growth and a more widespread material affluence that reinforced a naïve belief in perpetual and penalty-free economic expansion. A near pathological consumerism fed a reckless materialism so that the U.S., for instance, with six per cent of the world's population was producing and consuming over one-third of the world's goods and services by 1979. And yet there was discontent, especially among youth. For in the midst of this affluence many moral contradictions were apparent.

From the mid-1960s into the 1970s a new generation of organizations emerged which created a tide that dragged along the older established ones. The moralistic preservationists and the utilitarian conservationists now had to share the stage with the new activists who became skilled lobbyists and public opinion leaders. The resulting environmental movement was certainly not, of course, all of one piece. As one of the largest movements in human history it took root in various countries and drew on diverse political traditions. It was bound therefore to comprise a variety of ideological tendencies. Before and during the 1960s a number of organizations emerged such as Nature Conservancy and the Sierra Club, and many similar associations who loved nature and wilderness. There we find the desire to preserve "the great outdoors." These parts of the movement led to the establishment of a variety of regional and national parks in several countries.

As this tendency dove-tailed into a broader environmentalism which includes Greenpeace, Friends of the Earth, and Pollution Probe. One difference between this movement and the older conservationists is that the former does not shy away from mass popular actions as a means of pressure of the power structure. The essential approach was, and remains, dealing individually with one crisis point after another. This approach tends to concentrate on bringing about small but urgent changes to the immediate order of things. Taken alone, however, these intense but circumscribed efforts tend to draw attention away from the need for changes in our society's basic institutions of power. The result is that *the larger picture gets lost*; the forest cannot be seen for the trees.

An arguably more coherent currency within the ecology movement is "political ecology." The main difference between environmentalism and political ecology is that the latter presupposes substantial and radical changes in our relationship to the natural world and in our society. Environmentalists take a managerial approach to the crisis in the belief that these can be solved without fundamental changes in present values or in the current patterns of consumption and economic production of goods and services.

Political ecology advances the idea that *the science of ecology itself cannot be divorced from, and indeed imposes, certain political conceptions.* For example, inasmuch as the ecological crisis affects the Earth as whole, isolated attempts to solve the crisis cannot but fail; there must be coordination of efforts on a global scale. Thus the Green parties throughout the world evolved ideas in part as a critical response to the limited impact of environmentalism as well as the failure of Marxism and social democracy to transform society. In addition to introducing programmatic innovations, Green parties which emerged in the 1980s also represent a certain departure from the traditional political parties in their emphasis on other forms of political culture.

Space does not permit a thorough review here of the Green parties, their experiences and influence, but the spectrum of Green views ranges from light green (principally reformers who advocate compromise and engaging in elections to "get things changed") to "dark Greens" ("fundamentalists," red-Greens, and anarcho-Greens) who synthesize radical politics, feminism and anti-militarism and emphasize grassroots activism combined with selective electoral participation understood primarily as educational activity. A principal critique of the Greens is that in the majority of cases they fail to develop a sufficiently profound critique of the limits of liberal democracy and parliamentarism. Consequently they do not possess a radical understanding of the dynamics of State power and the present system's capacity to co-opt forces of opposition.

We then have the eco-socialists, in their many varieties, which include the eco-social democrats, who seek to blend environmentalism and "democratic socialism." All social democratic political parties attempt to integrate environmental concerns into their programs now. However, the programs of these parties are anchored in the metaphysics of the State, and consequently they maintain that a necessary condition for environmental protection is the election of social democrats to central political power. The unsatisfactory record of these parties in various countries speaks for itself.

Included under this rubric of eco-socialism is the eco-Marxist attempt to synthesize Marxism and ecology. Remaining within a broadly conceived Marxist theoretical framework, eco-Marxists continue to focus on political economy. While taking their distance from Marxist theories which assume the limitless abundance of nature and the celebration of productivism, they attempt to move beyond reductionist analyses of the primacy of the economic. The eco-Marxists are still inclined to regard change at the point of production as the motor of all social and political change. In their analysis of the lamentable environmental record of the former State Socialist bloc, the eco-Marxists ascribe the blame to Taylorism and the wholesale importation of the Fordist model of industrial organization. Though they are critical of this form of industrial economy, eco-Marxists still remain uncomfortable with an accent on decentralization and the local as the locus of political action and social development.

By far the most sophisticated and interesting group in the eco-socialist category are the European libertarian eco-socialists, among whom are the authors of the eco-socialist manifesto *Europe's Green Alternative*.[5] They envision a continent of autonomous regions, rather than nation-states, which are economically decentralized, shaped by feminist principles and built upon social structures which are not based on the arbitrary exercise of power. They maintain that eco-socialist change cannot be brought about by the State and they advocate citizen control of the economy.

In many of their declarations and proposals these libertarian eco-socialists display an affinity with social ecology. They stop short, however, of embracing the municipalist approach to ecological and social change integral to social ecology. Although libertarian eco-socialists in Europe reject the nation-state in favor of a continent of regions, they fail to identify a specific configuration of social, political and economic institutions as the potential foundation for radical social and political change they set as their goal.

Rooted in a rich philosophical framework which is reflected in its politics, *social ecology* is critical social theory both comprehensive and systematic. Conceptualized as a critique of current social, political, economic, and cultural anti-ecological trends, it espouses a reconstructive, ecological, communitarian, and ethical approach in its perspective of transforming society. The progenitor of the theory of social ecology is Murray Bookchin, who for over many decades labored to lay the foundation of this philosophy, in which history, technology and urbanism are interwoven.

Social ecologists advocate an outlook on issues which promotes direct democracy and confederal associations of citizens. As a body of ideas, social ecology envisions a moral economy based on its municipalization, which moves beyond scarcity and hierarchy, and seeks to move towards a harmonization of human communities with the natural world, eliminating exploitation of human by human, while celebrating diversity, creativity and freedom.

Social ecology suggests that the roots of current ecological and social problems can be traced to hierarchical and exploitative forms of the current organization of society. It contends that the systematic presence of hierarchy and exploitation cannot be resisted let alone replaced by individual actions such as the State management of environmental problems or by ethical consumerism but must be addressed by collective political activity grounded on a nuanced ethics and a radical democratic program of fundamental social and political change. The complexity of the relationship between people and nature is emphasized along with the importance of establishing mutualistic social structures that takes into account the need of a co-operative society.

Social ecology's social component comes from its position that nearly all of our ecological problems stem from social, political and economic problems. These problems in turn arise from the manner our society is organized, thus leading to domination through hierarchy and exploitation of humans by humans. Social ecologists argue that apart from those produced by natural catastrophes, the most serious ecological dislocations of the 20th and 21st centuries have as their cause economic, ethnic, cultural, and gender conflicts, among many others. Present ecological problems, it is maintained, cannot be clearly understood, much less resolved, without resolutely dealing with the need to radically transform society.

Having critiqued the current schools of environmentalism and political ecology and presented a framework of social ecology, I will now turn my attention to how social ecology is a grassroots practical response to the failure of the State management of the ecological crisis. To understand the importance of social ecology, however, it is crucial to first understand the place of the city in the environmental crisis and its political shortcoming and potentialities.

Since 2007, over half of humanity—3.5 billion people or 50.5% of the world population—lives in cities. By 2055, an estimated 75 per cent of the world's population will live in urban areas.[6] Cities today occupy just two per cent of the Earth's land but account for over 70 per cent of both energy consumption and carbon emissions.[7] Cities are, and will continue to be, at the nexus of the global crises related to economic recessions, energy insecurity, water scarcity or flooding, high food prices, vulnerability to climate change and natural disasters.

Cities and regional urban agglomerations, consistently undermined by nation-state governments for reasons of power politics, have been underfunded and underrepresented in the upper circles of the power elite that determine "national priorities." The result is that cities, big and small, have serious problems of political legitimacy. They are weak, face large-scale disinterest by citizens, and lack the will to transform themselves into democratic arenas for citizen participation in decision-making.

Still, there are a lot of issues that could potentially mobilize citizens to participate politically. How large-scale urbanization hollows out the sense of community of neighborhoods is one such issue. Collapsing infrastructure is another issue as are the daily impacts of climate change, inefficient public transit, water security, waste management, energy and fuel waste, overflowing landfills, flooding, water and air pollution and noise pollution, all with serious effects on public health. Capitalist urbanization, whether State sponsored or corporation driven, simply cannot handle the urban crisis, which in turn substantially aggravates the environmental crisis. Cities are locked into unsustainable modes of urbanization.

Over and above the cities' very heavy footprint on the Earth's environment, the economic role of cities must be considered, an issue that encourages mobilization around urban issues and the city's weak position in national politics. The city lies at the heart of capital accumulation and class struggles. In numerous books, geographer

David Harvey has showed how cities are a frontline for battles over who controls access to urban resources and who dictates the quality and organization of daily life. In an important recent book, *Rebel Cities*, Harvey singles out historical and contemporary examples where anti-capitalist struggles have been coupled with a desire to reclaim the city:

> The history of urban-based class struggles is stunning. The successive revolutionary movements in Paris from 1789 through 1830 and 1848 to the Commune of 1871 constitute the most obvious nineteenth century examples. Later events include the Petrograd Soviet, the Shanghai Communes of 1927 and 1967, the Seattle General Strike of 1919, the role of Barcelona in the Spanish Civil War, the uprising in Cordoba in 1969, and the more general urban uprisings in the United States in the 1960s, the urban-based movements of 1968 (Paris, Chicago, Mexico City, Bangkok, and others, including the so-called "Prague Spring," and the rise of neighborhood associations in Madrid that confronted the anti-Franco movement in Spain around the same time). ... More recently we have seen mass protests in Tahir Square in Cairo, in Madison, Wisconsin, in the Plaza del Sol in Madrid and Catalunya in Barcelona, and in Syntagma Square in Athens as well as revolutionary movements and rebellions in Oaxaca in Mexico, in Cochabamba (2000 and 2007) and El Alto (2003 and 2005) in Bolivia.[8]

Throughout the book, it should be noted, Harvey sympathetically acknowledges the analysis and insights of Bookchin. Sadly the political implications of this analysis are side-tracked by established Left orthodoxy. The city as a geopolitical terrain for the challenging of global capitalism and the State seems to have bypassed most of the Left, including the anarchist Left.

These contradictions of the urban world—its ecological challenges and political problems and the opportunities for anti-capitalist struggle and citizen mobilization—are crucial to understand why Montréal has been an important case of applied social ecology, and perhaps one of the most important to date. Montréal is an island city, with a population of approximately two million people, and the greater Montréal region adds up to 3 million in total. In this city, during the late 1960s, the urban new Left practiced a theory of community organizing and participatory democracy. Its activists worked to create forms of democratic grassroots organizations based in neighborhoods that would empower ordinary people. Thus, citizenship evolves into urban citizenship through an understanding of spatial relations.

Another equally important goal of community organizing was to generate a self-awareness and territorial identity. The movement further urged the radical decentralization of the city from City Hall to the neighborhoods. It argued in favor of establishing decision-making neighborhood councils of citizens. This attempt to democratize public life in Montréal referred to a need to democratize all power, including that dark area the central State closely guards for itself: the forming of defense and foreign policy, an area that the 1960s peace movement wanted to open up. The movement, in which I participated, wanted to change society for both global and local reasons.

During this decade in Montréal, we were influenced by the analysis and ideas of Henri Lefebvre who taught us the centrality of urban space in which the politics of daily life are mostly played out. We were also influenced by Paul Goodman through his critique of urban life articulated in *Communitas*, a book co-authored with his brother. Restorative and very relevant were the ideas of Jane Jacobs who, in a series of books and articles on neighborhoods and cities, dealt with the political economy of cities. Jane Jacobs also taught us that economic growth was mainly generated by cities and not by national economies over and above cities. By the end of the 1960s, we discovered the works and the personage of Murray Bookchin; he taught us radical history and ecology and plunged us deeper into the phenomena called urbanization, analyzing its negative effects in deforming cities today and, in particular, during the historical rise of industrial capitalism.

I n the fervent and revolutionary year of 1968, a major real estate company, Concordia Estates Ltd., announced that it would demolish a six-block neighborhood in downtown Montréal and build, in the name of urban renewal, the city of the 21st Century. Drawing inspiration and guidance from social ecology in part, a very militant urban struggle unfolded which involved door to door campaigning with information sharing, petition collecting, organizing public information meetings, demonstrations, squatting, sit-ins in the offices of the speculators, hunger strikes, occupations of emptied neighborhood residential buildings, arrests of some 59 activists, jail and a trial by jury which was won by those arrested.

The struggle ended without an initial success. But it started over again a few years later using a different strategy which kept a high level of mobilization of citizens, both young and old. This time the strategy used was to confront heavy traffic on residential streets. Once again the neighborhood came together to resist and fight, this time against City Hall. To be noted was the organizational form of the struggle which was with street committees, each with its personality and consciousness-raising perspective. The street committees would blend together from time to time into street occupations. The most celebrated street occupation took place in November 1978 in the middle of the municipal elections, when rush-hour traffic was blocked for some two hours. City Hall decided to have no one arrested.

Finally in 1979, eleven years later, having used all forms of struggle and coalition building, we won. With some $30.7 million of public funds we bought up most of the six city block neighborhood. The final edges of the struggle involved a fight with an internal group of aspiring yuppies. Recall that we wanted to create a cooperative community of non-profit cooperatives, based on affinities in various parts of the neighborhood. We wanted to abolish private property and profit making through real estate speculation. We wanted to restore the sense of community through actively engaged citizen participation whereby the principles of democratic self-management of property of buildings and land would become a real living daily experience. The yuppies wanted the opposite, private ownership of houses and real estate speculation. In a series of bitter fights we drove them into the ground, isolating them until they were marginalized and defeated.

Thus we established the Milton-Parc project—the largest non-profit cooperative housing in North America for low-income citizens based on a land trust wherein all the land was owned in common. Imagine an entire neighborhood where buying and selling of property is not permitted. This accomplishment co-exists alongside market capitalism. This process of social reconstruction resulted in a federation of 22 self-managed non-profit housing coops and non-profit housing associations, housing over 1,100 persons in 616 residences of various sizes in a heritage neighborhood in the downtown of the city.

Once this battle was behind us and the renovation work of all the 146 buildings was completed and we re-occupied our homes, militants asked the question: "What next?" We tried in the interim to build an explicit politics of social ecology and build a left-green municipal party, "Ecology Montréal," which presented candidates during the elections of 1990 and 1994; but the experiment ended in failure. In the elections, we had three of our 21 candidates who came second, but in an electoral system that is not based on proportional representation we hit a brick wall. It was also a political period when a politically left-of-center party ruled City Hall and the political culture of Montréal could not appreciate another political party further to the Left advocating social ecology and a party which proposed the radical decentralization of power through decision-making neighborhood councils with actively involved citizens. Even though our membership base included several hundred activists, Ecology Montréal could not break the barriers of the prevailing political system. So we had to re-think our strategy and program.

In 1994-95, we decided to enrich the political culture of Montréal by undertaking a program of ecological education including some social experiments and thus helped establish an Urban Ecology Center of Montréal based on social ecology. Its objective was to focus on all major issues of the urban question through the lens of social ecology. Several key projects and programs were established. Included in our approach was a major educational program during eleven months of the year, a bi-lingual alternative newspaper published every two weeks delivered free in the whole downtown core of the city; with a readership of 38,000, it championed experiments in roof-top gardens, alternative traffic designs, and persistent political engagement to influence various public policies at City Hall and in the boroughs. By 2006, the Urban Ecology Center had a staff of some twelve persons with a budget of $400,000. It is today a major actor in the larger Montréal region, having organized five citizens' summits from 2001, which brought together over one thousand citizens at the last summit in 2009, networking concerned citizens on a variety of social issues and actions across the city. Thus, the Urban Ecology Center helped create a self-conscious civil society in Montréal by bringing together citizen activists who advanced a citizens' agenda for "The City We Want," pushing it forward during that Fall's municipal elections.

Today, the Urban Ecology Center of Montréal has outreach in several other cities in Canada and a staff of fifteen with an annual budget of $1.5 million. Not only has it influenced the environmentalists to take seriously the urban problems surrounding them, but it has also influenced the political culture of the city. It helped legitimize the social movements and community organizations that constitute the core of Montréal's civil society; it raised the idea of human rights and the city so that a *Montréal Charter of Rights and Responsibilities* now exists as a legal city bylaw protected in the Constitution of the city. The Charter has received considerable international recognition through UNESCO and U.N. Habitat, as well as other international organizations, and has been emulated by Mexico City and other cities, thus expanding the program of the "Right to the City" movement world-wide. This Charter empowers citizens to engage in deciding on, as well as directly influencing, urban public policies *in between elections*. In addition, citizen rights are protected by the legal services of a municipal Ombudsman and the place of citizens in the process of public consultation is assured by an Office of Public Consultation. Both of these municipal institutions are publicly funded but arms-length from City Hall. Despite these institutional changes, many communities, as well as Milton-Parc, have continued to undertake grassroots civic struggles on a variety of urban ecological issues, often resulting in significant popular victories; regardless of what happens at City Hall, the work on the streets must continue.

The idea of participatory democracy is found everywhere in the popular culture in Montréal. Other neighborhoods practice it through important defensive campaigns against urban deterioration with a pronounced attention to social ecology in many instances. A fundamental re-definition of citizenship is underway whereby many citizens consider themselves first and foremost citizens of Montréal more than citizens of a nation. The envelope of democracy is constantly enlarged, with citizens initiating public policy instead of simply lobbying politicians. The whole idea of intermediaries is challenged as seeds of direct democracy have started to sprout.

More recently, all this activity has had an impact on the municipal government. A number of democratic reforms have resulted in openings that have been critically occupied in part by civil society. When recently more than 29,800 Montréalers signed a petition on the need for urban agriculture, demanding participation in decision-making and not simply supporting a statement making a request to politicians to change course on this or that given topic, a political electric current was visibly transmitted. The public desire to have citizens involved in economic decision-making and participatory budgeting with a movement directed towards economic democracy is slowly becoming an important political mix. People's impatience with the status quo and the political and economic establishment is clearly in evidence.

This deep desire for fundamental change massively burst forth with the general strike of students in 2012 which involved some 170,000 university and college students. On March 22, 2012, some 150,000 marched through the streets of Montréal against a government proposed increase in tuition fees. On April 22nd, Earth Day, however, 200,000 youth and others marched again in the streets of Montréal, but the agenda had widened into environmental and social demands in addition to a freeze of tuition fees. On May 22nd, more than 250,000 people from all walks of life, young and old, all colors and political stripes— left-nationalists, anarchists, trade unions, community organizations, and ecologists—marched together for a broader list of social demands. They also marched against a new repressive law, Bill 78, imposed by the provincial government, a significant imposition on civil liberties. On this march a huge number of marchers turned left instead of right at Rue Jeanne Mance and Sherbrook Street, thus committing a massive act of civil disobedience against Bill 78. On June 22nd and on July 22nd, mass marches again took place. Parallel to these mass marches, a social revolt began to emerge in scores of neighborhoods throughout the city as thousands of citizens at 8 pm every night came out onto their streets to bang pots and pans in protest expressing their sympathy with the mass marchers. Over 3,000 marchers were arrested in various acts of resistance as police used tactics imported from the US and other countries to repress the street actions. Solidarity actions with what was happening in Montréal and elsewhere in Quebec spread to New York, Chicago, Paris and other cities. The earlier Occupy movement and the anger it expressed against the plutocracy was integrated in this new social revolt and it re-emerged with a bang.

The point in recounting the year 2012 in outline form is to demonstrate that this social revolt had deep roots in the community organizations that are implanted here and there. It is important to note that this social revolt was anchored in a communalist sentiment and identity. Throughout the strike and its accompanied actions, all decisions where taken in general assemblies in each college and university, using the decision-making process of direct democracy. This politics was shown more generally during the mass demonstration in the streets on June 22nd when a pamphlet was widely distributed, titled *Manifeste pour une démocratie directe*, subtitled "Behind Representative Democracy, There is an Oligarchy Hiding." Authored by a number of anarchists affiliated to neighborhood associations, this pamphlet states: "The solution to get out of the current crisis is democracy, the only, true, real direct democracy—or self-management—in which citizens exercise power directly. We need to re-build general assemblies, popular councils, participatory budgets, self-managed cooperatives and the use of referenda so that our society can reorient itself from the grassroots and through horizontalism."[9]

On July 12th, Classe, the largest and most militant of the three student unions that drove the strike, published in a French-language daily the following remarkable manifesto, called *Share Our Future*:

> For months now, all over Quebec, the streets have vibrated to the rhythm of hundreds of thousands of marching feet. What started out as a movement underground, still stiff with the winter consensus, gathered new strength in the spring and flowed freely, energizing students, parents, grandparents, children, and people with and without jobs. The initial student strike grew into a people's struggle, while the problem of tuition fees opened the door to a much deeper malaise—we now face a political problem that truly affects us all. … The way we see it, direct democracy should be experienced, every moment of every day. Our own voices ought to be heard in assemblies in schools, at work, in our neighborhoods. Our concept of democracy places the people in permanent charge of politics, and by "the people" we mean those of us at the base of the pyramid— the foundation of political legitimacy. … Democracy, as viewed by the other side, is tagged as "representative"—and we wonder just what it represents.[10]

What follows in this manifesto is not only a critique of liberal democracy but a general analysis of the dimensions of social injustice, environmental degradation, the envisaging of a social alternative and the question of complete gender equality. The manifesto concludes thus: "In choosing to strike, we have chosen to fight for these ideas. We have chosen to create a power relationship. … Sharing this responsibility together, we can accomplish a great deal. … [At] a time when new democratic spaces are springing up all around us, we must make use of these to create a new world. … In calling for a social strike today, we will be marching alongside you, people of Quebec, in the street tomorrow."[11]

The red cloth square of the student movement, which adorned the garments of many thousands in 2012, has become an international symbol, often combined with a slice of black. Political culture has changed. Provincial elections were held with the strike ending. The government was defeated and the new center-left government froze the student fees but proceeded to backtrack, such as to increase the fees in the same way but more gradually as well as fanning xenophobia against migrants and Muslims; stirring little interest or credibility, its rule was short and it too was defeated in another general provincial election. The new conservative third government is carefully walking on eggshells. It has committed to a moratorium and indicated that it will bend to public will by objecting to the currently proposed pipeline coming through Quebec carrying oil from Alberta's tar sands. It has also told an oil company to shut down a proposed port on the St. Laurent River which was meant to export the oil from Western Canada. Small reversals and victories, but the storm clouds are still on the horizon. Especially with its aggressive program of austerity resulting in cuts across the board of education, healthcare, social services and public transport; this has recently sparked the fury of workers, especially in the public sector, and students and is fuelling a powerful anti-austerity struggle for 2015. At the writing of this article (in early March 2015), plans are already in place for an imminent student strike, recalling memories from 2012.

Before concluding, let me add a few new vital points. Several years ago, I help create the Institute of Policy Alternatives of Montréal (IPAM), an urban think tank, as a supplement to the Urban Ecology Center here. IPAM is focused on the entire metropolitan region of some 88 cities and towns of various shapes and sizes. In 2010, we organized an agora (a citizens' summit) on the need to envisage an urban development plan for the city-region as a whole. It worked and we thus influenced the drawing up of an overall overview which now includes major environmental issues, public transportation and housing concerns. The impressive feature of this and the follow-up experiences were that once again we proved to politicians and journalists that citizens are interested in the larger picture and want to influence public policy if given the opening to do so with their ideas. The agora idea has now become institutionalized in the bi-annual program of the metropolitan administration where progress, or lack thereof, is publicly scrutinized.

IPAM's regular roundtables also bring to the attention of civil society actors important urban issues. For example, the Quebec government decided some time ago to build two super hospitals and thus to close down five existing hospitals. One IPAM roundtable created a consensus that the five hospitals should remain in the public domain (the provincial government was leaning toward selling these off to the real estate industry) and that these sites should serve the common good, especially social housing. By 2014 this perspective has gained considerable traction with much agreement in the arena of public opinion and even amongst the local political elite. Here again, the important notion that prevailed was "No to private property," yet another step to the municipal or community ownership of land. Thus the ideological hegemony of private property has been challenged.

The undersoil of the new political culture is still fermenting. The politics of the sixties, nurtured by social ecology, created and re-creates a vital public sphere based on cooperation and community and it is driven by features of direct democracy. As Bookchin has argued, such politics does not exclude, and indeed requires, that citizens "take over the city" with a new municipal agenda, forming a new municipal administration of directly mandated elected delegates from the neighborhoods of the city. Montréal, thanks to the urban Left and historical circumstances, is the most decentralized city in North America, with its 19 boroughs, with borough and city councilors and 19 borough mayors, each with its own budget, open monthly to citizen scrutiny. Each council meeting begins with a citizen question period, which turns out to often be volatile.

All these changes have taken decades of community organizing, bringing citizens together in networking assemblies or summits, coalition building, spreading the vital importance of horizontal decision-making by citizens and remaining ever vigilant at the emergence of hierarchy and authoritarians. Transforming urban society and establishing a new harmony with nature, a social ecology perspective, is now on the agenda. This laboratory deserves to be duplicated rapidly elsewhere. It can be the birth of the new politics with the city as the geopolitical fulcrum. We have to go beyond websites, blogs, pamphleteering, book publishing and conference organizing. What is needed is that the new politics be experimented with on the ground. The road is long, however, and what is required is patience and the seizure of all opportunities to breech the power structure and open the doors and windows to the citizens of the city. This perspective marks us in different political colors to those of the eco-socialists, many of whom may even obstruct the way forward. What is needed is the political will to organize the new politics of ecology.

Why, then, "the Politics of Ecology"? What was critically reviewed in this essay was not only the failure of the state management of the environmental crisis but that the environmental organizations and movements in their varied responses and strategies have not delivered a coherent and realistic program for basic change in the dominant politics. In spite of their difference to the environmentalists, many political ecologists have only made marginal advances. Why, then, "the Ecology of Politics"? In the heat of the ecological and economic crisis of advanced capitalism in which we find ourselves, we turn urgently to examine those who claim to pose the alternative. Potent or feeble, successful or abortive, cooperative or divisive, in what state are the movements and their organizations, their ideas and their cultures? Are they articulating and demonstrating the way to rescue the life of our ecology and our democracy? "Politics," Bookchin maintains, "must be recreated again if we are to reclaim any degree of personal and collective sovereignty over our destiny."[12] Thus, by fusing grassroots community organizing with social ecology, the case of Montréal stands out and is worthy of emulation.

NOTES:

1. Gavin Schmidt and Joshua Wolfe, *Climate Change: Picturing the Science* (New York City: W. W. Norton & Company, 2009).

2. Ibid.

3. Philip Lowe and Jane Gayder, *Environmental Groups in Politics* (London: George Allen & Unwin, 1983). p.1.

4. Ibid.

5. Penny Kemp, *Europe's Green Alternative: An Ecology Manifesto* (Montréal: Black Rose Books, 1992).

6. UNFPA report, "The Power of 1.8 Million." (2014)

7. United Nations Department of Economic and Social Affairs, Population Division, "Population Distribution, Urbanization, Internal Migration and Development." (2011)

8. David Harvey, *Rebel Cities: From the Right to the City to the Urban Revolution* (London: Verso, 2012), 115-116.

9. Niclas Van Caloen, Pascal Lebrun, and Geneviève Lambert-Pilotte, "Manifeste Pour Une Démocratie Directe," *La Pointe Libertaire* (available at www.lapointelibertaire.org); my translation from French.

10. Coalition large de l'Association pour une solidarité syndicale (CLASSE), "Share Our Future: The Classe Manifesto" (available at www.stopthehike.ca).

11. Ibid.

12. Murray Bookchin, *Urbanization Without Cities: The Rise and Decline of Citizenship* (Montréal: Black Rose Books, 1992), Chapter Three.

ABOUT THE CONTRIBUTORS

EIRIK EIGLAD has been involved in a broad range of social ecology projects in Scandinavia for more than two decades, as a movement activist, writer, translator, and editor. Eiglad co-founded the New Compass collective. His writings include *The Anti-Jewish Riots in Oslo* and *Communalism as Alternative.*

DAN CHODORKOFF is the cofounder and former executive director of the Institute for Social Ecology in Vermont. For fifty years he has been actively committed to progressive urban and ecological movements. Chodorkoff is the author of *The Anthropology of Utopia* and the novel *Loisaida.*

BRIAN TOKAR has been a leading critical voice for ecological activism since the 1970s, and is the director of the Vermont-based Institute for Social Ecology. Tokar's books include *Earth for Sale, The Green Alternative,* and *Toward Climate Justice,* and he is co-editor of *Agriculture and Food in Crisis: Conflict, Resistance and Renewal.*

SVEINUNG LEGARD is an activist and researcher from Oslo, Norway. For twenty years, he has been involved in social ecology organizing in Scandinavia. Legard co-founded the New Compass collective, and is currently writing a PhD thesis on participatory democracy.

ADAM KRAUSE is an author, musician, activist and carpenter based in Milwaukee, Wisconsin. He has performed and recorded music for more than half his life, and has been heavily involved in the cooperative movement. Krause is the author of *Art as Politics* and *The Revolution Will Be Hilarious.*

MAT LITTLE is a freelance journalist, writing for *Red Pepper, New Statesman,* and *The Guardian.* He co-authored *Public Service Reform:*

But Not as We Know It! (with Hilary Wainwright). Little was active in Social Ecology London and recently joined the New Compass collective.

MARCO ROSAIRE ROSSI is a part-time writer and activist living Olympia, Washington, USA. Rossi has studied political science at the University of Illinois at Chicago and human rights at the University for Peace in San Jose, Costa Rica. He is the author of *A Politics for the 99%* and has published in *The Humanist* and *Z Magazine*.

JOHN NIGHTINGALE is a postgraduate researcher at Loughborough University, UK. His current research centers on radical and anarchist conceptions of solidarity, and how they relate to citizenship and cosmopolitanism.

JANET BIEHL is an author, copy editor, and graphic artist from Burlington, Vermont. Her books include *Rethinking Ecofeminist Politics*, *The Politics of Social Ecology*, *The Murray Bookchin Reader*, and the forthcoming *Ecology or Catastrophe: The Life of Murray Bookchin*.

ARNOŠT NOVÁK has been involved in anarchist activism in Prague since the beginning of the 1990s. He is a member of the autonomous social center, Klinika, and is nowadays mostly engaged in radical urban struggles. Novák teaches environmental sociology at Charles University in Prague.

JONATHAN KORSÁR has worked with popular education and social ecology since the late 1990s, and is currently a teacher at Färnebo Folkhögskola, Sweden. He is also an active member of Friends of the Earth Sweden, focusing on the transition to renewable energy, and democratic solutions to the energy crisis.

ERSILIA VERLINGHIERI is trained in applied mathematics. Focusing on participatory methodology, she works with grassroots planning groups to build an ecological future. Verlinghieri is currently a PhD candidate at the Institute for Transport Studies at the University of Leeds, UK, and a member of the Transnational Institute of Social Ecology and the Contested Cities Network.

MONICA CAGGIANO is a social ecology activist and holds a PhD in ecological economics. She has worked on a wide range of projects related to community development, rural and urban agriculture, and community-based economics. Caggiano now works at the French National Institute for Agricultural Research (INRA) in Paris.

SALVATORE PAOLO DE ROSA is an Italian activist and anthropologist, focusing on political ecology and the commons. He is currently a PhD candidate at the Department for Human Geography of Lund University, Sweden, and a fellow of ENTITLE, an international network for political ecology.

METIN GÜVEN has, since the 1980s, been involved in social ecology groups and other libertarian organizations in Turkey, Australia, New Zealand, and the US. Güven was on the editorial board of the Turkish social ecology journal *Toplumsal Ekoloji*, and has written for newspapers, magazines, and journals.

JOHANNA L. RIVERA is a human rights activist currently working for the Iraqi Civil Society Solidarity Initiative (ICSSI). She is trained as a pharmacist, but advocacy work has taken her all over the world, notably to the Middle East, where she has worked with civil initiatives for women's right, for non-violence, and for transboundary water rights. Rivera is now based in Oslo.

TOON BIJNENS is a Belgian activist focusing on questions of social justice in the Middle East. He holds an MA in Modern History and has worked in advocacy for Amnesty International and with local activists in Egypt and in Iraq. Bijnens is currently based in Erbil, where he works for the Iraqi Civil Society Solidarity Initiative (ICSSI).

CAĞRI ERYILMAZ is an assistant professor at the department of sociology at Artvin Coruh University, Turkey. As a social ecologist, his main areas of interests are social theory and methodology, environmentalism, popular movements, and rural sociology.

FEDERICO VENTURINI is PhD candiate at the School of Geography at the University of Leeds, UK, where he studies the relationship between modern cities and urban social movements. Venturini participates in the Contested Cities project, and is a member of the Transnational Institute of Social Ecology.

CAMILLA HANSEN is a democracy activist living in Oslo, Norway. She has been involved in organizations such as Attac and Women's International League for Peace and Freedom, as well as in the disability movement. Hansen is member of the New Compass collective.

DIMITRIOS I. ROUSSOPOULOS is a political activist, community organizer, and public speaker, and the founder of Black Rose Books. Currently he is president of the Task Force on Democracy of the City of Montréal. He has edited and written a number of books, including *Political Ecology*, *Public Place*, *Faith in Faithlessness*, *The Rise of Cities*, *Dissidence*, and *Participatory Democracy*.

Made in the USA
Charleston, SC
11 August 2015